Cultural Control and Globalization in Asia

When does inspired creativity become plagiarism? What is the difference between video piracy and free trade? Globalization has made these hot button issues today, and Pang Laikwan's *Cultural Control and Globalization in Asia* shows us why. Her analyses of, for example, stylized violence in the production of an Asian cinematic identity and *Kill Bill*'s copying of it versus attempts to control copying of DVDs of *Kill Bill*, are vivid and vital reading for anyone who wants to understand the forces shaping contemporary Asian cinematic culture.

Chris Berry, Professor of Film and Television Studies,
Goldsmiths College, University of London

This book makes a valuable contribution to discussions of global film culture. Through an original exploration of the role of "copying" in Asian (and American) cinema, Pang offers us new ways to think about issues ranging from copyright to the relations between global and local cinematic production. And through an equally original discussion of "violence" in cinema, Pang opens up a new perspective on the problem of the relations between images and practices of violence. It will be a welcome addition to those trying to "globalize" the study of media.

Lawrence Grossberg, Morris Davis Distinguished Professor of Communication
Studies and Cultural Studies, University of North Carolina

This book challenges the prevailing view of cinema culture, that Hollywood and the US creates, produces, and exports, with other countries importing, modifying, and sometimes pirating "original" American work. Instead the book challenges the construct of the so-called original ideas, which underpin the moneymaking activities of the creative industries, and for which ownership is secured through copyright. Culture is made up of, and constantly renewed through, processes of copying, which is particularly prominent in today's entertainment culture reinforced by globalization and capitalism.

This book introduces a truly interdisciplinary approach to study issues related to copyright in contemporary popular culture, particularly in relation to the current development of Asian cinema, and explores how copyright is appropriated to regulate culture. It examines the many meanings and practices pertaining to "copying" in the cinema, demonstrating the dynamics between globalization's desire for cultural control and cinema's own resistance to such manipulation.

The book considers especially the cinema of China, Taiwan, and Hong Kong, and film "piracy" in these places and other Asian countries, to show that ideas of cultural ownership and copyright are not as straightforward as they may at first seem, and that copyright is a highly contested realm in which cultural control is exercised and battled.

Laikwan Pang is Associate Professor at the Department of Cultural and Religious Studies, the Chinese University of Hong Kong.

Routledge Media, Culture and Social Change in Asia

The aim of this series is to publish original, high-quality work by both new and established scholars in the West and the East, on all aspects of media, culture and social change in Asia.

1 **Television Across Asia**
Television industries, programme formats and globalisation
Edited by Albert Moran and Michael Keane

2 **Journalism and Democracy in Asia**
Edited by Angela Romano and Michael Bromley

3 **Cultural Control and Globalization in Asia**
Copyright, piracy, and cinema
Laikwan Pang

4 **Conflict, Terrorism and the Media in Asia**
Edited by Benjamin Cole

Cultural Control and Globalization in Asia

Copyright, piracy, and cinema

Laikwan Pang

Routledge
Taylor & Francis Group
LONDON AND NEW YORK

First published 2006
by Routledge
2 Park Square, Milton Park, Abingdon, Oxon OX14 4RN

Simultaneously published in the USA and Canada
by Routledge
270 Madison Ave, New York, NY 10016

Routledge is an imprint of the Taylor & Francis Group

Typeset in Garamond by
Newgen Imaging Systems (P) Ltd
Printed and bound in Great Britain by
Biddles Ltd, King's Lynn

British Library Cataloguing in Publication Data
A catalogue record for this book is available from the British Library

Library of Congress Cataloging in Publication Data
A catalog record for this book has been requested

ISBN 0–415–35201–0

To KC

Contents

Acknowledgments

The book began as a casual conversation with Stephanie Hemelryk Donald two years ago. I had been interested in issues of movie piracy, but had not yet attempted anything more ambitious than individual articles. Stephanie, and later Peter Sowden of Routledge, gave me the strongest encouragement to develop my discrete ideas into a book-length study. Without their support, this book might never have been written.

Despite its published form, the book, I have to admit, is still a work in progress. One of my aims is to introduce a truly interdisciplinary approach to study intellectual property issues in contemporary cinema, and the related discussions recorded in this small book are best seen as reflections of a learning experience. This learning experience is built on help from many other people. I have to thank my research assistants, little joe and Felix Shum, who have aided my research at different stages in a number of important ways. My most sincere thanks go to those friends and scholars who generously gave their time to read and contribute constructive comments to the earlier drafts of my chapters: James Steintrager, Chris Connery, Arif Dirlik, Chua Beng Huat, Jon Solomon, Yu Xingzhong, and Mireille Rosello. I also want to thank the anonymous reviewers of *Modern Chinese Literature and Culture*, *Social Text*, *boundary 2*, and *Culture, Theory and Critique* who showed me the blind spots and flawed arguments of my earlier writings. Other scholars and friends who have supplied information and corrected mistakes at different states of my writing include Darrell Davis, Charles Leary, Dai Jinhua, and David Desser. I thank their generous sharing; all final mistakes, are, of course, mine. I am indebted to Rey Chow and Chris Berry for their scholarships and friendships – their encouragement has meant much to me. I am also thankful to my wonderful students and colleagues at The Chinese University of Hong Kong who make my teaching and research joyful. Among them, I am grateful to K.Y. Wong, Pan-chiu Lai, Leo Ou-fan Lee, Archie Lee, Ming-yan Lai, Natalia Chan, Lai Chi Tim, and Thomas Luk for their continual support and generous sharing of scholarship; I thank my sharp and diligent postgraduate students who struggled with me through readings that shaped my own scholarship. I would specifically like to thank Angela Wai-ching Wong, whose friendship I can always count on, and whose kindness to her colleagues and students I strive to emulate.

For editing and publication assistance I must thank my copyeditor Dawn Ollila for her elegant work smoothing over my bumpy non-native English in the manuscript's early stages; once again I thank Stephanie Hemelryk Donald and

Peter Sowden, who have given me the most professional and generous editorial and scholarly advice. I also thank John Clement and his staff, whose timely and professional works in the final production period are most appreciated.

Grateful acknowledgment is made to the following sources to reprint material in this book in edited form:

Chapter 3: "New Asian Cinema and Its Circulation of Violence," *Modern Chinese Literature and Culture* 17. 1 (Spring 2005): 159–87.
Chapter 4: "Copying *Kill Bill*," *Social Text* 83 (Summer 2005).
Chapter 5: "Mediating the Ethics of Technology: Hollywood and Movie Piracy," *Culture, Theory and Critique* 45. 1 (Spring 2004): 19–32.
Chapter 6: "Piracy/Privacy: the Despair of Cinema and Collectivity in China," *Boundary 2: An International Journal of Literature and Culture* 31. 3 (Fall 2004): 101–24.

An earlier version of Chapter 4 was presented in the Conference of "Hong Kong/Hollywood at the Borders: Alternative Perspectives, Alternative Cinemas" at the University of Hong Kong in April 2004. Parts of Chapter 4 and the introduction were given at Sarai's "Contested Commons/Trespassing Publics Conference" in New Delhi in January 2005. Conference attendants and fellow panelists gave me many wonderful suggestions that inspired my revision; I thank Gina Marchetti and Nitin Govil for their kind invitations to these two conferences.

Abbreviations

CCP	Chinese Communist Party
CCTV	China Central Television
CD	Compact Disc
CTEA	Sonny Bono Copyright Term Extension Act
DMCA	Digital Millennium Copyright Act
DVD	Digital Compact Disc
GATT	General Agreement on Tariffs and Trade
IP	Intellectual Property
IPR	Intellectual Property Rights
LD	Laser Disc
MPA	Motion Picture Association
MPAA	Motion Picture Association of America
NATO	North Atlantic Treaty Organization
P2P	Peer-to-Peer
PRC	People's Republic of China
TRIPS	Agreement on Trade-Related Aspects of Intellectual Property Rights, Including Trade in Counterfeit Goods
UN	United Nations
UNESCO	United Nations Education, Scientific and Cultural Organization
VCD	Video Compact Disc
VHS	Video Home System
WIPO	World Intellectual Property Organization
WTO	World Trade Organization

Introduction

Global control

One of the most fundamental ethical concerns in the recent discussions of globalization is the increasing power of the global system in all walks of life – control exercised on a global level. Saskia Sassen's description of the emergent system of global control is one based on the symbiosis of the global and the national, which makes citizens of different nations comply with the rules of the new global order (1991, 1994, 1996, 1998). Sassen's works demonstrate that the concept of "national" sovereignty remains valid in the "globalizing" world, but it changes forms to fashion a new geography of power that facilitates the penetration of global finance through national infrastructure. Through her careful readings of the various movements of humans and capital across nations, Sassen identifies three mechanisms that consolidate this new geography of power, which not only traverses but also reinforces national borders: the globalization of new territories materializing in specific institutions and processes, such as the offshoring of labor and clerical work; a new legal regime that governs cross-border economic transactions; and the growing number of economic activities taking place in electronic space (1996: 5). Sassen's work on globalization has had a broad-ranging impact on the discourse on globalization across disciplines, because her models help us understand how existing national interests and international relationships do not reject but rather facilitate the new global system, which not only continues to protect but also reinforces existing hegemonic powers.

There are two dimensions, or weaknesses, of Sassen's model that are pertinent to my study of copyright. My first concern is Sassen's sociopolitical bias in her analysis of global control. As a socioeconomist, Sassen's discussions largely treat those phenomena engineered by governments or powerful organizations, instead of the controls exercised in and felt by subjects in the looser cultural domain. She suggests that the profound influence US popular culture exerts on global culture is a manifestation of cultural globalization (1996: 20), proposing that contemporary culture cannot be independent from the global econo-political system. However, many cultural theorists have already pointed out the impact of the media and communication technologies, as well as various cultural ideologies on globalization, in that contemporary culture is constantly interacting with, instead of being subsumed by, finance (Appadurai 1996; Tomlinson 1999). Cultural representations penetrate as globally as the exchanges taking place in economic or political domains, making any assumption that transnational cultural exchanges are only services of or responses to global finance, highly problematic.

Instead of taking the concept of control for granted, the specific issue I want to explore in this book is that of the "fantasy" of cultural control in the age of globalization. If Sassen's model is based on the observations of some very powerful social and political forces that exercise control through a highly organized global–national structure, then to what extent is this largely an imagination based on the assumed inert receptivity of culture? Or, more specifically, how "free" is culture under globalization? In what ways and degrees can culture, which has its own mechanisms by which to resist manipulation, escape the principles of globalization? Copyright is a fascinating area in which to study the impact of globalization on culture because it brings into focus what "culture" means to "global control," or the other way around, which leads to my next question.

If globalization is a loaded term implying the large amount of "control" this globalizing mechanism desires and gathers, the legal system should be a key site where such functioning performs. How can we link law and culture together? As demonstrated in her description of the second mechanism (a new legal regime), Sassen, like a number of other social and political theorists, points out the importance of a new legal regime working beyond conventional models of international law and politics to sustain the present global economy. Sassen describes this new legal regime as the particular form of legal institutions that have sprouted to support globalization. These institutions, like international commercial arbitration or credit-rating agencies such as Moody's and Standard & Poor's, mediate between the global system and sovereign states to maintain the global flow of capital (1996: 14–16). She also points out the increasing demand for highly specialized legal services to support increasingly complex large transnational corporations (1991: 93–111). According to this model, the participation of nation-states continues to be pertinent to the global order, because governments must respect and enforce the regime before the new order can be "grounded" locally. The concept of legal regime in Sassen's model is once again basically economic and political. As she largely ignores the field of culture as a semi-autonomous discursive site, she does not explain how culture can be controlled legally – this is a question we cannot take for granted.

The term international legal regime refers not to a fixed set of legal statements but some loosely defined implicit or explicit principles, norms, rules, and decision-making procedures pertaining to a particular set of international policy issues. The resultant development of institutions and norms within the international system does not necessarily require the existence of formal international organizations. Unconstrained by specific concrete bodies of agents and institutions, the legal regime "has the capacity to incorporate within this framework the plurality and fragmentation of the international response to 'global' problems on a range of issue" (Jayasuriya 1999: 432). The new legal regime is, therefore, a discursive network comprising not only different types of organizations but also new legal concepts and social norms that can be conveyed and negotiated globally.

Kanishka Jayasuriya, however, contends that even today the regimes are still mostly seen as composed of states bound by international treaty, based on a more traditional contractual model of state relationships (1999: 432). As shown by Sassen, the legal regime is embodied in specific rating companies, which work very closely with national governments for each other's interests. But being a legal regime in the domain of culture, copyright has a strong propensity to unbundle the notion of sovereignty from territory. Cultural influences have always been transnational or ultranational, and the practices of culture are embedded in constantly changing social and economic structures. Copyright crystallizes the possibilities of envisioning a global order that, although still contracted by national sovereignties, is able to incorporate within its framework the plurality and fragmentation of international situations. The diffusing dimension of culture, more than other sociopolitical domains, may help propel, instead of merely resulting from global deterritorialization. If most legal regimes still work closely with national governments, copyright – which rules culture – is probably the most autonomous one from national sovereignty.

Taking these two points together, I would argue that culture is more resistant to global control than many other domains, precisely because it is always difficult to define boundaries in cultural sense. Copyright, being a global regime designed to regulate culture, most pertinently reveals the difficulties of cultural control. Daily financial transactions are subject to global regulation largely because the practices can hardly be separable from the legal regime – they mutually condition each other. Copyright, in contrast, exercises less control than other legal forms, but over a broader range of culture. On the one hand, the international copyright regime increasingly defines the concept of creativity and regulates all cultural practices in contemporary cultural industries (Towse 2001: 35); on the other hand, copyright infringements are pandemic. While copyright is as complex as any global legal regime, specialized legal services are often not solicited where these cultural exchanges are actually taking place. Large publishers or media groups might have their own consultants on copyright issues, but the people who perpetuate "copying," like us making photocopies, unloading images, writing in reference to other works, performing music publicly, are remote from copyright law. If the new global order makes many previously unimagined transnational exchanges possible, the territorial boundaries of culture have always been transient, making any attempt at legal control extremely difficult. We copy in spite of and without regard for copyright.

It may be too easy to assert that copyright is largely an alien system superimposed on the realm of culture not so much to regulate culture itself as the capital to be gained from it. This book will explore the validity of this claim. We do know that constant negotiations between culture and capital make copyright a highly contested structure relentlessly and painstakingly justifying its legitimacy. We must address and recognize the power of copyright as an international legal regime, but we cannot equate acts of copying, which copyright is designed to regulate, to economic transactions within the global capitalist order. I believe that copyright communicates between the globalized culture industry and the actual cultural activities and transactions in extremely diversified and often irregular manners; and sometimes the control of copyright simply fails. In cultural and cinema studies, we have not paid enough attention to the legal control of culture. However, I am hesitant to take copyright too seriously, or to go so far as to assume that copyright actually dictates how culture works, although there is no doubt that contemporary culture can hardly be free of the influences of capital. In this book I do not take the approach of the political economist and elaborate on how major cultural institutions and media conglomerates run their businesses according to the rules and practices of powerful organizations like General Agreement on Tariffs and Trade (GATT) and the World Trade Organization (WTO). Instead I want to focus on actual happenings in our present globalizing cinema culture on the ground level, which are so complex as to mock the philosophical tidiness of the legal regime.

Specifically, I aim to study two different categories of copying in cinema and their interaction. I call the first type of copying *idea copying*, which refers to the copying of themes, styles, ideas, characters, or plots. They are acts or phenomena we call plagiarism, or appropriation, or simply tribute and homage. The second type is *direct product copying*, or simply *piracy*. The two categories of copying seem to concern vastly different issues and belong to two different domains of studying. The first category, idea copying, could easily be conceived as "influence studies" in traditional literary or film studies, in which scholars present concrete textual evidence to show which filmmakers influence, adopt, and transform other works – and how they do so. The second category of copying falls under the rubric of legal studies, media studies, or sociology – disciplines that treat the production, circulation, and reception of creative works as fixed products. Scholarship on idea copying is therefore often mostly textually oriented, whereas that on product piracy concerns larger social effects and structures. In other words, the two kinds of copying do not interact in our current scholarship.

But when it comes to Intellectual Property (IP) issues, we have no choice but to rely on interdisciplinary approaches (Lawrence Liang 2005). Both types of copying are under the control of the copyright regime, and I want to study them in reference to each other, with an eye to a new understanding of the current copyright regime. Here I propose two systems of influence to which both kinds of copying contribute and are subject to. First, our present global modernity has a strong tendency to level all cultural differences. Second, in spite of the unidirectional global control of copyright owners over copyright users, there are many undercurrents that are intractable and extremely diffuse. My task is to bring them together organically in order to show how cultural criticism can more proactively engage with the current copyright regime, in the sense that we can further explore what the regime highlights and represses, and where it succeeds and fails.

To further examine the two major systems of influence addressed above – global modernity and cultural diffusion through copying, in the following pages I will first examine them individually in the common framework of "identity vs differences," which are so complex that a single legal system like copyright can never systematize them. This introduction is meant to provide a general theoretical framework in which to ground subsequent analyses, and clear elaborations of specific concepts and phenomena will appear in the chapters that follow. I choose to focus on the discussion of "difference" in this introduction because copyright tremendously exploits the concept of originality in order to control and regulate the production and circulation of culture. The US Supreme Court has made it clear that "originality remains the *sine qua non* of copyright" (Halpern 2003: 150), in the sense that the individual expressions copyright protects are supposed to be original. But reading copyright's obsession with originality from another perspective, only the original – and therefore the absolutely different – can escape its control, because it is free from any previous influences (I will elaborate more on this chain of influences in the next section); yet such a concept of "newness" does not exist. If copyright is meant to promote new works, it also tames the propensity of the "original" – how can we develop a system of control if what is new necessarily follows no predetermined path and tends toward dissolution (Vattimo 1988: 105)?

The diffussion effects of copying

Although copyright is often described as a superimposed regulating system that alienates culture, the object of its control is central to culture: the act of copying is perhaps the single most important cultural activity. Copying and culture cannot be separated; cultural boundaries can never be rigidly drawn because culture is necessarily transformed by copying, which takes place everywhere all the time. As John Frow demonstrates, "... the paradox of the relation between first and second authors [defined by copyright] resides in the fact that all first authors are themselves always second authors, indebted to their predecessors in an endless chain" (2000: 183). "Copying" is the major driving force of culture, which informs both individual creativity and cultural heritage.

Few would disagree that mimesis is one of the most important concepts in Western literary and art criticism, with roots that can be traced back to Plato and Aristotle. The concept of mimesis has generated extensive discussion in the disciplines of literature, philosophy, and art in the last two millennia, crossing so many disciplinary boundaries as to be beyond the scope of this small section. But the concept of mimesis is extremely helpful to our understanding of the dynamics of identity and difference in the practice of copying. The tensions between identity and difference are central to the making of culture, and they make any clear demarcations of legal and illegal copying highly problematic.

Within Western aesthetics, mimesis is understood to be a representation of reality, so that it is broadly associated with any art that aims to signify or embody reality (Auerbach 1953). This definition can be traced back to Plato and Aristotle. In *Republic*, Plato criticizes poets for relying on mimesis and delivering poor and unreliable knowledge through their poetry. Plato argues that poetry is an imitation instead of a quest for real knowledge – as opposed to philosophy, which can lead to real wisdom (1974: 421–39). Plato's criticism of poetry as a mimetic act is both epistemological and moral, accusing the imitation – literature and art – of being ignorant of both reality and truth. Aristotle argues otherwise, as he values the praxis of artistic "creations" through mimetic acts (1970: 15–27). According to Aristotle, imitation is natural to man, and the human being is the most imitative creature in the world. Both define art as mimesis, but Plato considers the artist an imitator, whereas Aristotle sees him or her as creator. As Arne Melberg claims, "Aristotle made the poet into a 'second maker', with the same stress on both words" (1995: 47–8).

Linking mimesis to creativity and artistic agency, Aristotle introduces a concept of authorship that cannot be found in Plato.

For Plato, mimesis is passive, but for Aristotle, it is active – as it is through such active mimesis that the artist can assert a creative agency (Else 1986; Melberg 1995: 10–50). But their theories converge in their common belief in the production of difference during the process of mimesis. Plato is critical of mimesis because it produces difference, yet Aristotle celebrates mimesis for the same reason, as difference allows the artist to assert his or her individuality. According to Aristotle, the end products of mimesis are inevitably marked by the idiosyncrasies and efforts of the imitators. Although mimesis is considered an artistic act with the aim of perfectly replicating its object, differences are always produced.

This classical reading of mimesis has been attacked as uncritical formalism in some recent scholarship, because it naïvely sets up a direct connection between representation and reality (T. Cohen 1994). In fact, one can argue that one common agenda of the poststructuralist project is precisely to challenge such simple "mimetic" thinking. One of the central ideas in Martin Heidegger's *Being and Time* (1996), for example, is the argument that art is realized not through a harmonized matching of idea and appearance, or of representation and reality. The relation between a work of art and reality is not one of the former trying to conform to the latter, but one of unfolding, so that the conflicts between the work and reality are never exhausted. Heidegger's criticism does not reject mimesis as a process but as a product, so that by avoiding a reflectionist reading of art, we continue to wrestle with the process of mimesis as a core mechanism of culture. In other words, the concept of difference continues to define Heidegger's critical reading of mimesis.

I would argue that the acts of "becoming similar" always involve the efforts of coming to terms with difference, as some anthropologists demonstrate that overcoming mimesis helps people to discover kinship, confirm otherness, and affirm hierarchies.[1] Michael Taussig puts it plainly: "The ability to mime, and mime well, in other words, is the capacity to Other" (1993: 19). Mimesis is a unique human faculty to connect oneself with the Other, and the concept attracts the attention of some contemporary theorists interested in language because of the possible connections between the "differing" effect of mimesis and that of language.[2] Many poststructuralist scholars maintain that mimesis, particularly in the capacity of language, is a core dimension of humanity, which produces differences through painstaking but futile efforts to become the same.

Identity-difference dynamics are in fact core to the discussion of commodity culture and globalization. Analyzing our commodified entertainment culture, Theodor Adorno raises the classic model of the culture industry, which comprises dynamic interactions between "pseudo-individualization" and "standardization" (1991: 302–5). In popular music, according to Adorno, "standardization" allows listeners to identify immediately with new songs by recalling songs they have already heard, but through some slight variations from the norm – "pseudo-individualization" – the listeners forget that what they hear has already been heard for them. According to Adorno, all commodities are products based on similarities to and differences from previous commodities, and it is impossible to think of any cultural products as entirely new or old. The concept of trendiness is built precisely on the interplay between the familiar and the new that will best attract consumption.

Globalization adds the dimension of cultural difference to the culture industry's product diversification. While it is true that global culture has largely become homogenized, we should not equate the global penetration of Western culture with the automatic and total eradication of local particularities. As the term "glocalization" suggests, just as the global modifies the local, local practices have had a determinate impact on the global (Robertson 1992: 8). Glocalization deterritorializes by making people's life more "translocal" (Gabardi 2000: 33–4), so that the fluidity of global identity is dialectically constructed by the presence of discrete cultural identities. There are two common global corporate strategies: to tailor select commodities to local markets by changing their packaging or content – as demonstrated by the HSBC's claim to being the "World's Local Bank"; and to package "exotic" products for the consumption of the entire world – the most obvious example being Hollywood's appropriation of Chinese kung fu. The dynamics of "pseudo-individualization" and "standardization," therefore, also play out as cultural differences qua similarities. Cultural differences are both dissolved in and reinforced by the global commodification of culture.

Therefore, discourses of consumerism and globalization reinforce each other by presenting cultural products with interplays of identity and difference, making individual commodities more attractive to world consumers. This might particularly be so in the case of cinema, which is one of the most culturally complex products, and always demands different degrees of cultural deciphering. If the aforementioned scholarship on mimesis has demonstrated that the making of difference is inherent in human culture, today's commodity culture only reinforces this essential aspect of humanity, but with specific patterns and specific interests.

We thus return to our discussion of copyright. Concepts of mimesis can be related to today's copyright discourse on at least two levels: the chain of creation and technological change. While Plato and Aristotle hold different views on the value of mimesis, they see mimesis as a continuing process and do not privilege any one mimetic moment over another, so that all mimeses are passive to Plato while all are active to Aristotle. Copyright discourse also considers culture to be a chain, so that a work might borrow from existing works and influence works to come. The permission of the copyright holder must be sought if an existing work is to be copied, and this principle in theory applies to the creation of all new cultural works (to be discussed in Chapter 1). This means that, in theory, all copyrighted works are part of an endless chain of creation and copying. However, by focusing on the rights of the copyright holders rather than those of the users, copyright law tends to radically freeze the act of creativity at the moment when the product is introduced, conferring on it the status of intellectual property. As I will illustrate in Chapter 1, copyright is often conceptualized as existing at the moment of a work's creation, just as, in some theologies, the soul enters the body at birth. But we know that no cultural items can be "new" as such, and the extreme privileges copyright owners currently enjoy are sometimes unwarranted.

Furthermore, does today's new digital reproduction technology still allow for difference? Aristotle's artistic agency may no longer apply to today's copyright infringement cases, because often it is not human hands that do the copying – the "second maker" is no longer a person but a machine that deprives the copied work of any artistic aura (Benjamin 1968). Plato's denial of artistic agency in mimesis might better apply to contemporary digital culture, in which plagiarism is a matter of cut-and-paste that seemingly involves no human labor or intellect. Plato's philosophy is criticized for being indifferent to artistic values, but in an age of digitalization and extreme commercialization, maybe we can expand our understanding of copying or a work of art from one of purely aesthetic notions to focus on other social and ideological issues pertaining to its reproduction. In general, I believe that the production of "difference" is still a valid concern in contemporary reproduction technology as long as a "different" product is the result. However, the mediation and alteration process is no longer invested only with artistic values but also with many economic concerns, cultural values, and structures of feeling that are pertinent to our everyday culture. As I will show in the following chapters, the "differences" produced in pirated movies are often most significant not in an artistic sense but in their reflections of their embedding social/economic structures.

A recent book piracy case serves to demonstrate why we should expand our attention from artistic agency to other discursive matters to understand copyright infringement. Just before New Year's Day, 2005, Hong Kong police uncovered a case of book piracy, which today is nearly nonexistent. More than a thousand pirated copies of books by famous fortune-tellers were found; these books were the products of several different printers (*Mingpao* 2004). The covers of 2004 editions were replaced and the books were sold as 2005 editions. Some 2005 editions were copied in their entirety, but other more "creative" pirates rearranged certain pages to distinguish the pirated versions from the original volumes. The fortune-telling messages printed in the pirated copies, therefore, might be completely random and thus not reflect the actual predictions of their famous authors. This, I think, is an interesting case to foreground the issue of "authenticity" of the original, as – given the nature of fortune-telling – the original and the pirated versions could be equally random and inauthentic. Maybe by the end of the year some will find the pirated book more accurate than the authentic one. Obviously, in this case, differences were produced, although their significance no longer lies in the Aristotelian sense of human agency but in the nature or commercial value of both the original and the pirated versions. If so many theorists have found mimesis a fascinating concept because of the "differences" produced, my study is also based on similar interests, but I understand "culture" more broadly than art in its traditional sense.

Global modernity

Culture's will to copy, as mentioned earlier, is particularly fueled by the globalization process, which drives the world to desire similar but different products, to acquire similar but different tastes. Therefore, copyright's mission to systematize and regulate copying and culture is both structurally necessary and doomed to fail. It is a mistake to see the copyright regime simply as a functionalist tool with a transparent rationality, because it is caught up in the complex network of desire for "cultural control" in contemporary societies. This copyright Empire – if I may borrow the concept from Michael Hardt and Antonio Negri – is not stable; it is constantly and laboriously reshaping itself to cater to the loose and transient field of culture on the one hand, and all kinds of power discourses participating in this new global system of control on the other. In other words, in this copyright Empire, the international hierarchies of the people who hold copyrights and those who do not are shaped by complex legal and economic systems, so that the copyright regime is contested and unstable, yet highly homogenized and closely regulated. To understand the convoluted mechanisms of the copyright regime between its homogenizing mission and culture's resistance, we begin with two different models dealing with global cultural transactions.

In response to the post-Second World War postcolonial development and globalization, the United Nations Educational, Scientific and Cultural Organization (UNESCO) has addressed the urgency of cultural rights. This "right to culture" is mainly a response to the cultural imperialism of the past and the present global homogenization engineered by the mass media and commodity society. The concept of "culture" is therefore framed as the distinct "common heritage" of different groups of people. Specifically, UNESCO associates the right to culture with the right of the people to protect their own cultural identity and language, their national and international cultural heritage, and their moral and material interests in works of culture (Hamelink 2003: 10–21).

There is also the WTO model, which conceptualizes and regulates cultural exchanges according to the logic of capital, so that transnational cultural movements are desirable instead of barricaded. While the United Nations and most other international organizations operate on a voting system, the WTO relies on consensus to develop transnational agreements, which is claimed to be a fundamental democratic guarantee (Panitchpakdi 2001). However, this consensus-governance model has reinforced the structural power of developed countries, who can easily veto proposals they object to and coerce small states to accede to their global schemes. While the UN voting system and UNESCO's concept of cultural rights seems to recognize differences among cultures, the WTO's mechanism of consensus levels cultural differences, ensuring different nations move towards one hegemonic system.[3]

We know that both systems are inadequate to bring about a solution to today's extreme global inequality. While we can easily criticize the WTO for being US-centric, UNESCO's assertion of cultural rights is fragile. Some contemporary Marxist thinkers have reminded us of the danger of the almost cliché claim of "multiple modernities" – different cultures and nations seeking their own ways to achieve wealth and power – which the UNESCO version seems to imply. Arif Dirlik criticizes that such ideas run the risk of "slippage from an insistence on the contemporaneity of all societies . . . to the potential or actual 'modernness' of all such societies" (Dirlik 2003: 280). Dirlik demonstrates that by relativizing culture, one can easily dismiss the underlying capitalist global-hierarchical structure that privileges certain countries. Frederic Jameson also writes, sarcastically:

> Everyone knows the formula [of alternative modernities] by now: this means that there can be a modernity for everybody which is different from the standard

> or hegemonic Anglo-Saxon model. Whatever you dislike about the latter, including the subaltern position it leaves you in, can be effaced by the reassuring and "cultural" notion that you can fashion your own modernity differently, so that there can be a Latin-American kind, or an Indian kind or an African kind, and so forth.
>
> (2002: 12)

Both Dirlik and Jameson remind us that the world is still largely unequal, which is the result of capitalism. There might be different paths to modernity, but a clear system of hierarchy is in place. UNESCO's defensive rhetoric is made possible by dichotomizing a totalizing global power from the cultural realms that it desires to rule, thereby running the risk of idealizing the latter as stable and clearly demarcated, and also giving the illusion that individual groups of people can acquire economic and cultural wealth by curtailing the control of the homogenizing global powers. On the one hand, the WTO's mechanism of leveling all cultural differences and breaking cultural boundaries only reinforces a global capitalist hierarchy, which promotes the diffusion of certain Western values and living styles while it punishes the free and uncontrollable circulation of technology and capital around the world. We know that certain Western values, like individualism, may not travel freely, but some legal concepts do – for instance, Jacques Derrida uses the term "globalatinization" to demonstrate how certain Christian concepts, like forgiveness, are now widely circulated and adopted in international politics (1998: 29–30; 2001: 32). To return to Sassen's argument, if the new legal regime is a construct essential to the foundation of the emergent global system, such circulation of legal–moral concepts across cultures might be more powerful than specific finance-rating agencies.

Copyright is clearly one of those Western legal concepts regulating the current global hierarchy, allowing only the "legal" circulation of ideas and creativity and criminalizing those evading the capitalist order – all in the name of protecting cultural diversity. In other words, copyright echoes the concerns of both the WTO and UNESCO, proposing a "top-down transcultural structure" to promote one's "right to culture." As I will discuss in Chapter 1, today's copyright regime is inseparable from the WTO's global ascendancy. But the founding principle of copyright is supposedly based on the promotion of cultural diversity. One question this book explores is the relationship between the two senses of the world "culture" – culture as cultural productions and culture as national/regional cultures – within the framework of copyright. To propose what is perhaps a premature thesis here: copyright levels culture in the name of culture.

The American government has identified information-based industries as being among the country's most competitive international sectors. These industries were given a prominent position in US foreign economic policy, especially in Washington's attempts to promote free trade around the globe (Sum 2003). "Copyrighting" culture, therefore, is connected to the political economy of capitalist development in general and the United States' national interests in particular. If the United States is the cultural Empire, this Empire is maintained largely through the global copyright regime's ensuring that all players in the culture industry comply with its rules, thereby guaranteeing profits from the exportation of copyrighted property around the world. The global adoption of copyright concepts should also be considered acts of copying embedded in specific political conditions, in that everyone is trying to mimic the same proprietary manners in order to survive in the capitalist world. Echoing Dirlik's and Jameson's concerns, in terms of copyright there is no "alternative modernity" as such. For most of the developing countries, globalization, which promises material abundance only as remote rewards for the present suppression of local demands and cultural diversity, is too far away from the empty slogans of democracy and egalitarian civil society, reinforcing instead of diffusing the existing hierarchy. The global IP regime, of which copyright is a part, is one of the key discourses regulating this hierarchy: copyrighted or patented materials circulated from the developed countries to the rest are strictly defined by the reversed paths of capital and other interests of the developed countries.

As I mentioned, awareness of the determinant role played by politics and economy in shaping copyright discourse should not take away the materiality of the subject of control – culture. The painstaking and oftentimes unsuccessful efforts of the US government to legislate and enforce copyright laws around the world only prove how difficult it is to "tame" culture, and also demonstrate the significance of the study of copyright, which explores how these different discourses interact. I hope to illustrate that the nature of copyrightable materials and the diffusing globalization tendency make this global copyright order particularly difficult to maintain; or, borrowing the self-justifying rhetoric of Hardt and Negri, copyright demonstrates Empire's very logic of crisis, so that "[t]he creative forces of the multitude that sustain Empire are also capable of autonomously constructing counter-Empire" (2000: xv). While Hardt and Negri remain largely speculative, actual instances of copyright infringement demonstrate the structural weakness of the current IP regime. Assisted by the US government's diplomatic means, Hollywood invests lavishly in various copyright enterprises – including the colossal Motion Picture Association of America (MPAA) and its international counterpart, the Motion Picture Association (MPA) – to coerce other states to comply with its copyright principles and policies, prove infringement, and sanction copyright violators. In spite of their astronomical budgets, the MPAA and MPA are far from being able to achieve a reasonable degree of control over the global distribution of Hollywood films. Pirated movies abound on the Internet (in the developed world) or on cheap Video Compact Disc (VCD) copies (in developing countries). Contrary to the rosy picture some political economists paint of the power of copyright, major studios and record companies are expressing real anxiety about the threat of piracy.[4]

The discourse of copyright is always about the legitimacy of border crossing, as it carefully draws strict barricades to prevent others from stealing one's intellectual property. John Frow argues that while the rhetoric of globalization is about the removal of regulatory controls, Intellectual Property Rights (IPR) regimes demonstrate the opposite, in that they institute severe restrictions on cultural flows, thus threatening the public domain that is supposedly protected by IPR laws (Frow 2000). But Frow does not elaborate on the reversed logic, that the painstakingly harsh restrictions might indeed be results of the diffusive tendency of globalization and culture, which makes all boundaries difficult to maintain. I am not trying to posit a linear causal relationship prioritizing globalization's volatility; I would only like to state that copyright regulations and present deregulations are two parts of a dialectic. No doubt global copyright discourse works largely to protect and maintain a global hierarchy controlled by copyright holders, who are concentrated in the West; but the many failures and ambiguities of the legal system, and its constant competition with other discursive systems, also demonstrate how fragile and desperate this model is. One of the main indicators of Iraq's "liberation" after the arrival of the American troops was, ironically, the screening of pornographic films – which were simply taped from satellite television channels – in local theaters (Pax 2003). Different sets of criteria for modernity are competing against each other in this case, in that both copyright and modern ethics are seemingly happy to retreat a little bit to make way for "political freedom." Copyright is both powerful and powerless.

Copyright and cinema

Clearly, our global order is more porous than anything a clear-cut West–rest dichotomy could embrace. No one can really provide a macro-level theorization of globalization, as it necessarily manifests and signifies differently in different contexts. Globalization also often entails opposing functions, and in the specific domain of moviemaking it strengthens the hegemony of Hollywood while constantly creating new possibilities for others to usurp its power. To understand the complexity of copyright in actual cultural practice, contextualization is essential. I focus on cinema – specifically Asian cinema – because cinema is still the most complex work of art and the most expensive entertainment culture; furthermore, its specific production and distribution modes complicate copyright concepts that are usually taken for granted: ideas, originality, and authorship. Films now circulate among such culturally and geographically diverse markets traversing different classes that any single and totalizing view of fixation and reception must be thrown into question. We will come back to some specific situations in the following chapters. Here I would like only to emphasize that no single power really controls the entire film culture – even with the help of copyright.

Here is an example. While copyright discourse has always been considered an American tool to expand and protect its cultural industry, the changing copyright environment also works to harm American film production. In general, US legislative culture is leaning toward a thick copyright protection. More and more recent cases show the tendency toward idea protection (which will be further discussed in Chapter 1) through the introduction of the concept of "total concept and feel," which suggests that while particular ideas cannot be protected, a pattern of ideas can be, because the pattern is itself an expression (Vaidhyanathan 2001: 105–16). This is leading to increasing numbers of copyright accusations in the United States in recent years, resulting in a general reticence among film producers. Lawrence Lessig quotes the grievance of an American filmmaker who complains that under the current thick copyright control, filmmaking is becoming impossible:

> The film *Twelve Monkeys* was stopped by a court twenty-eight days after its release because an artist claimed a chair in the movie resembled a sketch of a piece of furniture that he had designed. The movie *Batman Forever* was threatened because

> the Batmobile drove through an allegedly copyrighted courtyard and the original architect demanded money before the film could be released. In 1998, a judge stopped the release of *The Devil's Advocate* for two days because a sculptor claimed his art was used in the background.
>
> (2001: 4)

The obsession with copyright leads to what Lessig calls a "suffocation of creativity," which is only one side of the Janus-faced plight Hollywood is currently facing: on the one hand, Hollywood studios are constantly troubled by domestic copyright lawsuits to the extent that, as Lessig argues, it is lawyers instead of filmmakers who control movie production (2001: 4); on the other hand, American studios are also pursuing tough worldwide anti-piracy campaigns in the name of protecting Hollywood's interests. From their perspective, Asian cinema poses some of the biggest challenges to the ideology and power of the current US-centric copyright discourse. Asian cinema has been a major source of inspiration among Hollywood filmmakers, and Asian countries are probably the greatest potential markets for Hollywood products. The ways copyright is practiced and infringed in Asia testify to the difficult yet urgent task of controlling an unruly culture.

This also explains my interests in the seemingly obsolete concept of "national cinema" in this book, which distantly echoes Sassen's interest in exploring the validity of national sovereignty in the present global system. In trying to uncover the complex politics of copyright and copying, this book inevitably confronts the concepts of national and transnational cinemas so controversial in contemporary cinema studies. I present examples of actual movie piracy and the survival tactics of different film industries throughout Asia as windows to the cultural and political dynamics between Hollywood and these Asian countries. Copying takes place at many levels in transnational cinema, ranging from the supposedly benign and productive "idea borrowing" to criminal piracy, which helps us to reconsider assumptions of copyright in general. Cinema deserves our fullest attention because it is still the most globalized cultural form, and its basic visual logic and narrative influence the development of many new media.

I agree with Jameson and Dirlik that "global modernity" should be singular, not plural: in spite of its various manifestations and fragmented expressions, these "diversities" are grounded on the same set of global conditions, regardless of the cultural roots different cultures lay claim to. However, I want to unearth some difficulties this global modernity has encountered in establishing and legitimizing itself, and I also want to keep this global system open in spite of its tremendous will to power. I hope that this book can demonstrate that any engaging analysis of copyright and piracy matters would reveal the intricate relationship between legality, culture, and commerce in today's capitalist-global world, and help us envision a culture with a higher degree of autonomy and resistance against hegemonic control.

About the book

As this introduction demonstrates, I use an interdisciplinary perspective to explore the concept of copyright as it relates to Asian cinema. In Chapters 1 and 2, I lay out the legal foundation of copyright, demonstrating its scope, power, and bases of legitimization. Those readers who already know the basics of copyright can skip Chapters 1 and 2. In the remaining four chapters, I demonstrate how cinema in Asia actually interacts with this legal discourse. The four chapters are grouped into two parts, which correspond to the two types of copying – idea copying and piracy – I mentioned in the beginning pages. In the first part I study the circulation and borrowing of ideas among different national cinemas; in the second part I focus on actual product piracy. The two ways of copying circulate on two very different circuits of cultural exchange, and I want to study the complicated relationships between them, using them to illustrate how problematic it is to apply concepts of copyright to any ethics of cultural creativity.

In Chapter 1, I outline the basic principles and impact of copyright legal discourse, and demonstrate how copyright is closely connected with some of the more distressing and complex matters those of us studying contemporary culture now face. This chapter is designed to give lay readers a general understanding of copyright, with the chief aim of explaining its relevance to cultural and social studies. I examine three major principles and contested areas that are central to the idea of copyright: ideas vs expression, originality and authorship, and fixation.

In Chapter 2, I continue to illustrate the basics of copyright, focusing not on its sovereignty but on allowable exceptions. There are only two major limitations on the exclusive rights of a copyright holder: the "first sale" doctrine and the concept of "fair use." They are exceptions to copyright rules, and they therefore demonstrate copyright's boundaries and limitations. Another key concept of copyright discourse is that of the public domain, which is an area copyright establishes in order to limit its own reach. In fact, the public domain is the most contested terrain in the copyright discourse, largely because it represents the area where the "ethics" of copyright advocates meet the "ethics" of the critics of copyright. These concepts deserve our careful analysis, as they demonstrate how copyright perfects itself by acknowledging, incorporating, or even creating its own limitations. Through an examination of the "ethics" inherent in copyright discourse, I also examine the ways in which copyright is transforming from a moral–legal discourse to a system of belief, which complicates its foundational principle of protecting and assisting the "public."

Chapter 3 shows how different Asian cinemas copy and circulate violence among themselves, questioning the limits of such basic copyright principles as expressions and originality, and also demonstrating how practices of copying made transcultural cinematic reception possible. Violence has become a major artistic inspiration and marketing niche for the branding of the New Asian Cinema. In the commercial cinema we see the fighting scenes of one film influencing another; among many new Asian art films we can also find a common style of presenting psychological and social violence. It is through such repetition of styles and violent content that the New Asian Cinema can be seen as having a quasi-unified transnational identity. Echoing my earlier discussion of mimesis, this chapter discusses how such copying of violence demonstrates the violence of the copyright discourse, which is designed to repress the mimetic tendency of culture. I also discuss how the transnational reception of cinematic violence might diffuse simple cultural dichotomies between the West and the rest.

Chapter 4 uses the film *Kill Bill* as a point of departure to demonstrate the many levels of exchanges copyright entails, in that the film – like most other Hollywood films – is itself a commodity widely pirated around Asia, yet it is also a creative work heavily inspired by previous Asian works. This case study also invites us to rethink the concept of Hollywood as a (trans)national cinema. The copyright regime reifies the national status of the commodity by criminalizing other countries pirating American products; the biggest irony is that the "Americanness" of *Kill Bill* is also defined by its shameless borrowing of works of other regional/national cinemas. The national identity of Hollywood is forged through transnational influences and transnational reception. Copyright discourse, however, chooses to be blind to the cultural traffic on the representation level and instead concerns itself only with the circulation of the final product.

In the Chapters 5 and 6, I use examples of Asian people pirating Hollywood movies to demonstrate the complex global politics of world cinema. If Hollywood has always been the biggest pirate in incorporating or plainly copying creative ideas from other national cinemas as I demonstrate in Chapter 4, in what ways can we critically study the widespread movie piracy in many Asian countries? Chapter 5 explores how digital technology provides the Asian people easy access to Hollywood films through piracy. Focusing on the VCD as movie carrier, I examine how ruthless and widespread movie piracy in Asia might offer an alternative way to view the global circulation and adoption of new technology. Asian people's systematic piracy of Hollywood movies might only demonstrate the products' global popularity. But at a time when we can hardly imagine a world cinema not dominated by Hollywood, can the Asian piracy scene provide us an alternative pathway to rethink the limits or limitlessness of Hollywood's global reign? This chapter also explores how "technology" is central to the development of copyright discourse, which is constantly redefined according to the latest technology available.

While Chapter 5 focuses on asking what Asian movie piracy means to Hollywood, Chapter 6 examines the meaning of movie piracy to the Chinese state and Chinese cinema. Chapter 6 demonstrates how movie piracy reveals the tensions between the Chinese state and the global market economy. After twenty years of complex development in China, the state and the market are now mutually constitutive yet fearful of each other. Cinema is an exemplary case in this regard, as the government's extremely tight surveillance on cinema reveals its immense anxiety about the market, making the concept of pure commercial cinema an impossible one. This irreducible distance between the government's ideological control and its audience's desire for varied entertainment directly promotes the piracy of Hollywood films in China. This chapter demonstrates how piracy is caught up in the power network of China as it merges into a global system, and of an authoritarian government struggling to cope with its evolving market economy.

1 Expressions, originality, and fixation

While copyright is arguably the single most powerful legal discourse governing commercial cultural activities around the globe, many of us studying contemporary culture are not familiar with its basic vocabulary and principles. This chapter is an overview of copyright fundamentals for the general reader, and it also clarifies specific concepts that are central to the arguments presented in later chapters. As a basic introduction, this chapter does not detail the history and related legal arguments of the entire copyright system. Instead, it focuses on the relevance of copyright discourse to the study of contemporary culture, and my illustrations of basic copyright concepts are drawn chiefly from legal-studies textbooks or handbooks (e.g. Johnston 1978; Miller and Davis 1983; Strong 1993; Fishman 1996; Elias 1999; J. Cohen 2002; McJohn 2003), selected academic writings, and on-line reference like the Wikipedia encyclopedia.[1] I want to demonstrate in this chapter how copyright, like many other contemporary legal discourses, is conceptualized and employed in the present commercial environment. From a cultural studies perspective, I find copyright to be caught up in its conflicting missions of protecting culture and maximizing profit: copyright becomes a platform on which different vested parties negotiate their interests, making it a highly unstable discourse.

TRIPs and the global IP system

The following account is meant to be an introduction to a global copyright regime, which, not surprisingly, revolves around US law, a legal system increasingly normative worldwide. Before elaborating on this copyright Empire, I wish to situate it in a larger global context in order to explain the connection between copyright and globalization. Copyright is one component of IPR law, which is arguably the most powerful and influential legal discourse in the new information economy. Most countries develop their IPR laws according to two sets of international conventions: the TRIPs Agreement and the World Intellectual Property Organization (WIPO) Copyright Treaty.

The Agreement on Trade-Related Aspects of Intellectual Property Rights, Including Trade in Counterfeit Goods (TRIPs Agreement) was added to the GATT at the end of the Uruguay Round of trade negotiations in 1994. TRIPs is widely quoted because it is probably the single most important international agreement pertinent to cultural globalization. After the Uruguay Round, GATT became the basis of the WTO. The ratification of TRIPs is a requirement for WTO membership; any country desiring easy access to the numerous international markets opened by the WTO must enact the very strict IPR laws mandated by TRIPs. TRIPs has become the common ground on which all nations base their own IPR laws. The UN also has its own body devoted to regulating and overseeing the global circulation of IP: the WIPO, which was set up in 1883 to ensure the worldwide protection of intellectual properties. But WIPO has been criticized by developed countries as slanting towards the interests of developing countries, which partly explains the development of WTO (Yang 2003: 77–8). The WIPO Copyright Treaty, adopted by the UN in 1996, stipulates additional copyright protections for the information age, specifically the protection of computer programs and databases.

The most powerful dimension of TRIPs and WIPO is arguably their international applicability. Both treaties are largely based on the Berne Convention for the Protection of Literary and Artistic Works (Berne Convention) – the first international copyright treaty.[2] The Berne Convention was developed at the instigation of such notables like Victor Hugo and was first adopted in 1886 (Starr 2004: 149).[3] Prior to the adoption of the Berne Convention, nations often refused to recognize copyrights held by foreign nationals, ostensibly to protect the best interests of their own people. But protection under the Berne Convention, and its revisions, is extended to works by nationals of any country on the sole condition that the first publication takes place in a Berne country: no registration is required (Johnston 1978: 226). Berne for the first time introduced copyright to an international scope; TRIPs and WIPO further bring the Berne Convention under the aegis of the WTO and the UN.

Under the global network of legal protection woven by TRIPs and WIPO, intellectual properties have become the most protected and valued assets. There are four components to IPR law: patents, trademarks, trade secrets, and copyright. A *patent* is granted to give the patentee – who has developed a new, useful, and nonobvious invention[4] – the right to make, use, or sell the invention to the absolute exclusion of others for the duration of the patent. The principle of a patent is to reward the investment of time, money, and effort associated with research. The limited term of a patent also encourages quick commercialization of inventions, thereby making them available to the public sooner. However, patents also often create unfair competition (Sell 2003: 64–7). The most controversial patent cases often involve agro-chemicals or pharmaceuticals, because they involve both astronomical profits for the biotechnology sector and the survival rights of citizens of developing countries (Curti 2001).

The original function of *trademark* was to indicate the origin of goods by identifying the craftsmen who produced them. As trademark might confer marketing advantage, the registration of trademark can protect the owner against the use of similar marks and any resultant confusion. A trademark may include any original combination of numbers, letters or other symbols, colors, or musical tones, and trademark law can be used to govern the advertising and product branding of a wide range of commercial activities. A *trade secret* is information that is secret, or is not general industry knowledge – such as the formula for Coca-Cola – which gives its owner an advantage over competitors. A trade secret, therefore, must have economic value.

These three types of IPR law relate specifically to manufactured goods, whereas *copyright* is much more abstract, as it covers the realm of cultural commodities. Copyright, as its name suggests, refers to the exclusive right of the author or copyright holder to make copies of the work; it also allows them control over derivative works. While different national laws might define copyrighted works in slightly different ways, in general, to secure copyright protection, the work must be "an original work of authorship fixated in a tangible medium of expression" (McJohn 2003: 10).[5] It means that a copyrighted work must be an expression instead of simply an idea, original and authored, and fixated in a tangible medium. These three areas cover almost all aspects of a cultural work – from the content of the work to its creation and publication, and they also demonstrate how far copyright's control can, or cannot, reach. The following sections illustrate the basic logic of these three criteria and their problems, and juxtapose legal concepts with more familiar concepts in cultural studies.

Ideas vs expressions

The major distinction between copyright and the other three types of IPR law lies in the concept of expression. While the other three types of law protect ideas, copyright protects expressions only – copyright's realm is the chaotic realm of culture. As Paul Goldstein states, "copyrights are much less fearsome than patents, which do protect ideas" (2003: 15). In fact, contemporary copyright debates and legislation often deal with the idea–expression dichotomy, which both legitimizes and limits the scope of copyright's cultural control. We can copy ideas but not the expression of them: while expression refers to the creative rendering of ideas, ideas cannot be privatized and owned by individuals; instead, they belong to the entire human race. In other words, the separation between idea and expression in copyright discourse is based on an exalted humanist ideal, which asserts that no one can claim the ownership of, and therefore economically exploit, a human thought, opinion, or concept – whereas human expressions are products of individual creativity, and should be protected and promoted.

This respect for public access to ideas while preventing the exploitation of one's creative expressions has two important implications for the general betterment of human culture. The first is that people's access to cultural products ensures the continual development of culture, which is achieved through the constant revisiting and re-examination of common universal ideas across generations and cultures. The second one is that by guarding the economic and artistic interests of individual creators, these individuals are given incentive to continue publishing and distributing new works.

In general, the dynamics of specific ideas rendered in infinite possibilities of expression mark the continuity and distinctness of human cultures. On the one hand, the sharing of ideas allows readers and viewers to understand cultural products made in historical moments and geographical spaces different from theirs, as the work and readers are connected by commonly understood ideas, which are supposedly historically and culturally transcendental. On the other hand, the constant renewal of expression encourages creativity and propels the progress of human culture.

Taken together, the constant rejuvenation of a set of ideas through new expressions allows cultural identities and individual authorships to differentiate against each other, while facilitating transcultural and transhistorical understanding. Many stories celebrate romantic love, but its expression in William Shakespeare's *Romeo and Juliet* differs from that in Cao Xueqin's *The Dream of the Red Chamber* in numerous ways, ranging from how lovers perform their suicides to how affections are communicated through poetry. But in theory, once knowledge of these expressive traditions is acquired, people of different cultures and different times can appreciate them both as masterpieces.

One problem immediately arises: How can one differentiate idea from expression? We will return to this idea–expression dichotomy throughout the book; here I outline two major practical and theoretical problems this idea–expression dichotomy faces today: one is economic, the other stylistic.

First of all, the principle that ideas are shared by all and should be accessible to all runs counter to today's late-capitalist economy, as new ideas are increasingly capitalized, aestheticized, and protected in order to generate profit. Commodities are generally fetishized by their "newness," and the competition for new ideas and expressions is particularly evident in the areas of advertising and Research and Development. In fact, the development of Western modernity can be seen as a history of exhibition and advertising; a commodity acquires "life" through new modes of display (Buck-Morss 1989; Richards 1991). Ideas and expressions become particularly important and non-differentiable in the area of product packaging and product promotion, as it is through a combination of the two that "life" is injected into commodities, and human desires – which are insatiable – can be triggered and fulfilled abstractedly through the fetishization of the "new."

The idea–expression dichotomy is most difficult to substantiate in the area where culture meets the information sector. In fact, a core foundation of the information age is IPR law, which establishes property rights and protects revenues generated from intangible commodities like expression and entertainment. The information-age market no longer deals in material commodities but in non-material ones like information and ideas. But the protection of information under copyright law has been highly controversial. The famous *Feist Publications v. Rural Telephone Service* case (1991) shows how the court system excludes certain information, or the organization of information, from the terrain of cultural expressions protected by copyright. To summarize the case: in 1987, a federal district court in Kansas, US, held that a white-page directory was entitled to copyright protection against a competing directory that reprinted many of the same names and telephone numbers, because the telephone company had spent time and money collecting those names and numbers. But four years later, the US Supreme Court overturned the lower court's decision, stating that there is nothing remotely creative about arranging names alphabetically in a telephone directory; therefore, the directory is not copyrightable.

In fact, the US Supreme Court decision to rule against the protection of databases is based on sound social considerations: the legal protection of databases can easily create a knowledge monopoly, thereby severely limiting the ways people can access and use information. This case is controversial because, by extension, the Supreme

Court ruled against the interests of the new information industry, which invests lavishly on packaging and organizing information in ways that are appealing to customers and user-friendly. Seemingly, it is not difficult to differentiate information and databases from cultural expression. Information is objective and factual, and provides the basis for knowledge; therefore, it belongs to the social domain. Expressions are subjective and creative, and provide entertainment or invite intellectual reflections, and therefore lie in the cultural domain. If copyright is meant to protect creative expression only, social facts and data should not be copyrightable. However, as the term "infotainment" suggests, information and entertainment increasingly rely on each other to raise their market values. Just as TV news programs are packaged as entertainment, other knowledge industries also need to present their products in an enjoyable manner. Today it would be difficult to find any form of information not elaborately designed and organized "expressively." The protection of information and databases is of utmost importance to the industries concerned.

In fact, today's cultural productions are themselves becoming too complicated to be properly governed by basic copyright vocabulary. One example is that of the virtual human – the digital clone of a living individual, such as actor Robert Patrick's liquid metal cyborg in *Terminator 2: Judgment Day* (dir. James Cameron, 1991). As long as the actor is not the creator of the digital clone, copyright laws only minimally protect the actor, who sometimes is extremely powerless to deal with exploitation of his/her clone; he or she must resort to database protection to provide legal protection of his or her images (Beard 2001). As a result of such rapid development of the digital culture and information society, industries and individuals have pushed new legislation to protect ideas and databases, resulting in the rapid expansion and overlapping of IPR laws. The European Union has already enacted laws to protect databases (Picker and Rual 2001), and the US Congress is also moving toward similar legislation, such as the 2003 "Database and Collections of Information Misappropriation Act" (Petty 2004). Many of these laws are not copyright laws, as they fundamentally challenge copyright's exclusive concerns in protecting creative expression. But information protection is clearly a matter of intangible materials, and no other domain of IPR law deals with it properly. Cases of non-expression protection, confusingly, often involve a complex web of trade-secret laws, unfair-competition laws, contractual obligations, and industry traditions, only to avoid the copyright law.

The use of other IPR laws to govern copyright issues reveals copyright's limits. By emphasizing the right of the public to access ideas, copyright prevents the entertainment and information industries from monopolizing culture; however, "culture" is one of the most profitable arenas in the new economy, and it constantly invites interested parties to trespass on its domain. This has created the confusing legal enviornment in which the basic idea–expression dichotomy of copyright remains unchallenged, while ideas can be protected as commercial property. In fact, one of the reasons for the very rapid and complex expansion of the IPR legal regime is due to copyright's explicit protection of creative expression only, so that negotiators of the culture industry need to promote other IPR laws to cover obvious loopholes. The rationale behind these legal developments is largely economic, explaining some of the controversies created around copyright issues that should be culturally based. The increasing reliance on other laws to tackle copyright issues only demonstrates the powerful internal contradictions within legal discourse.

In terms of form, the distinction between idea and expression is also highly problematic. Theoretically, no pure "ideas" can be communicated without some "expressive" form. When we want to explore the concept of "love," the idea must be conveyed in some formal vehicle, be it prose, poetry, music, or drama. This dilemma is particularly evident and problematic for those contemporary works whose playfulness of style is more important than the central ideas expressed in them. This is most clearly seen in the case of rap songs. On the one hand, music, more than any other vehicle of culture, collapses the separation between idea and expression. How can a musical "idea" be separable from musical "expression," if the "idea" in music is always abstractly constructed by learned cultural understanding of specific musical forms? On the other hand, the hip-hop tradition distinguishes itself from dominant Western musical forms by sampling, parodying, and remaking previously released music instead of producing original "creations," as such, of their own. Copyright law does not protect, but often stifles, creativity in rap music.[6] As Siva Vaidhyanathan laments:

> So by the late 1990s, rap artists without the support of a major record company and its lawyers, without a large pool of money to pay license fees for samples, had a choice: either don't sample, or don't market new music.
>
> (2001: 133)

Similar situations can be found in many other contemporary art forms in which "expression" takes precedence over "idea," like architecture dance.

No one can provide comprehensive tests to distinguish idea from expression, culturally or legally, although many have tried. "No one really knows [how to clearly differentiate ideas from expressions], though many a court has formulated an all-embracing theory, only to see it discarded by the next court" (Strong 1993: 14). The intertextual form of rap music is not the only cultural form that creates confusion; almost all forms demonstrate different levels of complexity in the separation of expression and idea: To what extent can an architect claim that his specific "architectural expressions" are original if buildings always involve technical and functional similarities? Can a movie character be copyrightable? There are always basic movements in dance vocabularies; to what extent can a combination of steps be considered a new idea? In what ways we can protect fan culture and encourage fans appropriating and reworking their favorite comic books? (Lessig 2004: 25–8.)

The list of potential questions goes on, and there are many real and spectacular cases that demonstrate the many practical difficulties of exercising this key principle of copyright. This idea–expression dichotomy rests partly on the assumption that certain core aspects of an idea exist and signify, irrespective of how they are expressed, so that love is love whether it is presented in *Romeo and Juliet* or in *The Dream of the Red Chamber*. But poststructuralist theorists have already taught us the opposite: there are no transcendental ideas as such – they are always caught up in the network of power existing among us. Representation and textuality are never naïve but political and polysemous (e.g. Derrida 1978; Hutcheon 1989; Barthes 1991); mutatis mutandis, idea and expression – or, to put it in a slightly different way, content and form – are always mutually conditioning, constantly interacting with surrounding sociopolitical discourses to define and change their meanings. This complex relationship between ideas and expressions is particularly emphasized in contemporary works with "postmodernist" elements.

We are also seeing some "postmodernist" tendencies in commercial cinema, specifically in the decreasing importance of narrative. Some scholars argue that today's Hollywood films have returned to a primordial form of commercial cinema – that is, cinema of attractions, as they rely less and less on narrative to anchor global or domestic audiences, particularly the younger ones who have grown up in the age of MTV. Film theorists like Tom Gunning and Miriam Hansen have demonstrated convincingly that the attraction of early films to spectators lay predominantly in the exhibitionist display of events and actions (Gunning 1989, 1994; M. Hansen 1994). When Hollywood entered its studio era in the 1920s, the cinema of attractions was gradually replaced by narrative films that stressed realistic motivations (Bordwell *et al.* 1985), but the collapse of the Hollywood studio system in the 1960s led the American film industry to revive the cinema of attractions, imbuing world cinema with sensational excitement (Hozic 2000; L. Williams 2000).

Today, more and more contemporary Hollywood films feature either a succession of visual and auditory shocks and thrills, or fragmented storylines or character traits that mock classical Hollywood cinema's respect for narrative and character unity. As Robert Stam claims, "In the postmodern 'allusionist'...cinema of Tarantino, causality and motivation are trivialized; here characters kill not out of any 'project' but rather through accident (*Pulp Fiction*) or due to a fleeting impulse or momentary irritation (*Jackie Brown*)" (2000: 318). The differentiation between ideas and expressions on the formal dimension is increasingly difficult. I would argue, which some might not agree, that viewers are attracted to, for example, the *Matrix* series more because of the spectacular digital effects and action designs than because of the ideas of human liberation or the computer network as ideological apparatus explored in the film. As current commercial films are increasingly moving away from Hollywood's classic form, which appeals to viewers with careful plots or reasoning, most of the copyright issues in today's commercial cinema involve matters of expression. Plagiarizing ideas becomes less economically attractive than wrestling with digital effects, action scenes, or characters' images. If industries or individuals are pushing copyright's range of protection to commodities other than expression, we are also seeing the increasing difficulty of finding any commodity that is not composed or packaged in some form of creative expression; thus every commodity is theoretically copyrightable.

To conclude this section on copyright's role in advancing human culture, I want to emphasize that the promotion of the richness of human expression is not only a legal concept but also a core concern in modern critical thought. According to Karl Marx, the individual proves himself an independent social being by demonstrating a rich expression and confirmation of social life. A socially conscious man "exists in reality as the contemplation and true enjoyment of social existence and as a totality of vital human expression" (1975: 351). To Marx, the authentic human is the one who is "rich in needs." But the truly "rich man" is not the possessor of money or someone who craves material wealth but "the man in need of a totality of vital human expressions" (1975: 356). The quality of one's expressions, according to Marx, determines the quality of one's being, whether alienated or liberated. The celebration of human expressions is also central to Heidegger's thought, whose foundational concepts of "becoming" and "*techne*" are based on his belief in the liberating power poetry and art brings to humankind. Poetry is freedom, and freedom can only be achieved through human creative expression (Heidegger 1971, 1977). Similarly, expression can also be seen as a key thread running through Deleuzian thought, in which the variations of different forms of human thought and art – and by extension, those of the entire natural world – can be seen as different expressions of different creative forces (Deleuze and Guattari 1994). Accordingly, copyright, like many other legal systems, is not designed to alienate humanity but, in principle, to protect its full development. Negative descriptions of the new global legal regime as necessarily political and commercialist might not do it justice. But, as described above, the legal system is a site of extreme contestations, and it is particularly prone to manipulation by the powerful. Copyright will continue to be a site of wrestling among many vested parties in the arenas of culture and economy.

Originality and authorship

While neither Berne nor TRIPs imposes any requirement of originality or creativity, nearly all countries require some level of creativity as a prerequisite for copyright protection (J. Cohen *et al.* 2002: 75). Generally speaking, the notion of "originality" in copyright discourse has two distinct components. The work must first be independently created by the author, and second, must involve some degree of creativity. Therefore, originality alone is not sufficient to qualify a work for copyright protection. Facts and theories are not copyrightable because they are simply "discovered" instead of "created," although they might be original findings. Scientific discoveries, mathematical equations, and academic theories are not copyrightable, but if they have economic value, one might seek other forms of IPR protection, such as trade-secret protection. It also explains why telephone books or other databases are in principle not copyrightable.

To fulfill this second copyright prerequisite, "originality" and "creativity" cannot be separated, hence the importance of the concept of "authorship" in copyright discourse. A person who has "discovered" an unpublished manuscript cannot own its copyright, because he or she did not write it, and has not been granted copyright by the real author. On the other hand, if a musician creates a piece of music that, by coincidence, resembles one created years ago, the musician can still claim copyright of the work as long as the musician can prove that he or she had never heard the first piece of music or does not intend to infringe its copyright. Creativity defines authorship. As Strong argues, T.S. Eliot's *The Waste Land* is clearly a copyrightable poem, even though many of its lines are taken from works that are in the public domain.[7] Its originality lies in Eliot's creative juxtaposition of these elements (Strong 1993: 4). Therefore, a derivative work, like a film adaptation of a novel, is copyrightable because adaptation requires artistic skill and effort, although the adaptation could still be an infringement of the original work if the film producer did not seek permission from the novelist. In this case, the two works maintain two sets of copyright. But in general, most derivative works, including translations, acquire a narrowly defined scope of copyright to avoid encroaching on the rights of the author of the original.

Copyright, therefore, can be seen as a concept developed to "secure special conditions, status, and recognition for the creative worker as author" (Lury 1993: 26). In order to claim a work is copyrightable, or to protect one's work against the charge of copyright infringement of another work, the work has to demonstrate the originality and creativity exercised by its author. This celebration of authorship seems simple and straightforward enough to demand no further clarification. But the complexity of this concept of authorship lies not only in the quantitative measure of "enough" originality and creativity, which oftentimes can only be settled in court, but also in how concepts like authorship or originality are constructed. As I mentioned in the introduction, copyright at its core concerns copies and not originals; our culture industry cares the most about copies, as it is through the sale of these copies that huge profits can be reaped. But the original and the author still matter, for they attract the people who buy the copies. Copyright works precisely to protect the author of the original, or whoever obtains the copyright, so that his or her interests are best served. In other words, by regulating the trafficking of the copies, copyright reifies the original and its creator. To view this idea in an opposite but equally valid way, in the name of protecting authorship, copyright's real object of concern is the copies.

In order to better understand how copyright conceptualizes authorship, we need to examine its history. The US copyright system, which is based on the English common law system, can be traced back to the seventeenth-century trade regulations set up by the Stationers' Company, to which all publishers and printers in the United Kingdom belonged. This system was not law but a set of trade rules within the guild, which served the interests of the publishers rather than those of the authors. In response to Stationers' trade regulations that heavily favored publishers, a new copyright system – the "Statute of Anne" – was enacted in 1710; it was designed to curtail the monopoly of the publishers and to highlight the rights of the author. The common-law concept of copyright has since its beginning negotiated the struggle between publishers' rights and authors' rights (Patterson 1968: 1–20).

TRIPs incorporated all of the Berne Convention's standards except that of moral right (J. Cohen *et al.* 2002: 57–8), giving individual countries latitude to balance publishers' rights and authors' rights. Moral right – *droit moral* – entitles authors to maintain control over what they create, and to keep anyone – even their own publishers – from changing their works in any way that might affect their artistic reputation. In general, US law tends to protect the publisher or distributor, while European copyright law sanctifies the rights of the author (Strong 1993: 129–30; Goldstein 2003: 135–61). The US moviemaking industry is particularly vocal in its opposition to the moral right tradition.[8] US copyright law includes the category of "works made for hire," for which the employer, not the employee, is considered the author. There have been recent court cases about the applicablity of the "works for hire" doctrine in university lecture materials: should the lecturer or his or her employer be the copyright owner of the lecture materials? (McSherry 2001: 101–43). Not surprisingly, it was an American film entrepreneur, D.W. Griffith, who first developed and practiced this contractual arrangement (Vaidhyanathan 2001: 101), and Hollywood continues to rely heavily on this "works for hire" doctrine. Moviemaking is probably the creative industry that involves the largest numbers of "authors" producing the widest variety of creative components – music, set designs, editing, costumes, and so on – in one single work. A film's copyright owner is often the studio; as employees of the studio, the playwrights, art directors, and costume designers cannot claim copyright for their own creations. The *droit moral* tradition is antithetical to the current practice of film production companies, who buy screenplays from writers and retain the right to make any changes they see fit.

This tug-of-war between publishers' and authors' rights in terms of economic return does not provide us more in-depth understanding of the concept of authorship. In modern critical thought, the notion of authorship itself has been heavily criticized, both in the Marxist tradition and by poststructuralist critics. According to Marx and Engels, the concept of authorship implies a celebration of creativity, contributing to the myth of the autonomous, individual artistic genius. This myth is further reified by capitalism's division of labor, so that the ability of the masses is suppressed by the exclusive concentration of talent in particular individuals (Marx and Engels 1970: 109). Copyright allows a small number of artists to become superstars, thereby concentrating social resources in a few hands. Raymond Williams states more clearly the direct relationship among authorship, copyright, and capitalism:

> In the modern period there is an observable relation between the idea of an author and the idea of "literary property": notably in the organization of authors to protect their work, by copyright and similar means, within a bourgeois market.
> (1977: 192)

In the Marxist tradition, Williams criticizes the bourgeois concept of the author as an autonomous individual, who in fact is always a social being, which means that the contents of his or her consciousness are necessarily socially produced. This view is also echoed by Michel Foucault, who argues that an author, as we understand it, is not the individual writer but a historically unstable function caught between forces, discourses, and power. He dates the emergence of authorship at the point at which writers entered the system of property that characterizes our society, so that the term "author-function" might be a more accurate term than "author" to describe the discursive effects of authorship (Foucault 1977).

The recent conversion of many post-Socialist countries to capitalist economies presents many controversial cases that demonstrate how concepts of individual authorship are intertwined with sociopolitical maneuvering. The IP system could not be tolerated in a planned economy under the rule of the Chinese Communist Party (CCP). When all the privately owned land and enterprises were allegedly nationalized by the late 1950s, private ownership was theoretically impossible, and so were all IPR laws (Alford 1995: 56–61). The entire cultural sphere became a huge public domain. As the 1963 *Regulations on Awards for Inventions* (*Faming jiangli liaoli*) clearly state: "All inventions are national assets, any individuals and organizations are not allowed to apply for a monopoly. All the organizations across the country, including collectively owned enterprises can use them" (D. Yang 2003: 22). In fact, this socialist notion of common property is allegedly complementary to traditional Confucian thinking, which also values intellectual sharing and has historically developed an artistic vocabulary (Alford 1995: 19–28; D. Chow 2003: 410–11). However, after the introduction of the Open Door Policy, when the cultural market became a lucrative one, and imported concepts of copyright began to gain currency, legal cases against copyright infringement also began to emerge. For a socialist country like China, can legal doctrines like copyright be retroactive to a period when the concept was not in use? Peter Jaszi argues that modern copyright law fails to come to terms with the reality of even more obvious forms of literary and artistic collaboration in the West (1994: 50). The copyright law of the People's Republic of China (PRC), which was not fully enacted until 1990 (Feng 2003: 65–7), inevitably was handicapped to deal with collective creation which was norm to Socialist China. Just two decades earlier, property – particularly IP – was a concept severely criticized and deliberately suppressed under Mao, and claiming property rights at that time was criminal. Any attempt to retrace IPR to this period is a violent forgetfulness of history, fabricating a certain rationality of the law, which in fact cannot transcend the specific historical circumstances that engender it (Feng 2004: 65). But how can any comprehensive copyright system in China afford to ignore the protection of any work created before 1990?

Concepts of authorship are not only historically but also culturally specific. Peter Feng's criticism of the *ex post facto* practice of copyright law in China can be extended to a postcolonial critique, questioning those using Western legal concepts to criminalize actions that are not considered crimes where they are committed. Marilyn Randall uses the case of Yambo Ouologuem's *Le Devoir de violence* (*Bound to Violence*), which earned the important French Prix Renaudot before it was labeled a plagiarism, to demonstrate how the case highlights the postcolonial problems of Western copyright law. "Either an intentionally dishonest act of an untalented African student in Paris, or a brilliant politically committed gesture of reverse colonialism . . . , the novel now stands as an exemplar of postcolonial oppositional discourse" (1999: 136–7). Randall states that instead of being a legal doctrine that rules supreme, copyright should be seen as a discursive strategy for gaining dominance in a struggle for cultural power (1999: 139). Feng's criticism highlights the temporal (in)effectiveness of copyright, while Randall emphasizes spatial and cultural distance. Together they remind us of the specific confines of current copyright discourse, and how problematic it is to treat this discourse as global and transcendental.

In fact, even within the tradition of Western civilization, the idea that an author has some natural right to his or her creations has always been a constructed one. Many scholars argue that copyright is an outgrowth or the ground of the Romanticist conception of the author, whose creativity is seen as individual rather than collective (Woodmansee 1984; Rose 1988). According to Gilbert Larochelle, Immanuel Kant – perhaps the first Western philosopher to develop a general theory of authorship – proposes the new normative framework of the intellectual property, synthesizing the two originally separate entities – owner and property – together in the creative work, so that the author and the work for the first time become indivisible in the newly developed legal and moral concept (Larochelle 1999: 122–4). This concept of intellectual property jointly developed by writers, philosophers, and economists in the eighteenth century discursively establishes an artificial link between the author and the work, which has not been systematically challenged until the twentieth century.

One of the most widely circulating poststructuralist slogans is that of the death of the author. Roland Barthes announces that only when the author enters into his own death does writing begin (1977: 142). Via Levinas, Jacques Derrida urges his readers to kill the Greek father as the ultimate authority of writing as a form of unity (1978: 89). Challenging Kant's convergence of the author and "his" work, both Barthes and Derrida demonstrate the opposite, that the writer can never fully control the text. Adding the dimension of "writing as difference" to Kant's epistemology, they argue that all writing is polysemous and continually unfolds to escape control. While Marxist theorists concentrate on the external social circumstances that influence a work, poststructuralists maintain the internal structure of differences in textuality and believe that all meanings are based on their prior existence and their ongoing reproduction. The Marxists and the poststructuralists merge in their common belief that no author can claim complete control of his or her works, so that concepts of property are always problematic with regard to representations and textuality.

It seems easy to infer the uselessness of Marxist and poststructuralist thought in current copyright disputes: without the concept of authorship, how can we protect individual creators whose works are increasingly controlled and exploited by big corporations? It is unrealistic to promote such abstract concepts as "writing as difference" in the game of capitalism, whose maneuvering is based not on abstract principles but on the careful calculation of the balance of interests among various parties. But these critical thoughts can provide a radical model that demonstrates the artificiality of the calculations on which copyright law is based. This artificiality is built upon the assumption that, first, culture can be practiced and quantified economically, and second, the ontological concept of authorship is not only natural but can be measured and divided. While the conflicts between, for example, the rights of the publisher and the rights of the author are often based on negotiations of the division of the work's ownership, these imaginative calculations can never be fair and complete because a cultural commodity is also a social and textual product: it is implicated by and in many other social discourses, and its own differentiation always escapes the control of the author and the publisher.

The "originality" doctrine, like the "idea–expression" dichotomy, might be morally sound, but it is thorny both in its philosophy and in its practice. The most problematic dimension of the "originality" requirement in our late-capitalist economy is the intimate links between creativities and profits. Original creative works – if they are profit-generating – are often caught up in elaborate industrial maneuvering and marketing packages, meaning that the efforts invested in the work comprise not only the author's labor and creativity but many other economic and aesthetic investments. While copyright, as discussed earlier, is designed to establish the legitimacy of an author, distributors create the "works made for hire" doctrine and different kinds of contractual agreements to allow an author to transfer all rights in a work to someone else, which indirectly, or practically, eliminates the entire construct of authorship.

Marxist and poststructuralist critiques of authorship demonstrate how many loaded economic and cultural issues we must ignore in order to arrive at any copyright deliberation. Simply conceiving the legal development of copyright as a set of rational considerations balancing, for example, author's rights against publisher's rights, radically simplifies the complex discursive field of competing powers, and also explains the many controversies created around copyright and its constant remaking. In the global campaigns of major Hollywood studios and record companies fighting against pirated movies and songs, the real motive has little to do with the concept of originality. These cultural commodities have to be popular enough to be deemed worth pirating; therefore they are not particularly original. What matters for cultural commodities is less the authorship than it is the capital invested in the packaging and marketing of the original products. We will come back to issues of piracy in the following chapters.

The fictitiousness of originality and authorship is particularly evident in cinema as a mass entertainment. Auteur theory came to dominate film criticism and theory in the 1950s and 1960s, when theorists like François Truffaut (1954) and André Bazin (1967) attempted to elevate the status of cinema from an entertainment to an art in its own right, and they identified key directors as creative artists with their own stylistic marks on their films. However, very few film scholars nowadays are engaged in auteur theory; it is considered obsolete and not applicable to actual moviemaking, which is more a commercial enterprise than a purely artistic endeavor, and cinema as a cultural activity involves many more agencies than just the director. The dominating theoretical approaches in contemporary film studies – psychoanalysis, cultural studies, and cognitive psychology – also discourage us from studying Romantic paradigms of creativity and individual freewill. Instead, the focus is on audiences and interpretations, which are relatively independent from the intention or control of the author.

Some of the following chapters will deal more specifically how to cope with the matter of authorship in cinema under the copyright framework. If the notion of authorship is obsolete in film scholarship, the exchange value of a director's name is still very high in the market place. Viewers are attracted to films based on the names of, say, Wong Kar-wai, James Cameron, or Pedro Almodóvar. The notion of national cinema also implies a strong collective authorial agency. For example, David Bordwell (2000) argues that Hong Kong cinema is unique in that it manifests some kind of auteurism of the city-collective with the specific blending of art and commerce, implying a collective identity/authorship of the vast numbers of films produced in the city. While both the concepts of auteur and national cinemas are under some theoretical attack, they are still widely circulated in movie markets. What I would like to emphasize here is that the notion of authorship and originality in contemporary culture is not an ontological given nor an ethical obligation, but a function, as Foucault has argued, that is embedded in specific discourses and power. The many debates about the definitions of authorship and originality only prove that these concepts in their pure forms do not exist. In copyright discourse, what matters is really not original authorship as such, but how much each cultural creation is original or a repetition, and how much a new work bears similarities and is indebted to preexisting ones.

Fixation

This leads us to the third criterion of copyright, which no longer concerns the conception of the work but its ability to circulate: fixation differentiates between published and unpublished works.

While the other three types of IP protection can be granted only after the works are successfully registered, copyright comes naturally to the author when the work is created. Theoretically speaking, there is no need to obtain approval, a prior art search, or registration by any agency to qualify for copyright protection. The Berne Convention generally assumes that copyright requires no prior form of registration, and it leaves the decision about whether to require fixation to each of the member countries; neither the WIPO nor TRIPs mentions fixation (J. Cohen *et al.* 2002: 65). In fact, TRIPs states clearly that copyright must be granted automatically, and not based upon any "formality," such as registration or systems of renewal.

In principle, unpublished works should receive the same amount of protection as published ones; but we can imagine the difficulties of enforcing the protection of pure ideas not fixated in tangible forms, as, for example, in the case of a musician trying to accuse others of stealing work that is still in his or her head. Therefore, an author's rights to his or her unpublished works are curbed in many countries. There is still a requirement in the United States to deposit two copies of a copyrighted work with the US Library of Congress, although US law also honors the principle that copyright is granted with no formality required, however contradictory that may seem.

There are currently two systems in US copyright law: "common law" protects the right of an author to all of his or her creations, published or not; and "statutory" copyright is secured upon publication under federal law. But US federal law very severely restricts common law protection of unpublished materials (Miller and Davis 1983: 279–81; Strong 1993: 3). In order to be a signatory to the Berne Convention, the United States revised its copyright act to exclude deposit as a necessary condition of copyright protection. But the deposit requirement is still maintained on the statutory level because registration and deposit do have significant legal consequences, as an owner cannot sue for copyright infringement until he or she has official evidence that the work was created before the infringement (Elias 1999: 147). The two laws seem to contradict each other, but they are enacted to satisfy two different legal principles: that copyright needs no registration, and that fixation serves important evidentiary functions. Copyright law is full of contradictions; this double-standard on registration is only one among many. We will further examine copyright's volatility in the next chapter.

The means of fixation can be varied: a musical work can be fixated on a piece of sheet or a compact disc (CD), but in general having a commodifiable and communicable form is a precondition of copyright protection. This demand for fixation reveals most clearly that copyright is not a philosophical doctrine to be used in speculative situations but one designed to regulate real commercial activities. As I mentioned in the beginning of the chapter, to qualify for copyright, the work must be an original work of authorship fixated in a tangible medium of expression. Of the three qualifications, "expression" and "originality" are abstract principles, while "fixation" is a material quality that allows the actual copying to take place. Copyright, therefore, does not end but begins with fixation, as the real concern of copyright is not creation but infringement – not the definition of authorship but the regulation of product reproduction and distribution. It is only after the work has been fixated in tangible form that it can be copied.

It is also in the area of fixation that technology emerges as one of the factors most challenging to existing copyright laws. When the player–piano roll was developed shortly before the turn of the twentieth century, then-current law failed to protect the musical compositions it represented due to this novel fixation mode that the law did not grasp (J. Cohen *et al.* 2002: 65). The development of radio broadcasting also introduced a completely new environment of fixation and royalty collection that the law at that time failed to comprehend (Streeter 1994). In the entertainment industry, new technologies are developed to provide new sensations, constantly exploring new terrains through which to expand the entertainment experience. In other words, one duty of the entertainment business is precisely to challenge the meaning of "fixation"; the law is doomed to lag behind. We will talk more about technology in Chapter 5.

This problem of "fixation" is particularly obvious in the digital age, which is known for its tendency against standardization and tangibility in order to achieve the greatest degree of interactivity. We can assume that in interactive video games the same interaction may never recur. So are these "expressions" stable enough to be copyrightable? Interactive computer media seem to evade all forms of fixation in order to achieve infinite possibilities of virtuality, which might force the entire copyright law to be reconceptualized. But this interactivity, according to Lev Manovich, is based on a modern desire to externalize, objectify, and therefore to fix the mind: "The very principle of hyperlinking, which forms the basis of interactive media, objectifies the process of association, often taken to be central to human thinking.... In short, we are asked to follow pre-programmed, objectively existing associations" (2001: 53). Manovich points to the myth of interactivity, and he reminds us that digital media are not liberating but fixing our minds by asking the computer user to follow the mental trajectory of the designer. Both the minds of the player and the designer are standardized instead of set free. Digital technology only reinforces and facilitates the modern desire to capture one's subjectivity (Debord 1995; Crary 2001). The computer program, no matter how different it is from existing cultural forms, is a means to control human minds through fixed cultural expressions. To put it another way, regardless of the extent of technological development, the concept of fixation will not be outdated in modern society, as objectification and manipulation continue to be the most basic driving forces of modernity.

2 Copyright's limits and ethics

In the previous chapter, I demonstrated the three major criteria that define the scope of copyright protection. Almost all cultural works meeting these criteria can be copyrighted and therefore are protected by law. As Strong claims: "Once the three basic requirements of fixation, originality, and expression are met, the law's protection, though not universal, is extremely broad" (1993: 15). One might be surprised to note the large number of cultural works that meet all three of these seemingly highly restrictive criteria, and the law confers on the copyright holder a wide range of exclusive rights to the product, including the right of reproduction; the right to make derivative works; distribution rights; performance rights; and display rights.

There are only two major limitations on the exclusive rights of a copyright holder: the "first sale" doctrine and the concept of "fair use."[1] In addition to these two major exceptions, a specific space is also maintained in copyright law – the "public domain," over which copyright deliberately relinquishes its control. In this chapter I will examine these exceptions and how they delineate copyright's scope of manipulation. These exceptions demonstrate the limitations and the limitlessness of copyright discourse in its dialectical fashion, as it is copyright law itself which grants and defines these exceptions, so that even the exceptions are legitimized and confined by official discourse. By recognizing its own limits, the copyright law attempts to be all-encompassing. These tolerable exceptions also indirectly reflect the intolerable: anything beyond the borders of fair use and the public domain is not an exception but a real threat that must be annihilated at all costs. A discussion of the ambiguities of these exceptions in copyright law brings us to the second part of the chapter, in which I examine the ways in which we can understand copyright's "ethics." As I have illustrated thus far, copyright law is based on sound ethical principles with the aim of balancing protection and freedom, giving contemporary culture an optimal commercial environment to grow. Many of these principles are based on Enlightenment ideals, although copyright law is also one of the most turbid and contrived of today's major international regimes. I will discuss in the second part of the chapter how we can come to terms with the contradictory nature of the law.

"First sale" and "fair use"

"First sale" and "fair use" (or "fair dealing" in the United Kingdom), demonstrate two major ways copyright balances the interests of copyright holders and other users – the buyers of the copies, and subsequent authors who refer to, or are inspired by, the original work. The "first sale" doctrine applies to persons who acquire ownership of copies of the work, but it does not apply to those possessing the copies only temporarily. Therefore, it applies to a buyer of a Digital Video Disc (DVD) but not a person who has paid a rental fee to view it temporarily. The "first sale" doctrine authorizes the buyer to continue to sell or transfer the ownership of the copy he owns, but he or she is not allowed to copy the work, which infringes the rights of the real copyright holder. In other words, I can sell my DVD copy to my friend, but I cannot copy it without the permission of the copyright holder. The underlying principle of this "first sale" doctrine is to differentiate ownership of a physical copy of the work from the ownership of the copyright. It guarantees the permanence of the rights of the *copyright owner* but still provides the *owner of the copy* some limited rights. To be more precise, a *copyright owner* possesses all five aforementioned exclusive rights to his or her works; the *owner of a copy*, however, is only given distribution and display rights, and therefore is not allowed to reproduce, perform, or make derivative works out of the original. It must be noted that the first sale doctrine is not universal. Responding to the protests of the record industry and of publishers of computer software, the US Congress amended the related section of the copyright law to make the "first sale" doctrine inapplicable to the commercial rental of records or computer software, so that an owner of computer software or a CD cannot rent, lease, or even lend it to anyone else without the permission of the copyright holder (Strong 1993: 121; Halpern 2003: 146). We must recognize that copyright is a highly volatile legal system characterized by a continuing balancing of strongly represented interests, which we will further discuss in the second half of the chapter.

The "first sale" doctrine demonstrates the relationship and the basic differences between intellectual property and traditional property: intellectual property can be reproduced, but traditional property cannot – at least in terms of its intrinsic value. In general, traditional property rights conceive ownership of property and ownership of rights together, so that all rights are transferable through sale. But copyright law separates ownership of the copyright from the good it embodies, because the good is reproduced, which could be done in an infinite fashion, instead of produced – tying to a specific "creative" labor:

> Imagine that each purchasher of a copy of a Batman comic book also acquired the copyright as well. Then someone wanting to make a movie, television series or clothing collection based on the comic book might have to obtain permission from millions of individual copyright holders in order to avoid infringment.
>
> (W. Landes 2003: 134)

In order to produce a derivative work, its producer needs to request permission only from the copyright holder, instead of the numerous owners of the item. By separating copyrights from the rights of owners, the copyright holder can still control and financially benefit from his or her work no matter how many copies have been made. Copyright cannot be shared by those who acquired the copies: copies can be limitless while there is only one author. Due to the non-material nature of cultural works, it is highly problematic to equate ownership of copyright to ownership of goods.

Therefore, the "first use" doctrine, strictly speaking, is really not an exception to copyright; it only recognizes different kinds of rights given to different categories of owners. The concept of "fair use," however, is a core component in the overall philosophy of copyright discourse, yet it is also much vaguer than the "first use" doctrine. Those uses generally considered qualifying as "fair use" are "criticism, comment, news reporting, teaching (including multiple copies for classroom use), scholarship, or research" (McJohn 2003: 90). These broad categories are not determinative; the courts in the US usually consider four more factors to decide if use of a copyrighted work without permission is fair use or an infringement: (1) Is the new work of a commercial nature? (2) Is the original copyrighted work a highly protected creative work? (3) What is the amount and substantiality of the portion of the original work being used? and (4) What is the effect of the use? (McJohn 2003: 90.) But these factors are still extremely subjective, making "fair use" a notoriously troublesome doctrine, also making publishers and authors or artists extremely hesitant to rely on this doctrine to justify any use of copyrighted material without the consent of the copyright owner.

This slipperiness of the "fair use" doctrine, ironically, constrains instead of guarantees exceptions to copyright, as only the courts can decide its applicability on a case-by-case basis. Doctrines similar to "fair use" cannot be found in the Berne Convention, and TRIPs mentions it by highly limiting its use. TRIPs provides that members should, in their domestic laws, confine limitations or exceptions to copyright owners' rights to "certain special cases which do not conflict with a normal exploitation of the work and do not unreasonably prejudice the legitimate interests of the right holder" (J. Cohen *et al.* 2002: 54). The high restrictions implied in this phase demonstrate that global copyright regimes like TRIPs fear that nations might use various legal means to exploit the concept of fair use to curtail international copyright: the diversified national interpretations and enforcements of principles like "fair use" can topple copyright's global control. Fair use can be a site of contestation where the global demonstrates and acts against its anxiety, so that "local" diversities are severely regulated in spite of our popular "glocal" model. From another perspective, it is also through fair use, then, that individual users around the world might escape these global manipulations.

Comparisons between the two exceptions in terms of their meanings and effects can be made on two levels. If the "first sale" doctrine reveals the differences between intellectual property and traditional property, "fair use" demonstrates intellectual property's specific mode of production caught between cultural incentives and economic incentives. While copyright is meant to provide sufficient economic incentive for authors to continue to produce new works, too strong a copyright regime (meaning very limited fair use is allowed) might bring about the opposite, discouraging authors from creating new works that might bring accusations of copyright infringement. From a cultural perspective, the more mutual references among works, the more cultural dialogues are probably realized. Therefore, many critics promote fair use in the name of a more energetic culture of creation. "Satire and parody are particularly deserving of substantial freedom – both as entertainment and as a form of social and literary criticism" (Rinzler 1983: 26). Many in art circles also want to grant artists the right to appropriate the work of others, based on the aesthetic or political values added (Randall 2001: 153–7). But on the other hand, if "fair use" is unrestrained to the extent that economic incentives to the creators become too small, there is a danger of discouraging investment, and our contemporary culture – so embedded in the capitalist system – might fall apart. A major consideration in determining "fair use" is its effect on the original author's economic market. In general, "fair use" is a battlefield on which the limits and the philosophy of copyright are imprinted yet challenged.

However, if the "first use" doctrine is only an economic compensation to buyers who are not entitled to copyrights, the allowance of "fair use" can also be understood from an economic perspective of capitalist efficiency, making "fair use" less subversive than it seems. A major concern of today's copyright development is that as the Internet develops to facilitate royalty collection, "fair use" might be completely taken over by "fared use," in that all use of digitally delivered material can be recorded and its users can be charged for it (Towse 2001: 15). At the moment when this global digital jukebox is not yet available, fair use can be seen as less a means to encourage cultural dialogue than a practice to give up collecting cost-ineffective royalties. Imagine a situation in which all, however minor, references to existing cultural works are priced according to the amount of copying performed and the impact of that copying. How colossal this regulatory system would have to be to determine and collect royalties, considering the many arbitrations and enforcements involved! The "compulsory license" in the music industry is one way to simplify royalty collection: once a composer authorizes a recording of his song, others are free to perform and record the same song, as long as they pay the original composer a standard fee (Gallagher 2002). Compulsory licensing laws allow a musician to perform and publish a previously recorded song without getting the permission of the copyright holder, who continues to collect standard royalties. Radio broadcasters do not need to obtain permission from the copyright holders to play a song, but must pay usage fees to the copyright holders based on how often a particular song is played. But compulsory license is in general an exception to copyright law, because it gives the recording artists less copyright control over their own works (Lessig 2004: 57). In general, the cumbersome exercises to ensure the collection of all "fair" royalties are too costly to be effective, so minor fair uses are exempted. If there were a machine, like a perfected form of the web, that could accurately record and measure all cultural appropriations and references in detail, the royalty collection system would become much more effective, and fair use might disappear. Seen in this light, fair use is really not that subversive; it is allowed only because said use is generally considered trivial.

The public domain

This brings us to a more prominent area of contestation in copyright discussions: the "public domain," which, to a larger extent than "fair use," has been considered a haven built into copyright discourse to safeguard creativity and the public interest. While "fair use" is still considered an exception that is at the mercy of official discourse, the public domain is supposedly autonomous and free of copyright interrogation. Therefore, while "fair use" is rigidly confined by the law, in the "public domain" the law deliberately relinquishes its control. "Fair use" is elaborately discussed in many copyright laws, but the "public domain" enjoys much less attention within legal discourse because it is a space in which copyright does not interfere. In contrast, the "public domain" attracts the attention of many copyright critics, who often argue for its expansion, which would grant public access to more cultural works.

In general, the public domain comprises the body of works in which no person or organization has any proprietary interest, so that the public can use them and copy them without any legal consequences. The public domain is a concept applicable to all four IP categories, as items in the public domain are not owned by individuals but the public, and therefore lack the status of intellectual properties. As John Frow succinctly describes:

> The concept of public domain is the conerstone of all Western intellectual property regimes. In the case of patent law, "nature" has been the key area reserved for the public domain, and there has also been a strong emphasis on the publication of patentable knowledge; in the case of trademark, it is language itself that is reserved, and in the case of copyright, it is, above all, ideas. Yet the concept is a purely residual one: rather than being, itself, a set of specific rights, the public domain is that space, that possibility of access, which is left over after all other rights have been defined and distributed.
>
> (2000: 182)

The key defining feature of the public domain is the absence of legal protection. Items in the public domain include ideas that do not have patents, trademarks, or trade secrets; mathematical formulas and other abstract ideas; and, generally, creative works not yet fixed – those items not meeting the copyright criteria mentioned in the last chapter. There are also copyrightable items available in the public domain. A copyright holder can explicitly disclaim any proprietary interest in his or her work, granting it to the public domain by providing a licence to this effect. For example, many government works are in the public domain. In the public domain there are also works that were created long before copyright laws were passed, and works whose copyright terms have expired. The first category is rather clear-cut and invites little confusion, with a few exceptions – such as certain cases in post-Socialist countries where copyright laws are practiced *ex post facto*, as discussed in the previous chapter. But the second category is an extremely controversial one, because the length of the copyright term indirectly determines the size of the public domain – the shorter the term, the more items enter the public domain. Copyright's limited duration also demonstrates the differences between intellectual properties and traditional properties. An owner's possession of a traditional property should be permanent as long as the owner does not transfer ownership to someone else, whereas the required term limits of copyright ownership indirectly assert that no IP can be exclusively and permanently owned by individuals (Epstein 2004). The public domain is the ultimate destiny of all copyrighted works. Under TRIPs, copyright terms must extend 50 years after the death of the author. A work made for hire or an anonymous work generally has a term of 75 years from the date of its first publication. But in the United States and many other countries, the terms are expanding. In 1998 the US Congress passed the Sonny Bono

Copyright Term Extension Act (CTEA), which extended the term of copyright protection by 20 years, so that works created since 1978 are copyrighted for "life plus 70" rather than the former "life plus 50," and works made for hire receive 95 years of copyright protection.

CTEA is largely a result of the Walt Disney Company's extensive lobbying in 1998. Disney's copyright to Mickey Mouse, which first appeared in the cartoon "Steamboat Willie" in 1928, was due to expire in 2003, and Disney's rights to Pluto, Goofy, and Donald Duck were to expire a few years later. Rather than allowing Mickey and friends to enter the public domain, the Disney group told Congress that they wanted an extension bill passed. The result was CTEA (Sprigman 2002). While the constitutionality of the Act has been challenged, as shown in the *Eldred v. Ashcroft* case (2003), the US Supreme Court has rejected such appeals (McJohn 2003: 73–4). As large corporations continue to press for longer copyright protection terms, we are seeing the shrinking of the public domain.

The public domain implies public access – all items therein are available to all. While the public domain implies the forbiddance of private ownership, which runs counter to capitalist logic, it is also here where copyright ethics are most vigorously debated. As Paul Goldstein succinctly describes, "Intellectual property's divide between private property and the public domain is a legal artifact, not a natural phenomenon. The line shifts not only with the views of particular judges but also with national boundaries and with cultural attitudes" (Goldstein 2003: 10). This constantly shifting line is always a result of intense negotiation, defining the scope of copyright's cultural control.

The public domain has often been considered the haven of creativity, where culture can develop without the interference of the capitalist economy. Frow uses the example of recipes to demonstrate why we can enlarge the present public domain without worrying about the discouragment of creativity. Recipes "cannot be copyrighted because they are 'methods'; yet there is little evidence that this lack of protection inhibits the creation and publication of new recipes" (Frow 2000: 183). He argues that the public domain is a site of resistance to the private property regime, one which imposes limitations on the circulation and usage of knowledge and cultural materials. He concludes in his article that his reservations about the closure of the public domain are grounded in traditional Enlightenment values of critique, of an open public sphere, and of the scientific ethos of the free sharing of knowledge. He believes that it is in the public domain where the totalizing tendency of globalization can be resisted through the use and transformation of knowledge and information carried out on multiple local levels (Frow 2000: 184).

In this academic epoch baptized by poststructuralist thinking, Frow is courageous to admit his Enlightenment values, which in fact ground the general ethics of most copyright critics on both sides: Goldstein separates copyright scholars into the camp of the pessimists against that of the optimists. While the optimists characterize the present copyright regime as being rooted in natural justice, and entitling authors to all the benefits they deserve, the pessimists emphasize the restraining effects of copyright that encroach upon the general freedom of the people to express themselves (Goldstein 2003: 10–11). Looking at it from another perspective, the values of both camps are in fact similar in their common concern for rights, although one emphasizes the rights of the authors while the other cares more about the rights of the general public. Because of the concentration of copyrights in the hands of large corporations, liberal critics and scholars tend to be copyright pessimists, who advocate for a larger public domain to benefit the common people. As the public domain is supposedly an area in which legal copyright protections are absent, it should also be a space where – as many critics believe – capitalist control fails to reach. This assumption is well supported by the fact that only those large corporations investing lavishly in extensive legislative lobbying can manipulate the law, as demonstrated by the aforementioned Disney case.

As Ronald V. Bettig demonstrates in his close study of cable television's incorporation into the filmed entertainment copyright system, various class factions and industry coalitions organized individuals inside and outside of the state apparatus in order to promote their interests through state action (1996: 117–44). Although the actions led to some changes in the existing industrial hegemony, which lost some power as a regulatory-based monopoly, Bettig considers the transformation to be one of internal structural changes in the capitalist class, with the effect of promoting, instead of challenging, the larger interests of capital as a whole. Bettig concludes:

> The law and nature of intellectual property are essentially based on capitalism. Here the options of the state apparatus were even more limited. Despite the contradictory nature of the policymaking, legislating, and litigating processes, the pressures and limits imposed by capitalism determined the outcome that cable operators ultimately be held liable for retransmission of copyrighted filmed entertainment.
>
> (1996: 144)

This general state of pessimism characterizes the position of many critics of IPR laws, who find that in spite of the claimed openness and rationality of the present legal and policy-making structures, the benefits to the general public are often at stake if capitalist interests are involved. By promoting the enlargement of the public domain, critics cast their vote against the present legal system, reducing it to an object of manipulation by the dominant capitalist class. The public domain is then idealized as a site of resistance – a space where free dialogue can take place and culture can thrive.

This reading of the public domain closely echoes the underlying values of Jürgen Habermas's theorization of the public sphere as a place where human rationality can be exercised, and through which civil society can be established. Geoff Eley describes the basis of the public sphere according to the following criteria: public good distinguished from private interest; the clear demarcation of state and society; the constitutive role of a participant citizenry; and the shaping of public policy and its parameters through reasoned exchange, free of domination (1992: 292). These criteria can all be applied to the public domain. The public sphere is idealized as the site where Enlightenment values (echoing Frow's ideological ground to understand the public domain) can be realized. But the public sphere is also vulnerable to the hegemony of consumer culture, which easily corrupts the substantive reasoning immanent in the space. As Habermas demonstrates, when bourgeois newspapers became the medium of a consumer culture, they lost the public function they had originally assumed in the eighteenth century (Habermas 1989: 139–40). As I mentioned earlier, this anxiety among critics of the public sphere is commonly shared by public domain advocates, who generally idealize the public domain as a space free of control by consumer culture – it is art, knowledge, and creativity that occupy the public domain, not commodities as such.

Therefore, there is a convergence of the basic values of the public sphere and the public domain: both are spaces where the erosion of private interests is resisted for the public good; they are areas the state and other hegemonic powers cannot reach; they encourage individual participation; and ideas are freely circulated and transformed. If the public sphere is a social ideal, the public domain can be understood as a parallel notion in the cultural realm. Although they are two different concepts and historical entities, they coincide in their attractiveness to scholars for their promises of emancipation from hegemonic forces.

While the public sphere has been roundly attacked by scholars, specifically for its homogenous assumptions and effects, the idealization of the public domain has not been systematically criticized. Feminist scholars, like Joan B. Landes (1988) and Miriam Hansen (1991), have criticized Habermas's ignorance of the gender denial of the public sphere; Eric Clarke (2000) criticizes the confinement of the public sphere from the gay and lesbian perspective. Oska Negt and Alexander Kluge (1993) argue that the public sphere is homogenized in terms of class constituents and is based on capitalist order. In general, critics of the public sphere argue that a demand of absolute equality is itself hegemony. These criticisms seemingly do not apply to the public domain, which involves abstract ideas instead of human beings. But the Enlightenment values of the public domain treasured by Frow and others like him reside also in the active participation of the people, who enter the domain not by physically walking into it but by depositing and using materials freely. Therefore, freedom of access is also a fundamental principle of the public domain, which, as shown in the criticisms of Habermas's concept, inevitably begs the question of legitimacy.

The public domain is an artificial space created by law, so that the space exists and makes sense only among those who already abide by the law. The public domain matters most to entities such as publication houses, which constantly visit it for "free" items. But through the endorsement of the publication companies, these images circulate widely in the mass culture and our everyday life. Items in the public domain acquire certain reified values via these lawful agencies. Those of us who do not know what the public domain is value different images according to criteria other than copyright. The public domain is not created, for example, for the pirates and the ignorant, who of course can still use works in the public domain, but they would use them regardless of the domain. For them, the public domain becomes an issue only when law enforcement is involved. If Habermas's public sphere is hegemonic in its demand for equality, the public domain is hegemonic in its lawfulness. An idealization of the public domain runs the risk of taking all the basic and exclusive rights of the copyright holder for granted, but it might also privilege those inside the public domain against those outside, as if only the former can benefit the continual development of human culture and society. In both cases the endorsement of the public domain only reinforces copyright's cultural control.

This brings us to the issue of piracy, which will be extensively discussed in Chapters 5 and 6. I want to mention piracy briefly here because the legitimacy and the scope of control of copyright as a legal discourse rests precisely on the lines of demarcation between piracy and the public domain. Both piracy and the public domain are areas where the legal protection of IP does not reach. But the two are also dichotomized in their legal status: the public domain is at the mercy of the law, while piracy is simply against the law, so that the concept of piracy has been appropriated as alternative cultural tactics to challenge the hegemonic (Samuelian 1998). The flourishing of piracy or any kind of IPR infringement can be read as a result of legal failure: the invocation of an unreasonable law often sanctions a kind of lawlessness. The relation between specific legal system(s) and piracy is a complicated one, which I will discuss in detail in the following chapters. I do not want to romanticize piracy as a subversive transgression of a hegemonic law: it would be naïve to read movie piracy simply as an upright and romantic act of looting Hollywood, as the power structures and ideology involved are more convoluted. But I do want to point out that any endorsement of the public domain, which can actually be seen as the "other" of piracy, is also an endorsement of the copyright legal regime.

Precisely because of the intimate relationship between the public domain and copyright law, many anti-copyright movements do not resort to the concept of the public domain to make their statements. In the case of art, the 1980s witnessed the rise of a generation of appropriation artists who freely appropriate art without abiding by copyright law, with the aim of criticizing the current art world – which they view as corrupted by the commodification and copyrighting of art. This politics is crystalized in the 1988 "Festivals of Plagiarism" held in various European and American cities. The festival pamphlet, entitled *Plagiarism: Art as Commodity and Strategies for Its Negation*, is a manifesto in favor of plagiarism as a weapon against the domination of capital in the arts (Randall 2001: 230). As Marilyn Randall writes, "The visual arts in the twentieth century have a long history not only of appropriation, but of lawsuits ensuing from such practices" (2001: 253). These appropriation artists equip their works with a clear political agenda, and the significance of their conceptual art lies precisely in the copyright lawsuits and related disputes the works generate. Another recent international project of "piracy activism" is the "Kingdom of Piracy" project originated in Taiwan. "Kingdom of Piracy" is an online, open work space to explore the free sharing of digital content – often condemned as piracy – as the net's ultimate art form. But the project has been moving its base from country to country, as it has been termed illegal by governments (Medosch 2005). What is intended is not to enlarge the public domain, but to invite people to discuss the legitimacy of the law itself.

The recent "copyleft" movement is intimately linked to the legitimacy and limitation of the public domain. Copyleft is a licensing system which allows every user of a copy of the "copylefted" work to use, distribute, and modify it; the most famous example of a copylefted work is the Linux operating system. Any works derived from a copylefted work must themselves be copylefted, creating a viral network that becomes an ever-expanding realm of works with no copyright registration. Copyleft is a potentially subversive new practice for two reasons. First, unlike piracy, copyleft is strictly legal, making creative use of the current IPR laws to develop a realm beyond the control of the regime. While copyleft is not yet a term used in law, it is used by activists as a legal tool to debate current IP concepts and practices. Second, because of its viral network, copyleft is a future-oriented concept. While there are also no copyright restrictions applied to works in the public domain, a person making a new work deriving from works in the public domain can copyright his or her new work, although not the portions that are in the public domain. Once copyrighted, the resulting derivative work is not relegated to the public domain. But – as stipulated by its license – the derivatives of a copylefted work can never leave the copyleft domain, so one copylefted work can produce an infinite number of future copylefted works.

While many copyright critics are enthusiastic about the expanding scope and influence of copyleft (Söderberg 2002), copyleft might not be as subversive as is claimed because it has no capacity to challenge existing and future copyrighted works, and, not surprisingly, most authors choose copyright instead of copyleft licenses for financial reasons. Also, while the copyleft viral network might point to an expanding volume of works with no copyright concerns, the production of copylefted works still needs to conform with copyright principles whenever copyrighted works are involved. Like works in the public domain, copylefted materials are on a lone island in a vast sea of copyrighted works, and foreseeably will have only moderate impact on the global expansion and accessibility of copyrights. Richard Stallman, founder of the Free Software Foundation, does not conceive of "copyleft" as a criticism of copyright as such, but only as a specific "use of copyright law to assure that open source code remains 'open' even when it is modified and redistributed by subsequent developers" (Hartnick 2004). While we should be happy to see more freely available but licensed cultural works, their marginal existence does not necessarily challenge the present dominant practice (Mustonen 2003). As echoed in Stallman's statement, copyleft might probably be a supplementary vehicle to add to and strengthen the public domain in particular and the copyright regime in general.

Copyright as ethics or copyright as belief?

The above discussion of the critical discourse of copyright brings us to copyright's own ethics. In the second part of this chapter I want to take leave of the relatively dry and intertwined copyright laws and their principles, and ask a more fundamental question: is copyright a reflection or a realization of social morality, or is it just a positivist law – a legal system defined independently of evaluative terms or propositions? On the one hand, copyright is seemingly based on an elaborate system of humanist concerns, and has the aim of providing an optimal commercial environment to protect creativity and nourish cultural development (Landes and Posner 2003). But in actual practice, copyright does not fit nicely into the category of natural rights; it is enforced less because it is just and can promote basic human goods on its own than because it is designed to facilitate and balance the changing interests involved. The nature of copyright law makes it difficult, if not impossible, for individuals to find or to construct an unambiguous moral compass (Halpern 2003: 145–6), and the equivocal relationship between copyright and ethics makes the law particularly manipulative and incomprehensible. I am not trying to develop a normative theory of copyright law, which is a matter of legal philosophy (Netanel 1996; Brenner 2003; Epstein 2004, etc.). From a cultural studies perspective, I am more interested in understanding how concepts of copyright are actually conceived and practiced by ordinary people in their everyday lives, which are very remote from the legal platform, yet inevitably entangled with larger political and economic discourses that condition legislation and court decisions.

There are more and more cultural activities falling into the control of copyright in one way or another. With desktop publishing and other kinds of digital reproduction becoming so accessible, copyright has become a matter of concern not only to publishers or designers but to all of us who consume and appropriate cultural commodities non-commercially. Consider the many everyday practices that might violate copyright: teachers screen films in classrooms without any permission; students copy and paste materials from various sources as homework or projects; people make more copies of books, newspapers, and magazines than they are allowed; we copy materials from the Internet for our own web pages; music is heard everywhere, although there are many places that do not pay proper royalties; not to mention the many infringements we knowingly commit, like downloading music from the web and watching pirated movies. Like any other law, copyright fails to completely rationalize and regulate social reality. But this inefficiency is particularly evidenced in copyright because, as I have discussed, copyright is situated in the crossroad of culture and economics, and it involves too many players with their own interests and needs. One can argue that modern copyright discourse is designed to guarantee the maximum capital return for producing and distributing new cultural works (Landes and Posner 2003); yet one can argue just as convincingly that the main objective of copyright discourse, through practices like fair use and the public domain, is to protect cultural freedom against the domination of capitalism. Lyman Ray Patterson simplifies this complex topography: "The problem of copyright today is how best to reconcile the interests of three groups – authors, who give expression to ideas; publishers, who disseminate ideas; and the members of the public, who use the ideas" (1968: 224–5). I would argue that the specific demands of these three groups, whose interests are highly heterogeneous to start with, cannot be settled, say, just on economic terms; copyright also involves cultural values like freedom and access, as well as political dynamics such as those between national sovereignty and transnational legal regime. These extremely divergent concerns sometimes overlap, but more often they conflict with each other, and fair negotiation among all parties is extremely difficult if not simply impossible.

While all laws are sites of dispute incorporating and negotiating different interests, copyright is particularly contested because the territory being fought over is itself extremely vague and elusive. As I mentioned in the introduction and will continue to explore in the following chapters, the cultural realm is the most complex and dynamic arena of human activity, and it resists any monolithic form of control. The involvement of many other vested parties trying to own and control culture through the manipulation of copyright results in the denseness and sometimes irrationality of the law to the minds of the common people. Copyright rests on a set of wavering principles. While some legal scholars explain that copyright is difficult to define because it is a heritage with a volatile history (Patterson 1968), others describe it as one of the most forward-looking contemporary laws (Lessig 2004). As the past and the future often hold conflicting information and ideas, such complaints from a judge are not surprising:

> Patents and copyrights approach, nearer than any other class of cases belonging to forensic discussion to what may be called the metaphysics of the law, where the distinctions are, or at least may be, very subtle and refined, and sometimes, almost evanescent.
>
> (Miller and Davis 1983: 1)

Situated within such a dense discursive network, copyright strives to present itself as a logical and sensible system of law based on a set of ethics agreeable to the majority of the people. The actual terms of this ethics include the celebration of creativity, people's universal right to access ideas, and the protection of ownership. These principles sound reasonably comprehensible on their own, but when built into the legal system their interactions and negotiations are convoluted, and the details become too ambiguous and case-specific to be easily grasped even by legal experts. As a result, charges against copyright infractions cannot be established according only to textual features, but rather are based on a combination of judgments involving social, political, aesthetic, and cultural norms and presuppositions (Randall 2001: 4). It is this overlapping of judgments and contingency that makes its "ethics" sometimes "unethical."

This explains why the Janus-faced copyright law is both extremely transient yet extremely accessible. On the one hand, its complex technicality, and sometimes "artificial" logic, is scandalous, alienating the people who are constantly subject to its control. The high level of frustration of a writer or an amateur designer trying to understand copyright lies in stark contrast to a driver's sense of control in his or her grasp of traffic laws. To many people, the reasoning of copyright is incomprehensible, unpredictable, and yet extremely powerful. On the other hand, the common ethics of copyright is as simple and as sensible as any everyday morality; very few would dispute the claim that it is wrong to copy a work without the consent of the copyright holder. The extremely complex rational aspects and principles of the law are radically simplified and mythologized by mismatched universal ethics, like the direct equation between copyright infringement and theft. One of the major components of the global IPR regime – education – resides outside the law. In most of these campaigns we are told that downloading music illegally from the web is the same as robbing the artists, buying pirated movie destroys the entire national cinema, and those who copy software must be put in jail. We are even told that piracy profits directly fund terrorist activities (Mikuriya 2004). The MPAA, the extremely powerful trade association of the American film industry, states on its web page:

> Pirate activities undermine every aspect of the legitimate filmmaking business since legitimate retailers cannot possibly compete fairly with pirate business.

> Pirate operations do not have the average expenses associated with the cost of doing legitimate business. Piracy negatively affects every rung on the ladder including the studios that invest in the film, the distributors, the retailers and foreign and local filmmakers.
>
> (2004)

These simple and assertive statements, common to all anti-piracy campaigns, made copyright's ethics unambiguous and authoritative, successfully covering up the highly unstable components that make up this legal regime. In the words of Charles Taylor, such ideas are no longer confined to the moral order, but have already infiltrated and transformed our social imaginaries (2004: 23–30). The representations of such social imaginaries can be found within Asian cinema. For example, in the Hong Kong teenage film *Spacked Out* (*Wuren jiashi*; dir. Lawrence Lau, 1999), thirteen-year-old Cookie is pregnant, but her irresponsible teenaged boyfriend has disappeared to Mongkok to sell pirated VCDs. Negative value judgments are associated with both the seller and the buyer of pirated VCDs, which in this case is particularly reinforced by Hong Kong's filmmakers – whose own livelihoods are jeopardized by movie piracy.

As I mentioned in the introduction, "copyrighting" culture can be seen as a cultural Empire working to facilitate capitalist development in general and US interests in particular. The moral high ground occupied by copyright owners effectively directs people's attention away from the many economic and political interests copyright owners enjoy. The extreme technicality of copyright, as demonstrated in previous pages, can be seen as the manifestation and result of its elusive and mythologized ethics, so that only the absolute ethics of copyright is accessible to the people, not its "rational" system. In other words, although presented as a natural law, copyright is heavily embedded in a positivist system; on closer examination, the seemingly secure connections between its ethics and its logic are obscured by its extremely convoluted arguments. This also marks the reversal of Max Weber's sociological law, as the ethics of copyright is becoming so dense that it is presented to the people not as a rational system but as a "truth," making copyright a "belief" system.

Weber characterizes the development of modernity in terms of the separation of substantive reason from monotheistic religious and metaphysical worldviews, so that modern epistemology is separated into three autonomous areas of knowledge, justice, and taste. The realm of justice, therefore, should be independent from the influence of the two other areas and any other authorities. Weber argues that premodern forms of popular justice are in general irrational, and do not achieve the highest degree of formal juridical precision but support the expediential and ethical goals of the authorities concerned (1968: 810). But modern formal justice guarantees interested parties the maximum freedom to represent their formal legal interests. "Juridical formalism enables the legal system to operate like a technically rational machine" (Weber 1968: 811). Although to Weber a completely systematized, unambiguous, and specialized formal law is still an ideal to be realized, it is its rationality and accessibility to the people that defines the superiority of modern law to premodern law. In fact, most moral philosophers describe morality in hierarchical terms: traditional and prudential moral values are inferior to rational values achieved through deliberations and reflections by autonomous and free moral agents (Frankena 1973: 7–8). However, copyright law, which is one of the newest systems of law in contemporary Western society, has become so complex that people's commitments to copyright principles are usually based on leaps of faith or unsupported ethical concerns instead of rational undertaking.

In criticizing some modernists' radical attempt to sublate art for the autonomy of aesthetics, Habermas argues that similar situations also take place in the legal domain. "(T)he activity of moral–practical argument segregated within the legal system ha[s] become so remote from everyday life that here too the programme of *elevation* implied by the Enlightenment [in the autonomy of the moral–practical] could be transformed into that of *sublation* instead" (1997: 50, italics original). This undercurrent of the modernity project, according to Habermas, becomes its own terrorism. It is ethics that legitimizes the law's technicality, but when the latter has transformed into such a complicated system that it can no longer communicate with ordinary people, its ethics also becomes its burden. If Vattimo believes that modernity's fascination with the new is characterized by secularization (1988: 101–3), copyright might only be a regression from modernity, which, in the name of an ethical means of promoting the new, tames the new and confines its production within a specific system with a high degree of control, so that all creations are locked in copyright procedure.

In general, it is very easy and tempting to "believe" in the terms of copyright without knowing what they really are. The problem, therefore, is the general public's failing to examine the principles and the scope of copyright's control while continuing to assert it as "truth." Such uncertainty is translated into myth, into a belief system where meanings collapse. As Michel de Certeau claims, in modern society what perpetuates a belief is not one's faith but one's inertia, in the sense that people no longer know the content of their belief but continue to hold it. He defines belief "not as the object of believing (a dogma, a program, etc.) but as the subject's investment in a proposition, the act of saying it and considering it as true – in other words, a 'modality' of the assertion and not its content" (1988: 178). De Certeau laments that religiousness is becoming easier to exploit: advertising is evangelical in this supposedly secular modern society, and politics has once again become religious (1988: 180–1).

In the case of copyright, examples demonstrating de Certeau's concerns abound. Many books and visual-audio materials contain a copyright notice asserting that no portion of the work may be reproduced or publicly screened for any purpose without the written consent of the copyright holder. But this statement is not accurate, as fair use and other exceptions to copyright are allowed by law. But the nature of our present legal system institutionally prevents non-experts from understanding these details, and the severe punishments lurking in the shadows of this gray area discourage all attempts at trespassing. Jane Gaines argues that IPR law is meant to be "*of* the community – and that is especially true of American legal discourse, with its emphasis on the common law and its evolution in custom and use . . . that is most like commonsense knowledge" (1992: 11–12, italics original). Gaines believes that, under the common law system, our understandings of IP should be drawn out of the reservoir of shared knowledge, norms, beliefs, and values in the culture – this respect for the commonsense knowledge leads to the necessary confusion in the IP regime. She also argues that this commonsense knowledge, although derived to benefit the class in power, can be borrowed by the unprivileged class to challenge the status quo. I believe that the fierce ethical tendency of the IPR regime demonstrates its painstaking attempts to tame the contradictions and confusions inherent in this potentially subversive common store of wisdom.

By turning copyright into a myth, it easily becomes a form of censorship. The earliest British copyright laws were in fact instruments of censorship – only members of the Stationers' Company could legally produce books. Many of the subsequent revisions to copyright legal discourse were meant to fight such monopolies, and attempted to ensure that no one could single-handedly "control culture" (Patterson 1968). William P. Alford also describes the copyright system in premodern China as a form of state censorship (1995: 12–18, 57). Sadly, modern copyright continues to retain some forms of censorship, which results in authors' reluctance to test copyright's limits. The risk of engaging in expensive legal cases prevents people from challenging copyright discourse in practice, and thus continues to reify copyright's omnipresent control. The real evil of copyright is not its details but the inability of the people to ask what these details are. Law is an exemplary dimension of what Louis Althusser termed an ideological state apparatus whose ultimate function is to lock the individual into an imaginary relationship with the real (1971). As the single most important legal discourse governing culture, copyright is most prone to this criticism, but it is through criticism that we can articulate a politics of subversion and redemption against such control.

According to Hardt and Negri, ethics is a particularly important part of the new global legal regime supporting Empire, which pushes the equation of the ethical and the juridical to the extreme. The notion of "perpetual peace" becomes not only a utopian ethic but an international right, subjecting people to Empire's control (2000: 10–11). Copyright demonstrates precisely this premise: as the notion of copyright has become an international right, people are willing to submit to its control. With its complex international politics, copyright ultimately justifies its "Empire" through its claimed ethical bases. It is naïve to treat copyright simply as an ethical issue, separating the law-abiding from the "criminals." If the public domain is central to all IPR discussion because these laws are ultimately set up to protect human rights instead of individual rights, the tortuous and dense logic of copyright prevents the public from participating in its making or interrogating its development.

If the copyright regime is as much a system of myth as a system of rationality, we need to read it and engage with it accordingly. Myth might be a poetry of truth, but precisely because it is poetry, it is only through our interpretation and participation that truth can come to light. As I mentioned in the introduction, the act of copying is essential to our humanity. While the new reprographic and digital technologies give us new possibilities in engaging with different acts of copying, the copyright regime deters us from engaging with our mimetic faculty, without which we cannot reach the Other. An underlying aim of this book is to propagate our continual multilevel engagements with and understanding of the acts of copying, and thus to continue to practice culture. De Certeau's concept of culture might once again be of help here. He points out that some people find cultural actions ineffective if they are not part of a social struggle. De Certeau finds this view myopic:

> In a festival, as in an artistic creation, something exists that is not a means, but that is sufficient unto itself: the discovery of possibilities, the invention of encounters, the experience of these departures for "other places" – without which the atmosphere becomes stifling and seriousness amounts to everything that is boring about a society.
>
> (1997: 118)

In the following four chapters, we will analyze how we can discover possibilities, invent encounters, and experience otherness through a culturally embedded reading of copying. I believe that the various kinds of copying taking place in and around Asian cinema can help us rediscover cultural issues the present copyright regime governs, hides, or simply fails to address. If the last two chapters have bored you, I hope that some concrete engagement with film culture in the coming chapters will show that culture is indeed more exciting than law. We will start with violence.

3 Violence and New Asian Cinema

In Chapters 1 and 2, I provided an overall picture of copyright discourse, illustrating the principles and the problems behind its cultural control. I also have pointed out that copyright's simple ethics betrays its deep roots in the capitalist system, which makes copyright unapproachable as an ethical system to understand contemporary culture. Despite its seemingly irrefutable principle of "thou shalt not steal," copyright is in fact an extremely complex set of laws, discouraging us from critically and experientially engaging with the practices and meanings of different cultural copyings. A major aim of the book is to demonstrate the distance between this legal regime and the actual cultural scenes, and that there are still many forms of copying actually taking place with which copyright fails to come to terms. Beginning with this chapter, I contextualize copyright's philosophy and implications in actual instances of copying that take place in cinema. And I will take leave of the legal vocabularies and arguments and concentrate on the film culture. In this chapter I examine a common marketing and artistic practice of recent Asian films – the mutual copying of action and violence. I want to illustrate how a careful examination of this practice of copying could cast new light on our reading of copyright and allow us to re-examine the meanings of authorship and creativity. I am specifically interested in the theme and form of violence because it tests the limit of the idea–expression dichotomy – is violence an idea or an expression? The production and reception of violence also demonstrates some predicaments of transnational popular culture in which copyright is developed. I hope that this chapter can provide a unique perspective from which to understand how globalization engenders a unique inter-Asian cinema permeated with violence, and how this violence can in turn help us re-examine the core principles, and their failures, of copyright's control.

The New Asian Cinema

The last decade has seen the rise of a new cinematic brand name: New Asian Cinema. A number of young Asian directors have been identified as leading this new wave. Wong Kar-wai is one such filmmaker, who "in the late 1980s and early 1990s emerged as the most daring and inventive stylist in the new Asian cinema" (Fuller 2001). It is also widely believed that "the most promising [recent films] come from Asia, the continent at the head of a new cinematic movement" (Jalladeau 2000).

But other than the names of a few filmmakers, or references to some very general new cinematic "sensations" (not even specific cinematic styles) or non-exclusive common themes like sexuality (Chakravarty 2003), no single scholar or critic has yet given New Asian Cinema a more unified and systematic description. Similar problems are faced by scholars for Latin American cinema, African cinema, or even European cinema, which to a large extent are also fantasized entities not unified by language and politics (Bakari and Cham 1996; Stock 1997; Nowell-Smith and Ricci 1998). But these categories of "continental" cinemas are often upheld against the hegemony of Hollywood or to address some connected social experience of similar cultures. The case of the New Asian Cinema is even more difficult to conceptualize: it transcends national and cultural lineages, it diffuses the boundary of mainstream and alternative cinemas, and most importantly many of these films collaborate deeply with Hollywood. In short, any simple political, commercial, or cultural categorization of this new cinema phenomenon is not only artificial but also doomed to be unconvincing. Instead of defining what this New Asian Cinema is, in this chapter I investigate the ways in which some of these films position themselves in the emerging global film culture – many Asian films, ranging from the most commercially oriented entertainment to art films meant only for film festival buffs, share an obsession with acquiring some kind of global recognition. And this global recognition, as I will argue, is achieved precisely through copying.

What draws my attention is a certain slipperiness between culturally specific expressions and transcultural influences that can be detected in this loosely defined cinema, which I think can help us rethink copyright's idea–expression dichotomy. As I mentioned in the introduction, copyright discourse stipulates that while expressions belong to individual authors, ideas belong to the entire human race. This logic might be extended to a transcultural dimension – that different cultural expressions are based on a common universal pool of basic ideas, with examples like love, anger, beauty. Different cultural expressions might be mutually incomprehensible, but ultimately they are connected through these common ideas. Is it really the case, particularly for today's globalization project that is based largely on cultural translations? I would like to explore the transcultural connections that built the New Asian Cinema in order to question this idea–expression dichotomy. My question is whether we can understand today's increasingly transcultural exchanges and receptions, which are approved by and support the current copyright regime, as translations of universal ideas through and between individual cultural expressions. Or, what are the elements that connect individual film cultures and film audience? Are they ideas or are they expressions?

I want to demonstrate in this chapter that it is the wide transcultural copying of expressions, more so than of ideas, that defines our global cinema. The fundamental concern of today's copyright logics that expressions are personal possessions and should be legally protected is in fact contradictory to the very real practices of globalization, as today's global culture is made up of extensive copying of expressions. If we want to examine and be critical of copyright, we must first understand the term culture and its double meanings: culture as individual cultural works and as communal expressions: Asian films are both individual commodities and cultural expressions of a collective. The contemporary discourse of copyright is developed mostly according to the former, that individual cultural products are distinctive and possessible. But in order for films to be understood by the diversified world viewers, cultural differences are very much at stake. Copying of expressions, or "styles," might be the key to bridge cultural differences and translate untranslatable "ideas in the project of cultural globalization, which gives rise to the current copyright regime in the first place." The issue of style, I believe, is the cultural blind spot of copyright, as it does not understand that culture is based on copying, which is most dramatically reinforced and speeded up by capitalism.

Chinese films of the past two decades, from the mainland's Fifth Generation to the aforementioned Wong Kar-wai and Taiwan's Hou Hsiao-hsien, are definitely crucial to the branding of this New Asian Cinema, and one could argue that they are running threads connecting extremely diversified films. But this new cinematic trademark has worldwide appeal not for its culturally pure constituents but for its transcultural makeup. There is something in these films that can be lifted by other Asian cinemas to recycle in their own cultural contexts, and film viewers around the world can also identify with them. The significance of the films of these famous Asian directors is probably their cultural slipperiness, notwithstanding recent film scholarship that celebrates their embeddedness in their own cultural specificities and political agendas. The chief aim of this chapter is to examine this dilemma, studying how some of these new Asian films echo both cultural specificity and transcultural elusiveness. To fully reveal the construction and the cultural implications of this new cinematic branding is far beyond the scope of this chapter; herein I only hope to investigate violence – one key, but not exclusive, element that runs through many of these new Asian films. The common theme and form of violence, I believe, can help us investigate how these culturally and generically diverse films can be grouped together, and how these Chinese and Asian films can be both culturally specific and unspecific.

Criticizing violence in an international context

I begin this investigation of the violence circulating among Asian films with a discussion of how media violence in general is understood in the context of global media, and how seductive the concept of violence is in our understanding of the East–West cultural relationship. The representation of violence has been a recurrent topic in media studies, as many theorists worry and argue that a steady diet of media violence influences and distorts viewers' conceptions of social reality (Carter and Weaver 2003: 1–20). Media effects research often links media violence to the viewers' personal vulnerability to crime, highlighting the social harm of media violence (Weaver and Wakshlag 1986). Extending this line of thought to cultural globalization, critics often condemn the importation of Western moral ills – such as promiscuous sexuality, violence, and extreme individualism – to the rest of the world through mass media, because it damages the local cultures on the receiving end (Kamalipour and Rampal 2001: 1–4). Cinema quickly becomes an evil sign of the West, which, according to conservative groups around the world, necessarily portrays violence and corrupts people (Thompson 2001). Even sophisticated cultural theorists like Arjun Appadurai believe that violence projected in cinema "is the spur to an increasingly rapid and amoral arms trade that penetrates the entire world" (1996: 41)!

The most dangerous aspect of cinematic violence, according to many scholars, is not its image but its narrative. According to William Rothman, most film violence is narrative-driven, which in turn is endorsed by a certain ideology – the major force fueling the violent nature of Hollywood's films is ultra-individualism. "In American movies, it is a moral imperative to quest for human fulfillment, even when that means refusing to accept the strictures of conventional morality; self-realization is a greater good than social acceptance" (Rothman 2001: 43). The confrontation between the individual and the social that permeates American ideology legitimates and is legitimated by Hollywood's violence, demonstrating the mutual conditioning of social reality and cinematic representation. Rothman's differentiation of violence between its image and its narrative already points to the complex issue of violence as expression and as idea. We will come back to it.

Asian cinema has also been branded as violent, and fans in the Western world love the films. This is most evident in the words of authors and editors of Asian cinema guidebooks, like Thomas Weisser (1994) and Stefan Hammond and Mike Wilkins (1996), who find that Asian cinema's blatant and novel representations of violence are extremely attractive to Western viewers. Not surprisingly, such receptions enrage some scholars. Ackber Abbas complains,

> [W]hen the Hong Kong cinema is praised (interestingly enough, more often by foreign than by local critics), it is for its action sequences, its slick editing, its mastery of special effects . . . . To praise the Hong Kong cinema in these terms is not only to prize it loose of its very specific cultural space; it is also to place the kung fu films . . . as the examples par excellence of an emergent international Hong Kong cinema.
>
> (1997: 18)

Abbas finds it indispensable to retell the significance of Hong Kong cinema through a batch of less violent films, which he calls the new Hong Kong cinema. In another context, Wimal Dissanayake also attributes the decreasing social significance of the later works of Oshima Nagisa, who is famous for his representations of violence, to the surrendering of his earlier Japanese self-positioning to a universal one conflicted by Western orientations and impulses (1996: 152). To many scholars, Western viewers devour the violence presented in Asian films regardless of the films' embedded social context, which in the end only harms the authenticity and the creative vigor of these cinemas.

Interestingly enough, while critics condemn the West's global exportation of media violence, Western audiences supposedly cannot get enough of the violence portrayed in East Asian cinema. The two seemingly opposite discourses locate different sources of media violence, one in the West and the other in Asia. But both postulate a negative view of violence and globalization with the West as the center: in one case the West is the producer of violence while in the other case it is the consumer, yet in both cases Asians are victimized. In fact, as Rothman argues, filmic representations have always been considered violent in nature, considering phases like "film-shooting" and the strong ideological power early filmmakers, like Sergei Eisenstein, gave the medium (2001: 41). It is often persuasive to analyze the "violent" nature of cinema through an Orientalist discourse: on the one hand, Western media export violence and force it on Asian viewers; on the other hand, Western viewers exploit Asian subjects by watching them suffer and hurt (Steintrager 2005).

In general, it is easy and tempting to posit binary oppositions between the Oriental and the Occidental in analyses of media and cinematic violence. Since the monumental colonial theories of Frantz Fanon and Edward Said, we have become used to the discourse of violence in the study of the East–West relationship, which always implies political power differences between the two cultural and geographic locations. In the case of cinema and other mass media, which themselves can be vehicles of violence, the victimization of the non-West is particularly convincing and alluring. This chapter is not meant to challenge this formula – in our increasingly globalizing Asia, the cultural domination of the West is irrefutable. However, a major problem of critiquing media violence in a binary East–West international relationship is the emphasis on the social effects of violence over violence as a style of representation, so that violence is understood more as an idea than an expression, or an expression with definite effects. While violence is a structure of power with social effects circulating within a culturally and geographically predetermined hierarchy, it can also be seen as an empty signifier that floats around the world in metonymical ways.

In the case of the new Asian cinema, although its violent images are not devoid of Orientalist assumptions, we might be able to avoid simply reading the violence featured as a direct result of the Western market if we can read violence as not just a theme but also a style. This new pan-Asian cinematic identity is not only a stereotype constructed by the West, but is also deliberately built and celebrated by Asian viewers and filmmakers. While many viewers in the West might have exoticized and eroticized the violence featured in Asian films, many Asian viewers also indulge in the violence, sometimes considering their own Asian films better than, say, Hollywood films precisely because of the more energetic and flexible style. There is a clear tendency among individual East Asian filmmakers to mimic each other, forming a loose identity of pan-Asian cinema both in the festival circuit and in the global commercial film market. And it is the circulation of violence that most effectively builds the transcultural identity of this New Asian Cinema. This tendency can be detected not only in the commercial cinema but also in alternative films. Not simply seeing violence as a tool to anchor the sensational identification of global viewers, some Asian filmmakers are also interested in analyzing social or psychological violence of their own communities through a common stylistics of representation. In other words, I want to show in this chapter that the inter-Asian copying of violence is both an idea and an expression – the mechanism of cultural copying is more complex than that formulated by copyright discourse.

Going beyond Hong Kong action films

It is clear that violence is one of the most profitable and popular themes in commercial cinema, and its increasing intensity could be linked to the increasingly diversified markets films have to serve. According to Frederick Wasser (1995), the rise in irresponsible depictions of violence in American films can be explained by the need for Hollywood to service a global audience with easy-to-understand action movies. The global audience is too infinite to be knowable, and violence seems to be an easy way out. This argument can also be applied to the marketing concerns of many contemporary Asian cinemas, which are reaching more viewers around the world through various new distribution networks like Internet, DVD sales, and cable TV. While Hollywood may rely on the spectacular representation of violence to appeal to Asian viewers, Asian cinemas also attract world viewers with violence. But the two strategies are not parallel: in this racially predisposed global entertainment market, Hollywood can claim a global identity, yet Asian cinema must differentiate itself from Western cinema and find an alternative identity to legitimize its commercial and cultural projects. Chua Beng Huat (2004) understands the advent of a trans-Asian popular culture commercially. He argues that the construction of a pan-East Asian identity is a conscious project for the producers of East Asian popular culture, based on the commercial desire of capturing a larger audience and market within Asia. Reading the phenomenon from a cultural point of view, Lori D. Hitchcock states that the increasing popularity of Asian films in Japan reveals an ideological shift in Japanese society toward identification with other people in Asian locales, particularly Hong Kong, as they "occupied with the same questions of non-Western, (post)modern, and local/global identities" (2002: 71).

Hong Kong action cinema occupies a crucial position in this formation of a new pan-Asian cinematic identity, which can differentiate itself from Hollywood, yet potentially develops a new transnational Asian identity. Some emerging Asian film-makers openly acknowledge in their own films their indebtedness to Hong Kong action films. The Japanese film *Go* (dir. Isao Yukisada, 2001) and the South Korean film *Once Upon a Time in High School: Spirit of Jeet Kune Do* (Maljukgeori Chanhoksa; dir. Yu Ha, 2004), for example, both highlight the status of Bruce Lee as the ultimate transcultural Asian masculine ideal. Hong Kong action cinema has obvious cultural distinctions; however, the universal sensual enjoyment of violence also facilitates an easy identification among viewers from different cultural backgrounds. As I mentioned elsewhere

> This aesthetics [of Hong Kong action cinema], emphasizing choreography design, dexterity of action, and editing craft impregnates a specific type of male representation that displays fanciful actions and a refined body, which can be contrasted with Hollywood's standard hard-boiled representation of masculinity.
> (Pang 2002c: 334)

Hong Kong cinema fleshes out a new masculinity that, on the one hand, appeals to both Asian and world viewers because it is different from traditional Hollywood representations, and, on the other hand, easily travels and becomes a transnational style.

In fact, in the West, where "Asia" is a more comprehensible cultural and commodity form than individual Asian cultures are, distributors and investors are also attracted to construct a new Asian cinematic collective largely based on the already familiar stylistics of Hong Kong action films. Contemporary Asian cinema is a diversified entity; marketers and critics need to construct a seemingly unified image and brand them with generic terms, and action is a convenient category with which to link culturally diversified film contents. One critic writes: "In the last ten years . . . a new kind of filmmaking has sprung up in the Orient – less populist than classic chop-sockey, yet still massively violent" (Mason 2002). Theaters advertising make claims such as this: "On the last Sunday of every month, Subway Cinema hosts a screening of an Asian movie that'll blow your mind" (Subway Cinema 2004). And last but not least, film festival organizers also promote these films: "In recent years, Asian cinema has produced energetic and vibrant popular and art house films, which have gained acceptance around the world" (James 2004). From critics to distributors, these mediators portray a common image of New Asian Cinema characterized by action and speed, shocks and excitement – as if Asian cinema is the primitive Other of the civilized American and European cinemas.

Taiwanese scholar Ding-Tzann Li accuses Hong Kong cinema of being hegemonic, as its domination in the Asian cinematic market jeopardizes the survival of many of the smaller national cinemas. But all fifteen "hegemonic" Hong Kong films Li identifies are action films (1998: 132–5), despite the fact that Hong Kong cinema produced films in many different genre types during the period Li discusses. Li's obviously biased sampling can be explained by the fact that Hong Kong cinema is known around the world, both to critics and viewers, primarily for its action films. Jackie Chan films play anywhere in the world, whereas most dialogue-based comedies stay local. The extremely popular films of Steven Chow, for example, generally fail to break into non-Chinese markets. But his *Shaolin Soccer* (*Shaolin zuqiu*, 2001) did, as he deliberately associates his film with Bruce Lee and the action tradition, which is the most globalized segment of Hong Kong cinema. *Shaolin Soccer* presents the two dimensions of action I have discussed: it features the playing of an "international" sport in the "Chinese" way. While soccer is supposedly a global sport, kung fu is distinctly Chinese. The combination of soccer and kung fu seems to produce an exotic version of a universal form. Speculatively, Steven Chow might justify his creation and stop others from making a similar kung fu soccer film by arguing that he appropriates soccer-playing as a universal idea but renders it with his own unique kung fu expressions. But obviously, this dichotomizing of a unique expression (kung fu) and a universal idea (soccer) is fragile, because the success of the film also hinges on soccer as an expression (action and speed) and kung fu as an idea (power, strength of will, hard work, and dignity). We might ascribe the global success of *Shaolin Soccer* to its action elements, but the action also signifies, communicates, denotes, and connotes. Obviously, it is very difficult to differentiate action as an expression from action as an idea.

The apparent universal appeal of action also encourages filmmakers to copy each other's violence. In general, this quasi-unified identity of pan-Asian action cinema is both discursively forged by critics or distributors and consciously constructed by filmmakers through mutual copying. While Japanese films of the 1950s and the 1960s influenced many Hong Kong filmmakers in the 1970s and the 1980s, no single Asian cinema can now be immune to the impact of Hong Kong action films. According to John Woo himself, the Japanese film *The Rascal* (*Narazu-mono*; dir. Ishii Teruo, 1964) had a major impact on *The Killer* (*Diexue shuangxiong*, 1989),[1] and in turn the influence of John Woo can be easily seen in many recent Japanese and Korean gangster films. The numerous bullets and punches shooting from one cinema to another weave a network of trajectories that connect different Asian cinemas, collating a pan-Asian violent cinema whose identity is fantasized through action, both as expression and as idea.

This quasi-identity of this transcultural cinema is contradictorily made up of, firstly, the culturally heterogeneous backgrounds of various national cinemas, and secondly, viewers' sense of familiarity with certain common styles of action films. We can take the Thai film *Ong-Bak* (dir. Prachya Pinkaew, 2003), a recent global hit, as an example to demonstrate how the global market welcomes culturally diversified products with familiar forms, encouraging the mutual copying of violence among different Asian cinemas. The film depicts the journey of a rural young man, Boonting (Phanom Yeeram), to Bangkok to find a sacred Buddha statuette called Ong-Bak that was stolen from his village. Along the way, Boonting combats his adversaries with astounding athleticism and traditional Muay Thai skills. As a low-budget film with an uncreative plot, the film mainly sells the power and brutality of Muay Thai. Muay Thai is a martial art combining kicking, kneeing, elbowing, and punching in a manner that is rather free – in contrast to, say, the more graceful and structured kung fu seen in Hong Kong cinema. Muay Thai is direct and brutal, and emphasizes efficiency and economy of movement – as opposed to the polished, twirling forms favored by the Hong Kong style of action cinema now dominating the world's cinematic logic of movement.

Ong-Bak has attracted much global attention precisely because it is an update of Hong Kong action films. Many of the film's international reviews compare the actor Phanom Yeeram with Hong Kong action stars ranging from Bruce Lee to Jackie Chan and Jet Li, and consider the Thai action scenes featured in the film to surpass those in the seemingly dated and hackneyed Hong Kong action cinema, now allegedly corrupted by the Hollywood system.[2] But many viewers may also note *Ong-Bak*'s obvious and extensive copying of Hong Kong cinema on both the levels of style and plot, from Jackie Chan-style acrobatic performances to the chop-sockey style of narrative seen in many Hong Kong kung-fu movies in the 1970s and 1980s – which often involve a rural hero fighting against modernization. As a reviewer asserts,

> Watching *Ong-Bak* I felt what it must have been like to watch the Hong Kong film industry when it first exploded onto the international scene all those decades ago, filled with bravado, pure balls, and unbound energy. Before Hong Kong became a bad mirror image of Hollywood, now lost in silly bliss with films like *The Twins Effect* and other CGI-burdened "kung fu" films, they were *Ong-Bak*.
> (Nix 2004)

It is this subtle play of similarities to and differences from familiar Hong Kong films that makes this Thai film both a member of the New Asian Cinema collective and at the same time a radically new offshoot from Hong Kong and Hollywood traditions. In other words, while the global market favors violence, viewers are particularly attracted to films with careful engineering of novel action scenes and references to earlier films.

In his classic study of Western poetry, Harold Bloom (1973) argues that new poems originate mainly from old poems; that the primary struggle of the young poet is to "clear imaginative space" for him- or herself through a creative misreading of great poets of the past. If Bloom's study is influential because it describes the universal predicament of all young artists, we can also read this "misprision" from the other end, in that readers are receptive to new works that reference familiar ones. As demonstrated in their writings, fans of *Ong-Bak* belittle Hong Kong films in order to highlight the fresh sensations of the Thai action film, and action scenes might be the most accessible and visible elements of commercial films for viewers to compare and contrast. A key to commercial success is these new films' ability to invite derogatory readings of earlier films that viewers originally liked – a disavowal of the established masters. *Ong-Bak* successfully attracts those Hong Kong cinema fans by telling them that it is like – but also better than – familiar kung fu films.

As I mentioned in the Introduction chapter, the mechanism of copying, or mimesis, always invites a complex interplay between similarities and difference. I have also illustrated that our global consumer culture effectively reinforces the classic dynamics of "pseudo-individualization" and "standardization." Cultural differences are both dissolved in and instigated by the global commodification of culture. I believe that the new "violent" identity of Asian cinema is a powerful case to illustrate this point – it demonstrates how contemporary culture makes use of cross-cultural copying to produce a product that can be consumed both globally and locally. For Asian cinemas, copying and surpassing the already standardized action designs can be an extremely effective strategy for breaking into foreign markets, as it marks the film's cultural uniqueness yet also retains a universally accessible cinematic expression. But the balance between familiarity and surprise must be carefully maintained so that consumers are excited – but not alienated – by the new product. In general, for world viewers who both desire and fear cultural differences, violence packaged in idiosyncratic cultural stylistics is very attractive, because it is often both accessible and inaccessible: inaccessible because of its claimed embodiment of cultural secrets, and accessible because it is so readily understood by all.

A key marketing strategy of many Asian cinemas in the global market is their ever-renewed renditions of violence, both as an expression and as an idea, with a careful calculation of the interplay between the novel and the familiar. While I have demonstrated how the stylistics of violence travels across cultures, I want to continue to explore how violence can also be a "culturally specific" idea. It must be pointed out that the brand name of New Asian Cinema is more than just a commodity. The mutual borrowing of certain stylistics and concerns among a group of culturally diversified filmmakers does not boil down simply to marketing calculations. Focusing on the theme of violence, I will continue to explore how some alternative Asian filmmakers attempt the reverse of their commercial counterparts – they try to question the ideology of violence by desensationalizing violence – with the similar aim of addressing a transcultural audience.

Representing social and psychological violence

A favorite topic among Asian filmmakers is social and cultural violence: modernity and modernization based on Western or global models can be seen as a form of violence directed against local life and people. Asked about the recurring theme of vengeance in his films, South Korean director Park Chan-wook (*Joint Security Area: JSA*, 2000; *Sympathy for Mr. Vengeance*, 2002; *Old Boy*, 2004) explains:

> With the development of civilization and the rise in education levels, people have had to hide their rage, hate and grudges deep within them.... The fact that people have to resort to another type of violence in order to subjugate their initial guilty consciences is the most basic quality of tragedy characteristic in my movies thus far.
>
> (Russell 2004)

Miike Takashi (*Audition*, 1999; *Dead or Alive*, 1999; *Agitator*, 2001) is another emerging Asian filmmaker who relies on violence to portray wider social ills. He also connects the violence in his films with that in society:

> I suppose film takes up the slack of what is not expressed in Japanese society. Obviously it is good that Japan is a safe place, but I wonder if there is something unnatural about the placidity of Japanese society. Anyway, it looks like we won't be able to hold onto that in the future.
>
> (Rees 2001)

The violence that permeated Hong Kong cinema and the Korean New Wave in the late 1970s and 1980s is often associated with local cultural resistance to modernization. As many critics have pointed out, Chinese nationalism is a red thread that runs through much of Tsui Hark's Hong Kong action cinema (*Zu: Warriors From the Magic Mountain*, 1983; *Peking Opera Blues*, 1986; *Once Upon a Time in China*, 1991) (Teo 1997: 162–74). Others argue that through the representation of psychological and physical violence, classic Korean New Wave cinema, as shown in *Chilsu and Mansu* (*Chilsu wa mansu*; dir. Park Kwan-su, 1988), "ultimately depicts a culture that denies the material success and personal security it tries to create" (Gateward 2003: 125). In general, while violence is a key selling point for Asian cinema in the world market, the violence depicted in much of the auteur Asian cinema is associated with local or national cultures' struggle to maintain their own cultural identity against modernization. Between the global market and one's cultural identity, violence is dialectically embedded in the modernization dilemma of many Asian cinemas.

While many of these auteur Asian filmmakers continue to use bloody scenes to assert their artistry, many others choose to explore the "ideology" of violence by avoiding from its blatant representation. The general ethics of our modern society, as demonstrated in the works of many media effects scholars, is still prejudiced against the representation of violence; filmmakers might easily be thrown into a moral dilemma: is their representation of violence becoming a form of entertainment? Cinema is considered by many to be a strong ideological apparatus, and filmmakers are held responsible for the messages that viewers receive. As mentioned earlier, inviting the viewers to watch, and probably to enjoy, violence can be a form of exploitation and moral corruption.

David Bordwell claims that "as if in rebuke to Hong Kong's brash sensationalism, Asian festival cinema slips steadily toward fixity and silence. Scenes of violence become awkward or opaque" (Bordwell 2000: 256–7). Bordwell's explanation of the dichotomization of Asia's commercial films and art films in terms of action and silence might be underdeveloped, but the tendency of alternative filmmakers to use a calm style with long takes and little action is obvious, in Asia as in the world. While commercial films rely more and more on action scenes to engage world viewers, many of the filmmakers hopping on the festival circuit choose to differentiate their works from mainstream movies by their extreme calmness. This is specifically the case for contemporary Taiwanese and mainland Chinese filmmakers, who are sullenly struggling against the overdose of Hong Kong action films in local markets and abroad. As Nornes and Yeh demonstrate, in order to compete with the highly popular Hong Kong films in its domestic markets, in the early 1980s the Taiwanese government's Central Motion Picture Corporation began to support young and promising local directors who were producing their first films – they became Taiwan's own New Cinema Movement (Nornes and Yeh 1998). We can safely assume that most of these new Taiwanese directors made films with latent or deliberate ideological opposition to the ultra-commercialism of Hong Kong cinema. But such deliberate suppression of sensationalism does not make violence disappear. I agree with Bordwell that the calm style is a prominent, if not dominant, stylistic form permeating the so-called new Asian "art" cinema. By suppressing social and psychological violence through the use of calm styles, filmmakers can avoid the sensational or spectacular dimension of violence that supposedly creates pleasure and invites real social violence. But it is also clear that many of these young Asian filmmakers continue to investigate the social and cultural violence of their communities. Tactics like long takes and still cameras can construct a safe haven for filmmakers to "investigate" violence rather than to "exploit" it.

An interesting case in point is the cinema of Hou Hsiao-hsien (*The Puppetmaster*, 1993; *Flowers of Shanghai*, 1998; *Millennium Mambo*, 2001). Hou himself admits that he always aims to represent Taiwan's terror and repression in his films (Ellickson 2002). *City of Sadness* (*Beiqing chengshi*, 1989), for example, engages violence as a theme and an expression allegorizing Taiwan's cultural identity and colonial experience (Nornes and Yeh 1998), but at the same time it differentiates itself from other Chinese commercial films by its extreme calmness. The result is Hou's "trademark" representation of fighting and political violence with long takes and long shots; often the violent scenes are replaced by other allegorical scenery that is extremely peaceful, such as nature scenes. *City of Sadness* prevents the audience from being absorbed by and enjoying the violence, forcing them to contemplate philosophically on the social meanings of violence instead of bypassing intellectual dimensions.

This specific style of Hou turns out to be pan-Asian. While Hou's serene, minimalist style is also indebted to other Asian – particularly Japanese – directors like Ozu Yasujirō, Hou's aesthetics have influenced a lot of younger auteur filmmakers (Bordwell 2002). In fact, Hou at one point admits that his goal was to create an indirect style that would belong to "the East" without specifying China, Japan, or even Taiwan (Udden 2002: 55), and he just made his first Japanese film *Café Lumiere*

(*Kohi Jikou*) in 2004 with subtle references to Ozu's 1953 masterpiece *Tokyo Story* (*Tokyo Monogatari*). His "pan-Asian" style partly explains why many young Asian filmmakers find Hou's style appealing. This repressed style of representing violence is also empowering due to the bipolar signification of violence: it is universally comprehensible and appealing, yet it can also be easily appropriated to allegorize culturally specific experiences.

While commercial films design novel action scenes and aesthetics to cover up the hackneyed effects and ideology of violence, many alternative young Asian filmmakers adopt Hou's style to investigate their own place-based cultural issues. For example, Kore'eda Hirokazu (*After Life*, 1998; *Distance*, 2001; *Nobody Knows*, 2004), perhaps the most sought-after new Japanese filmmaker in international film festival circles, has shown much respect for the New Taiwanese Cinema,[3] and his first feature film *Maborosi*'s (1995) references to the films of Hou Hsiao-hsien has also been widely observed by critics (Mackintosh 1996). As the first feature film of an unknown director, *Maborosi* surprised many by sweeping international film festivals – it won the "Osella d'or" at the Venice Film Festival, the "Dragon & Tiger" in Vancouver, and the "Gold Hugo" in Chicago. This film's success may not be unrelated to its clear reference to Hou's aesthetics, which dominated the international film scene at that time.

Kore'eda considers *Maborosi* to be a shocking film; however, he wants to differentiate his films from other commercial films featuring "fast cutting, loud music, blood spewing everywhere and gunshots permeating the scenes" (Feinsod 1996), which partly reveals and explains his strong indebtedness to the New Taiwanese Cinema. *Maborosi* depicts the psychological struggles of Yumiko in the face of the frightening childhood memory of losing her grandmother and of the recent death of her first husband. She rediscovers herself after moving to her new husband's home in a remote village on the Noto Peninsula, by the Sea of Japan. *Maborosi* is an extremely peaceful and calm movie, with static camerawork and extremely long takes that unequivocally remind us of Taiwan's New Wave.

While *Maborosi* can be meaningfully compared to many of Hou's early films like *Time to Live, Time to Die* (*Tongnian wangshi*, 1985), I will focus here on *City of Sadness* because of the success of the film around the international film festival circuits – its global comprehensibility. The repressed violence in *Maborosi* can be compared to that in *City of Sadness* on two levels. First, both films displace violence with representations of nature. Some Taiwanese critics consider Hou Hsiao-hsien politically soft precisely because of this film style. In *City of Sadness*, according to a local critic, "every time things go wrong politically, Hou shifts to mountains, seas, or fishing boats instead of showing the real violence. Social evils are displaced and misplaced by the beauty of nature and calm scenery" (Liao 1991: 130). Like *City of Sadness*, the calmness of *Maborosi* is also dialectically contrasted with repressed violence. In *Maborosi* we do not see either death, and we seldom see Yumiko express her suffering; the psychological violence is displaced and reinforced by the raging Sea of Japan and the harsh but beautiful weather of Noto. I will return to my discussion of the political implication of this particular style; here I want to reiterate that how to represent violence has become a moral question for individual directors, and many of them choose to forgo violence rather than risk violence becoming exploitation and entertainment.

Second, as in *City of Sadness*, the psychological violence in *Maborosi* is an allegorical representation of a social situation. By focusing on the liberating forces of nature, the director Kore'eda links Yumiko's personal suffering to a repressed collective experience of the violence of urban modernity. As Donald Richie asserts, "In *Maborosi*, Kore'eda rejects not only contrived storylines and editing emphasis, but the media-driven consumer madness of urban Japan as well" (2001: 241). If the repressed violence in *City of Sadness* refers to the general state of being of a people who cannot speak for themselves, *Maborosi* shares these allegorical representational tactics, connecting personal suffering to the common feelings and experience of a community. However, *Maborosi* also retains a strong individual psychological dimension that *City of Sadness* does not emphasize. According to Kore'eda himself, the film is about an undefined feeling of loss that permeates younger generations of Japanese, in that they all share a lack of certainty about anything.[4] The untamed sea and weather can be seen as metaphors for a certain longing to return to nature and to pure cultural roots uncorrupted by modernity, but nature as represented in *City of Sadness* does not have this nostalgic dimension.

Kore'eda also appropriates Hou's aesthetics of repressed violence as a means of purification and achieving personal freedom. There is a tradition in Japanese films of using violence to assert and defend a pure cultural tradition against modernity. Dennis Washburn argues that the aesthetic representation of violence in the classic Japanese film *Vengeance is Mine* (*Fukushu suru wa, ware ni ari*, 1979) is an effective and complex way for the director Imamura Shohei to assert an authentic Japanese culture in the face of the West and modernity. As the final stop-action shot of the film suggests, the violence of the protagonist is transfigured as a spirit of pure, irrational desire that seeks the arrest of time, amounting to a culturally essentialist statement by Imamura, who links the aesthetics of violence to myth-making (Washburn 2001: 229). Although Kore'eda and Imamura seem to have little in common stylistically, their interest in the exploration of the theme of violence might demonstrate a connection between them.

In *Maborosi*, the dual signification of violence – social violence and personal redemption – can be observed in the two contrasting deaths that haunt Yumiko. Her grandmother left the family because she wished to die in her own hometown, while Yumiko's husband's suicide is interpreted as his own return to freedom. Yumiko's grandmother's identity is rooted in a strong cultural tradition, while her husband's is that of a free subject. In other words, if Hou "elevates" violence on an individual level, making it a metaphor for the historical condition of a culture, Kore'eda both welcomes and resists this tendency of allegorization, maintaining both the public and private dimensions of violence. Although he copies the seemingly transcultural style of Hou Hsiao-hsien, Kore'eda deviates from Hou's political messages.

Like Kore'eda, many of the most sought-after Asian filmmakers in major film festivals are directly or indirectly influenced by Hou, whose style is highly adaptable to different political agendas. Comparing the violence depicted in the commercial sector and the art sector of the New Asian Cinema, we see that representations of violence, as an idea or as expression, can be both globally comprehensible and culturally diverse. This would explain why Asian filmmakers use violence, whether as a metaphor or as a sensational appeal, to construct cultural identities as well as to gain global renown.

The transcultural signification of violence

Violence is both an expression and an idea, and what it communicates to viewers can take the path of both commercial sensation and philosophical reflection. In spite of the film's claimed novelty, *Ong-Bak* is shockingly similar to the Hong Kong films it strives to supersede, both in terms of its action (Jackie Chan-style acrobatic movements) and theme (a heroism marked by collectivist ethics and traditional culture). *Maborosi*'s appropriation of *City of Sadness* also demonstrates the rich dynamics of similarities and difference. Although *Maborosi* employs a style similar to that of New Taiwanese Cinema to express Japan's own unique cultural conditions, the domestic concerns of the film are also largely comprehensible to global viewers because of its visual metaphors. The film ends with its narrative unresolved, suggesting that Yumiko's psychological struggle is radically private. But this radical privateness becomes accessible to viewers through the allegorization of violence. In a way, the easy symbolism of the violent sea and weather to represent Yumiko's psychological state mocks any effort to keep her struggles to herself. To global viewers, violence probably most easily manifests the cultural otherness they cannot access. In other words, the different forms and significations of violence cannot be categorized through simple dichotomies like idea–expression, culture–transculture, art–entertainment. What needs to be stressed, I believe, is the extreme malleability and richness violence as a transcultural form of representation contains: violence as idea and as expression are both transculturally accessible.

As J. David Slocum has argued, "One of the difficulties in making sense of film violence around the world is the extreme variability of the contexts in play and the methodologies therefore in use" (2001: 13). But this diversified cultural application is probably made possible by the fact that violence is transculturally appealing and comprehensible, so that in spite of its diversified cultural significations, violence is still probably the most accessible cinematic form around the world, particularly in its ability to conquer both the entertainment and the high-art markets. In general, violence is extremely fluid in meaning, yet it is also a fundamental part of humanity, so that it both resists and invites allegorization. The mutually conditioning transcultural and culturally specific dimensions of violence encourage individual Asian cinemas to copy each other's stylistics for the dual purposes of global marketing and identity assertion, simultaneously producing a pan-Asian cinema of violence and culturally distinct identities.

This might explain why Rey Chow finds the representation of violence a new ethnography common to Fifth-Generation Chinese films (1995: 143–5). Chow characterizes Zhang Yimou's films as a new ethnography: their cultural details suggest collective and hallucinatory significations of ethnicity. The power of these details lies not in their authenticity but in their mode of signification, which allows the films to be spectacular and imaginative writings about China. Violence is the strongest dimension of this "ethnographic" signification that is both spectacular and imaginative. The bruised body of the beautiful Gong Li in *Judou* (1990) shocks the viewers (R. Chow 1995: 166–72). Extending this argument a bit, the displaced representation of violence in *City of Sadness* or *Maborosi* serves the same purpose, compelling viewers to use their powers of imagination to come to terms with the meanings of and the reasons for violence. But the one dimension missing in Hou's style that Chow detects in Zhang's films is the "confrontational" power between the filmed subject and the viewer, and this stylistic difference might invite us to think about violence's transcultural significations beyond a rigid East–West hierarchy.

Both Zhang and Hou investigate and represent cultural violence in their early award-winning films, but the former focuses on woman as the bearer of suffering and foregrounds her pain, while the latter tries to push the violence as far away from the camera as possible to avoid viewers' fetishization of the violence. In a way, Zhang and Hou employ opposite visual politics to represent cultural violence, in that one exploits exhibitionism while the other denies it. Chow praises Zhang's blunt display of such visual confrontation as a profound understanding of the power of image. But a major area of dispute in Chow's criticism also lies here: this confrontation necessarily implies a polarized struggle for power between the viewer and the viewed. Metaphorically it can be extended to the confrontation between the West and China, and between male and female. This model runs the risks of ideologically predetermining the meanings and the impacts of representation in a cultural hierarchy, which she actually criticizes in her own works. While Hou's films might not engender the same kinds of powerful visual confrontation, the binarism of male/Western/viewer and female/Chinese/viewed is also more difficult to establish than it is in Zhang's films, at least according to Chow's arguments.

However, Chow's criticism also helps us to reread Hou, whose "transculturality" readily invites a politically indifferent voyeurism. Both refer to specific cultural experiences: Zhang's close-ups invite direct confrontation between the viewer and the filmed subject, while Hou's distancing effects protect the viewer by putting him or her in a safe position. As Chow discusses, in Judou's bathing scene, both Judou and the viewer occupy relatively vulnerable and rigid positions – they must participate in the direct gaze. However, Hou's long takes and distant shots defer any personal identification, so that viewers can reflect on the situations without personally identifying with, or being responsible for, the political violence. This explains some local critics' discomfort with the political softness of *City of Sadness*. Hou's distancing effects may in fact weaken the trans-Asian identity that is allegedly constructed in the New Asian Cinema. Watching social violence in Taiwan through Hou's pacified stylistics, viewers of another cultural background can easily study the situations, but only from a third-person position, necessarily diluting any political engagement.

Wimal Dissanayake argues that "Hou Hsiao-hsien displays no anxiety about appealing to Western audiences," which demonstrates his cultural authenticity (1996: 154). In fact, much of the scholarly criticism on Hou Hsiao-hsien's cinema to date has been culturally specific, praising his commitment to and skill in dealing with Taiwan's history and its problems. But Hou's stylistic representation of violence, which is too simple a symbol to allegorize the very complicated cultural experience and identity struggle of the Taiwanese, also invites viewers of other cultural backgrounds to objectify Taiwan; Hou runs the risks of self-subalternization and self-exoticization, for which Chow is critical of Fifth-Generation filmmakers in general

(1995: 148). The tensions between asserting one's cultural identity and inviting transcultural recognition persist.

Being the dominant socio-legal discourse regulating the realm of culture, copyright is completely ignorant of such dynamics of cross-cultural copying, because copyright formulates creativity and cultural productivity according to financial incentives and damages only; it is not equipped to understand copying as a mechanism which both constructs and destablizes globalization. To put it in another way, today's global copyright regime will never truly understand copying, because it is the numerous numbers and kinds of copying that make up the dynamics of globalization, the phenomenon that gives rise to the current copyright regime to start with.

In the words of a recent Filipino critic: "One of the pleasant surprises I've discovered in the Philippines for the last couple of years has been the rise in appreciation of Asian cinema. No longer are we heavily biased toward all things Hollywood" (Dolor 2004). The critic's celebration of the ability of Philippine viewers to accept cultural differences, not surprisingly, leads to a desire for a wider global recognition of Philippine cultural products, and of the Philippine identity. Dolor continues: "When can the Philippines produce something like these little masterworks? . . . Or maybe our fellow Asians cannot comprehend us the way we comprehend them." The critic is asking a question that obsesses many Asian filmmakers, critics, and viewers in general, who strongly desire the global reception of their films. As Dolor implies, film as a cultural product is conflated with one's nation in general and one's cultural identity in particular; one's national films breaking into foreign markets connotes acceptance of that culture, which also demonstrates the world's recognition and endorsement of one's cultural identity.

The dynamics between comprehension and incomprehension are central to the transcultural identification and commodification of New Asian Cinema, which, once again, brings us back to the "idea–expression" dichotomy. Global viewers are able to identify with films with cultural concerns and backgrounds they are unfamiliar with, not necessarily because they understand the ideas conveyed, but it is often the familiar style that effaces the cultural distance. While the Filipino critic accuses the Asian audience of not comprehending their films as Filipinos do for other Asian films, a careful orchestration of miscomprehension is in fact the secret that makes a film marketable in the global market: we understand yet we do not understand. It might also help us identify a fundamental issue related to copying that copyright discourse fails to highlight: we copy in order to connect, but we copy also to differentiate. If copyright discourages us from copying, how can we connect and differentiate onself from others, particularly within the globalization project? I hope that this case study can help us understand that cross-cultural production and understanding, which is a key objective or prerequisite of the globalization project, is always based on copying – or more accurately, ineffective copying. Those transculturally signified cultural specificities in turn run the real risk of being misrepresented. This politics of misrepresentation leads me to *Kill Bill*.

4 Copying *Kill Bill*

Chapter 3 emphasized the complex network of copying engineered in and associated with the loosely defined New Asian Cinema, demonstrating how transcultural (mis)understanding is made possible by different politics of copying. In this chapter I shift to Hollywood, and I would like to investigate how transcultural copying is also fundamental to Hollywood's movie industry. Despite the prevailing view that Hollywood creates and exports while other countries import, modify, or pirate these productions, I want to demonstrate how Hollywood also copies Asian films on different levels. This putative transnationality in the end conjures up a unified national identity. The discourse of copyright helps us to link Hollywood's (trans)national structure to its global hegemony: the "Americanness" of Hollywood film as a representation and as a commodity is often constructed through the exploitation and repression of its transnational components, making it accessible to world markets while maintaining its national brand. This chapter, therefore, also attempts to explicate the complex mechanism of copying in today's global cinemascape by examining not only the film's text but also the context of its global circulation. But here I want to shift my attention to Hollywood's indebtedness to Asian cinema. In a way, it is naïve for Hollywood and the copyright discourse serving it to believe that cultural products and legal discourse are universally applicable and culturally neutral; however, Hollywood's global domination is built precisely on this deliberate ignorance of cultural difference.

The nationalist copyright discourse

Holding a pirated VCD copy of *Kill Bill: Volume 1* (dir. Quentin Tarantino, 2003) that he found on a street in Beijing, US Commerce Secretary Donald Evans solemnly warned the Chinese government in his speech in the American Chamber of Commerce in Beijng, "We have been patient but our patience is wearing thin" (Evans 2003). Evans was on a mission to coerce the Chinese government to further open its markets to American products and services; this economic mission was a crucial feature of George W. Bush's reelection campaign, and Evans chose to attract the media's attention and solicit the American people's identification by picking up on a pirated Hollywood film as the ultimate symbol of China's disrespect for fair trade in general and the country's robbery of American wealth in particular. The VCD copy, according to Evans, was available all over Beijing, yet the film had begun its first run in movie theaters in the United States just two weeks before and was not yet available in US stores in video or DVD format. As Evans told members of the Chamber, "It didn't take long. In the last twenty-four hours, I was able to purchase a CD on the streets of Beijing" (Evans 2003). As Evans had arrived in Beijing only the afternoon before, his assertion simply implies that roaming the streets of the capital to locate a bootlegged version of a recent hit Hollywood film was the first, and probably the most important, task for this high-profile China visit. With this pirated film in hand, Evans could praise American creativity, criticize protectionism, defend globalization, celebrate market liberalization, and curse political authoritarianism all at the same time. The bootlegged *Kill Bill* VCD effectively condenses a basket of capitalist ideology into one sublime object.

Behind this sublime object is the American interest in governing the current copyright discourse. As Ngai-Ling Sum demonstrates, "new narratives such as the 'copyright story' and new data such as 'piracy statistics' enable the self and the others [of the United States] to be redefined. Once classified as 'copyright partners' or 'copyright enemies' (i.e. pirates), countries then either join the ranks of 'most-favored nations' or are placed on the U.S. 'Watch List' " (2003: 378). While Hollywood – as so fascinatingly revealed in *Kill Bill*, which we will discuss later – is itself a major pirate of global trends and tropes, it is always accusing other countries of pirating Hollywood works. The copyright discourse becomes a handy and powerful tool for Hollywood to reinforce its global interests; but, as I will demonstrate, it also always fails to fully control the global production and distribution networks of commercial cinema, precisely because a film is not only a commodity but also a complex system of representation.

Hollywood's nationality

Film scholars have repeatedly stressed the difficulties of conceptualizing the structure and practice of national cinema because of the transnational nature of today's cinema – in terms of financing, production, and reception.[1] Although widely used, the concept of national cinema is often more a convenient hypothesis than a real practice of film-making and film viewing. Andrew Higson argues that national cinema can be practiced only on the policy level, in the areas of censorship, state funding, and local economics (2000: 63–74). An uncritical use of national cinema is also often accused of being ignorant of "nation" as an illusive and oppressive concept (Willemen 1994). Academically, there seems to be only one legitimate rhetorical use of national cinema: as a hypothetical model against Hollywood (Crofts 1993; Berry 1998; López 2000). Hollywood, therefore, is always the opposite of national cinema, both in terms of its transnational nature and its hegemonic position as the enemy of all national cinemas. But relatively few have discussed whether Hollywood can be considered a "national" cinema. Focusing on *Kill Bill*, I want to complicate the national–transnational dynamics of Hollywood on two dimensions: its transnational textual influence and its global distribution, both of which are protected by US-centric copyright discourse. On the one hand, Hollywood films actively copy elements of other film cultures; on the other hand, Hollywood uses copyright discourse to criminalize others who reproduce their film products. To situate the global status of Hollywood textually and contextually, I am interested in the film as "copy" both as a representation and as a commodity product.

On the level of representation, if *Kill Bill*, or Quentin Tarantino specifically, represents the auteur creativity of Hollywood, this cultural imperialism is built on an effective appropriation or copying of transnational ideas (Semati and Sotirin 1999). American film producers often set for themselves the task of portraying an "America" that is a dreamscape for "universal" desires rather than a historic reality (Wasser 1995). As many theorists have argued, the mythologized American nationality portrayed in Hollywood films is made possible partly through a narrative structure that tends to produce plural meanings to suit different viewers. The "transparent" texts produced by Hollywood are considered highly polysemous, encouraging diverse populations to read them as though they were indigenous. These narratives have meaning to so many different cultures because they allow viewers in those cultures to project their own values, archetypes, and tropes into the films (Olson 1999). Instead of debauching a unified national identity, such diversification of meanings holds a fantasized Americanness together.

While these readings of Hollywood as a national cinema are inspiring, sometimes the formula is posited too easily, assuming a relatively automatic identity–plurality dialectic on the representation level. I believe that there are many other mechanisms at work that hold the unity of Hollywood cinema together. Some scholars have elaborated on aspects related to industry and distribution that construct Hollywood's global hegemony (Miller *et al.* 2001). In this chapter I want to add copyright discourse to the analysis. The underlying logic of the universal application of copyright is its indifference to the nationalities of the products and parties involved, yet both Hollywood as a cultural product and copyright as a global political discourse are marked by national interests. While Americans take legal action against everybody for infringing their copyrights, almost no producers outside the United States file lawsuits against American studios. In an interview I asked Lawrence Ka Hee Wong, Director of Film-Physical Production at Shaw Brothers, about the "Shaw Scope Wide Screen" title card that appeared in *Kill Bill: Volume 1* (L. Wong 2003).[2] Wong disclosed that Tarantino's Supercool Manchu Production Company did contact Shaws for permission to use the title card, and Shaws was so honored by this credit that it asked only for a symbolic royalty in order to release the copyright. Wong admitted that in similar cases Shaws would need to watch the film before they made the decision to release the copyright; but Shaws was so grateful for Tarantino's notice that it asked no more from him. In fact, as Wong revealed, Shaws originally wanted Tarantino's production company to recognize Shaws by putting the credit in words instead of indirectly through the Wide Screen title card. However, Supercool Manchu refused the request, and Shaws happily conceded.

Secretary Evans's arrogance and Wong's humbleness reveal one key feature of the present copyright discourse governing the film industry: America vs the rest of the world. Copyright discourse has a strong national bent: people believe that the United States is the leader of the copyright discourse, and thus should be held up as the standard to which all other countries' copyright protection should aspire. Unlike the situation in Hollywood, the increasing global popularity of Hong Kong cinema has not led Hong Kong's major studios, such as Shaws, to seek more legal copyright protection of their works. To my surprise, Lawrence Wong revealed that Shaws never seriously investigates whether the copyright to their works is being infringed, particularly by Hollywood productions. Hollywood, according to Wong, is a trustworthy enterprise, as demonstrated by certain Hollywood producers who properly sought copyright permission from Shaws.

This does not mean that Shaws has no concept of copyright. In fact, Wong complained that copyright protection in Hong Kong is very weak, and explained that Shaws therefore registers their copyrights not in Hong Kong but in the United States. The sense I got is that Wong believes that things related to copyright "always" work properly in the United States; Shaws consequently trusts the name of Tarantino so much that they allow him to do anything to their films. According to Wong, the only legal copyright case Shaws ever launched took place in 1971, when its major rival Golden Harvest brought Wang Yu and the Japanese star Katsu Shintarō together to make the film *The Blind Swordsman Meets His Equal*, a.k.a. *Shin Zatōichi: Yabure! Tojin-ken* (*Dubidao dazhan mangxia*; dir. Yasuda Kimiyoshi). Shaws filed a suit against Golden Harvest, saying that the production infringed on Shaws' earlier box-office hit *One-Armed Swordsman* (*Dubidao*; dir. Zhang Che, 1967), in which the title role is also played by Wang Yu. The case is relatively unique because it involved direct market competition between Shaws and Golden Harvest.[3] The irony is that the image of the one-armed swordsman is so frequently seen in *Kill Bill* that it almost becomes a parody, particularly in the case of the character Sophie, whose arms are brutally chopped off in a violent act that symbolizes the desire of The Bride (Beatrice Kiddo, or Black Mamba) to engineer the castration of Bill.[4] Arguably, Tarantino is consciously using and stealing the image and the symbolism of the one-armed swordsman for his own film, theoretically making him as "guilty" as Golden Harvest was thirty years ago. But, of course, Shaws' inclusion in *Kill Bill* is seen as an honor instead of an insult.

While Wong insisted that concepts of copyright are very weak in Hong Kong, he has complete trust in Hollywood. Shaws filed a copyright suit against its local market competitor, but it has always been insensitive or blind to its much larger market rival, Hollywood. One of the assumptions behind this cultural disposition is that the United States is the owner of copyright – not only the copyright of products but also the discourse of copyright itself; this presumed ownership was shown in the way that Evans appropriated supposedly universal copyright discourse as an American diplomatic tool. The United States as a nation and Hollywood as a cultural industry composed mainly of transnational corporations are conflated into a monolithic power that defines what copyright is.

Therefore, current copyright discourse circulating in commercial film industries is highly conscious of nationality, but only in one direction, involving American corporations accusing people of other countries of infringing copyright. While Evans's righteous indignation at the Chinese pirating of *Kill Bill* was indicative of American diplomatic policy towards China, it seems ludicrous for the government of the PRC to complain about Tarantino abusing the ideas and expressions of Hong Kong cinema in his Hollywood film. The apparent unidirectionality of present international copyright discourse lies in sharp contrast to the numerous cinematic influences and borrowing that make up American cinema itself. Under the protection of globally applicable yet US-centric copyright discourse, the United States is always the victim and, ironically, is allowed to seek revenge (much like The Bride in *Kill Bill*).

However, as I have declared in the Introduction chapter, I want to show that copyright discourse is less powerful than it proposes to be. A film is not only a commodity but also a complex system of cultural representation. One interesting example that demonstrates how representational politics complicate this "copyrighting" discourse of Hollywood is again shown by the "Shaw Scope Wide Screen" title card in *Kill Bill: Volume 1*. There are two title cards shown at the beginning of the film, one with the Shaws logo and the other a plain line indicating a tribute to the Japanese director Fukasaku Kinji, both of which point to the influences of Asian cinema on *Kill Bill*.[5] By not rendering the tribute to Shaws in words as it does to Fukasaku, the film is clearly playing with a politics of representation that hinges on viewers' familiarity with classic Shaws productions; only those familiar with the trademark and the jingle would connect with this shot of extremely short duration. The Shaws card sublimates and complicates the film's freewheeling cultural appropriations. It is clearly an indication of piracy; or more correctly, it is against trademark law. But in this case, Tarantino's piracy becomes an act of honor, because the title card is not only a trademark; it also marks a specific politics of representation. The card differentiates those Shaws buffs, like Tarantino himself, against those (probably the majority of its young Western viewers) who do not know Shaws films. And the film would be read very differently by those viewers who recognize the Shaws title card and those who do not. From Tarantino to Lawrence Wong and Shaws' fans, the title card is a kind of secret code. A unique feature of the two *Kill Bill* films is their ability to demonstrate how an act of copyright infringement becomes an homage, and how Hollywood attempts to own the copyright discourse and define how it works. I will elaborate on the complexity of Hollywood as a (trans)national cinema by focusing precisely on two levels of cultural circulation in *Kill Bill*: the legal copyright discourse defining and protecting the films' commodity status, and the politics of representation that allows it to be embraced by viewers all over the world.

Idea copying vs product copying

As discussed in preceding chapters, a major foundation of today's copyright discourse is the "idea–expression" dichotomy, which upholds people's universal right to freely access and recycle ideas but prevents anyone from using creative expressions without the consent of the copyright holders. However, I also have demonstrated that ideas and expressions cannot be easily differentiated, and this has created countless debates in and out of courtrooms.

Despite its legal complexity, many copyright-related issues concerning commercial filmmaking can also be comprehended by translating this idea–expression dichotomy to the differentiation between copying ideas and copying products, which I briefly mentioned in the Introduction chapter. In the previous chapter I demonstrated the difficulty of differentiating ideas from their expression in film; this is so complex a question that usually the court does not bother with it. In general, in commercial cinema, only exact product piracy or direct quotation of copyrighted items, like the furniture in *Twelve Monkeys* (see the Introduction), is considered infringement, while all stylistic borrowings or appropriations are considered to be borrowings of ideas.[6] In the case of *Kill Bill*, for example, all Asian influences, such as graphic violence and action scenes, would generally fall outside legal protection, because they are considered ideas, and Hollywood, in this case, can freely appropriate aspects of other cinematic traditions without worrying about being sued. Plagiarism, strictly speaking, is an ethical issue, not a legal one, as long as it concerns the infringement of an idea instead of its expression (Vaidhyanathan 2001: 33; Goldstein 2003: 8). Piracy is direct product copying, and is unrelated to the idea–expression dichotomy. Pirates are clearly parasitic to existing creative processes, as they supposedly introduce nothing new (except the pirating technology that I will further discuss in the next chapter) to the product. Hollywood's "copying" exists in a gray area, as films incorporate foreign ideas but render them with new expressions, whose reproduction and distribution rights are subsequently fully protected by copyright law. In turn, the Hollywood producers, with their borrowed ideas and new expressions, have all the legal and commercial rights they need to stop all kinds of piracy, from pirated videotapes or discs to Internet downloads.

The bipolar "idea–expression" foundation of copyright discourse can be further linked to the practice of Hollywood filmmaking in its basic production and distribution structure: copyright discourse allows producers to borrow ideas from other cinematic traditions at the production level, but it strictly prohibits un-authorized distributors (pirates) from benefiting from the sale of the products. This logic seems to make sense in light of the economy of today's culture industry, as most of the investment goes into production rather than distribution, due to high upfront costs and the relatively low cost of duplication. In the words of an economist:

> [Copyright protected] works all have in common what economists call a "public goods aspect" to them. Creating these works involves a good deal of money, time and effort (sometimes called the "cost of expression"). Once created, however, the cost of reproducing the work is so low that additional users can be added at a negligible or even zero cost.
>
> (Landes 2003: 132)

Hollywood itself exploits this financially uneven production–distribution system, as the major studios increasingly rely on smaller production houses to make movies more cheaply, while the major studios still directly control the distribution arms. As is widely known, among the three major sectors of the movie industry – production, distribution, and exhibition, Hollywood's most profitable component is distribution, specifically global distribution. While independent producers are responsible for the production of more films than major Hollywood studios, the majors are the only organizations that have a global distribution network, so the small production houses must collaborate with the major studios (McCalman 2004: 111). Because of the weight of profit in distribution, copyright law naturally focuses on the same areas.

While both the major Hollywood distributors and the pirates engage in the same relatively low-cost section of filmmaking – distribution,[7] copyright is currently designed to protect the interests of the Hollywood majors against the pirates. Not surprisingly, it is the transnational studio-distributors such as Miramax, rather than the smaller production houses, that are the most vocal about copyright protection. Combined with the US government's painstaking diplomatic efforts, major Hollywood studios invest lavishly in setting up various copyright enterprises, like the MPAA, to coerce other states to comply with copyright principles and policy, both on legislative and enforcement levels.

The originally nationality-blind "idea–expression" principle ends up fitting into and strengthening the present global wealth hierarchy, allowing Hollywood to continue appropriating and thereby reaping the benefits of any new ideas from other cultural traditions, while piracy – product copying – is criminalized. The way American diplomacy claims ownership of Hollywood production is clearly based on a national myth. Although Hollywood does tend to serve the interests of American audiences at large, the largest profits come from its international markets. Even in terms of investment and production Hollywood is also no longer "national" as such. The media conglomeration process begun in 1985 made all the major studios transnational, and today's Hollywood is composed of only a few global media conglomerates (Gomery 2000: 25). Compared to former Hollywood studios, these conglomerates are less committed in "American" productions but tend to work in countries with the right labor force and language but lower overall production costs. As many scholars have pointed out, there has been an exodus of production from Los Angeles to countries with lower production costs in recent years: "In 1999 . . . the U.S. was losing at least $7.4 billion and 24,000 jobs to runaway productions, the majority of which were going to Canada (81 percent) and to Australia and the U.K. (10 percent)" (Hozic 2001: 116). Hollywood's "transnationality," then, traverses both its production and its market, although it is still highly US-centric. It is true that Hollywood's runaway trend depends on peripheral nations, but the highest management resides in the United States (Miller *et al.* 2001: 63). This kind of "transnationality" often reinforces American control.

US-centric copyright discourse, therefore, is raised not against but along with the transnational Hollywood system. While Hollywood is a quintessentially global industry with a global market, the copyright discourse protecting its interests is nationalist in mind, as seen in Evans's equating American interests with *Kill Bill*. If the urgency and the meanings of the global implementation of a universal concept of copyright are built on Hollywood's tremendous global appeal, copyright is a system of actions always hoping, but also refusing, to homogenize the cultural differences upon which Hollywood feeds. The paradox is this: although based on universal principles and application, today's copyright discourse is extremely nationalist in its power structure and economic interests.

To return to the speech where Donald Evans held up the bootlegged *Kill Bill* disc as evidence of China's infringements on American national interests, would there be any difference if the disc he held was a piece of computer software with an American brand rather than a Hollywood film? To Evans and the political ideology he represents, a pirated film and a pirated computer program produce the same political signification: American interests being violated by another country. But as a film *Kill Bill* is culturally more complex than a piece of computer software, in that it is not only a commodity circulated transnationally, but also a system of representation itself composed of many transnational "information flows." An example may help illustrate the point: in 1990, Hong Kong received 9.8 percent of New York's total Federal Express exports, showing the strong tie between the two global cities in the production and exchange of higher-order information (Mitchelson and Wheeler 1994: 99). Sociologists have insistently pointed out that today's global economy is organized around command and control centers coordinating the intertwined activities of firms, which, according to Manuel Castells, can all be reduced to knowledge generation and information flows (1996: 109). The global cities, of which New York and Hong Kong are certainly two, play a key role in facilitating the flow of knowledge and information across nations, which constitute the bedrock of the new global economy (Sassen 1991). Using this analogy, *Kill Bill* can be seen as transnational on two levels: the film itself is one of these Federal Express parcels circulating and being used in different areas, yet the film is also a creative combination of many of these parcels, making Castell's analysis of information flows a bit too simple. Therefore, in order to understand the system of transnational circulation of Hollywood films, we cannot just read the film as an inert commodity being thrown around the world – we also need to examine the film's text itself, which reflects and manipulates these exchanges.

The eternal problem of Hollywood

The United States has become a strong cultural power partly because it was a pirate nation in the nineteenth century (Ben-Atar 2004). As Lawrence Lessig reminds his American readers: "Our outrage at China notwithstanding, we should remember that before 1891, the copyrights of foreigners were not protected in the United States. We were born a pirate nation" (2001: 106). Such active pirating practices were particularly important to the development of Hollywood in the beginning of the twentieth century, allowing it to become the largest film industry in the world. As Siva Vaidhyanathan demonstrates, Hollywood went from copyright-poor to copyright-rich during the course of the twentieth century, as it shifted from its free and easy adaptation of other works to become in itself a global enterprise highly protective of its own works (2001: 82). The copyright protection the US government is seeking globally does not mean that the American culture industry need not "consult" the works of others. Quite the contrary – Hollywood has always actively appropriated both the ideas and expressions of other cinematic traditions. As is well known, the US film industry has always imported cultural workers, ranging from German Expressionists and Hong Kong action choreographers, for their ideas and expressions. And it also constantly usurps ideas from other cinematic traditions. For example, the Indian director Shekhar Kapur accuses the Hollywood blockbuster *True Lies* of copying the conventions of the Indian film industry in its use of the fantastic (Wasser 1995). This rapid and effective appropriation of other cinematic traditions into its own might be, ironically, one major defining feature of Hollywood as a national cinema.

As a prolific culture industry producing hundreds of feature-length films annually, it is clear that Hollywood can hardly afford the copyright doctrine of "originality." Alan Williams identifies an eternal Hollywood problem: "Where to get the basic narratives for the huge number of films to be made each year?" (2002: 151) *Kill Bill*, consciously or not, foregrounds this eternal Hollywood problem by stating almost explicitly from which film sources it borrows. In fact, very few viewers would miss the "postmodernist" style of *Kill Bill*, which freely takes and parodies François Truffaut's *The Bride Wore Black*, blaxploitation films, spaghetti Westerns, Japanese samurai films, and, of course, Hong Kong action movies. And *Kill Bill* is very frank about this web of "intertextuality," as shown in the opening titles and the numerous pilfered soundtrack cues clearly directed at the Japanese and Chinese film traditions to which the film "pays homage."

As many audiences would notice, allusions to Hong Kong cinema in *Kill Bill* are everywhere. Bruce Lee is almost the god of the film, as seen in Uma Thurman's yellow jumpsuit and Asics Tiger shoes; the "House of Blue Leaves" sequence that clearly was modeled after the final scene in *Fist of Fury* (*Jingwumen*; dir. Luo Wei, 1972); the mask of the Crazy 88 team, resembling that of Bruce Lee in *The Green Hornet*; and the character Bill, who is played by David Carradine, who starred as Kwai Chang Caine in the US television series *Kung Fu* (1972–5), a series allegedly based on a concept by Bruce Lee. And Tarantino is very honest about the influence of Hong Kong movies on his work. In an interview, Tarantino has this to say about the final "House of the Blue Leaves" sequence ending *Kill Bill: Volume 1*:

> I didn't write it as a stand alone action scene. It was just like the whole rest of the script. I was kinda working my way through it, you know. But when I didn't have a middle section, what I would do is I'd think of something I'd seen in a cool Kung Fu movie. A cool moment that Samo Hung did in that movie or Yu Wang did in that movie and let that be the space in between. Then over the course of a year I'd constantly rewrite it and rewrite it until all those things I'd take from other movies were gone and it was all filled with *original* stuff, so that's how I did that.
>
> (Turner 2004, italics mine)

If Tarantino is a distinct cult figure representing American cinematic creativity, this confession tells us something about how Hollywood creativity operates. Although Tarantino claims authorship by asserting his "rewriting" process, the film itself betrays that Tarantino has introduced relatively little that is new to the sequence. Originality, according to Tarantino, is nothing but free appropriation and transformation, which are retouched to the point that viewers can no longer identify the originals. But an interesting statement *Kill Bill* made, in relation to the above comment of Tarantino on the film, is that we do see the originals everywhere in *Kill Bill*. As we all know, *Kill Bill* is choreographed by "Master" Yuen Wo Ping, whose *The Matrix* and *Crouching Tiger, Hidden Dragon* drastically redefined the filming of action in Hollywood. But Yuen, who himself is also highly influenced by Japanese samurai films and Hollywood westerns, also choreographed many Shaws films – the films to which *Kill Bill* pays tribute and which it copies. Although in *Kill Bill*, particularly in *Volume 1*, many of the action scenes are supposed to involve Japanese samurai fighting instead Hong Kong kung fu, the action is almost entirely identical to that seen in Yuen's earlier Hong Kong productions. For both Tarantino and Yuen, *Kill Bill* is a remake of Hong Kong films, and it constantly reminds us that it is in fact very difficult to differentiate between homage, parody, or simply knockoffs.

Hollywood cannot but continue to copy ideas and expressions from other cinemas in order to maintain its annual output and global domination. I think *Kill Bill* is a uniquely rich text, as not only does it present itself as a hyper-pluralistic film with so many sources of influence that a clear remapping of these influences is impossible and meaningless, but it can also be seen as a meta-cinematic text that reflexively comments on the mechanism of Hollywood. We can use *Kill Bill* as a case study through which to understand Hollywood, particularly its relationship to Asian cinemas, in terms of the circulation and appropriation of ideas and expressions in global cinematic discourse. If the eternal problem of Hollywood, as Williams claims, is to find new forms of filmic expression, copyright also becomes its eternal problem, as copyright supposedly prevents the free appropriation of cultural creativity. The biggest irony, of course, is that current copyright discourse ends up protecting Hollywood but not protecting the sources it appropriates.

While Hollywood actively appropriates and benefits from foreign cinematic creations or production environments, the American people watch fewer and fewer foreign films. David Desser illustrates a new cinephilic culture beginning in the 1980s when video stores sprang up around the world, and when new film buffs, like Tarantino himself, watched the many foreign films that ultimately turned them into a new generation of filmmakers (Desser forthcoming). Tarantino admits that he is largely influenced by the Hong Kong martial arts movies of Angela Mao and Li Hanxiang, both in terms of themes, such as female revenge, and film style, such as the bird's eye view; both of these can be found in *Kill Bill* (Turner 2004). Desser might be right that new carriers (including videos and later VCDs and DVDs) and the new Internet culture helped shape a new generation of cinephiles who are able to watch foreign films in a rather systematic fashion. But in general the American people are watching fewer foreign movies, at least in terms of theatrical attendance. In the mid-1970s, foreign films accounted for 10 percent of box office receipts. Two decades later, the number had fallen to 0.5 percent (McChesney 1999: 38). Regarding Hollywood's global reign, Peter Wollen once concluded:

> The problem with the American dominance of global cinema... is not that it prevents Britain (and other countries) from developing cultural identities for themselves but... it also threatens to deprive America itself of views of America from the outside. American dominance... [is] harmful not simply to everyone else in the global market but also, above all, to America itself.
>
> (1998: 134)

Tarantino is definitely one of those self-selected diehard fans of Asian cinema, and he spent a lot of time and effort studying and enjoying many Asian movies in order to come up with films like *Kill Bill.* But the new cinephilia Desser describes, in which Tarantino participates, remains the pursuit of a small population.[8] Most of the American viewers watching Tarantino's films know little about Asian cinema in general. Or what they have is a generic image of Asian cinema, composed of speed, violence, and exoticism, for which Hollywood is largely responsible. On the one hand, films like *Kill Bill* present a generic Asian aura that is packaged as a "cool" and faddish product, and which, therefore, is deprived of any cultural depth. On the other hand, large studios such as Miramax are purchasing the distribution rights to many Asian films in order to become not only the owners but also the translators of these Asian films for American audiences. Dialogue is rewritten and sections are cut with the aim of taming the "culturally difficult" portions for American audiences.

If *Kill Bill*, or Hollywood in general, benefits from its free appropriation of foreign cinematic practices, a major problem that results is a cultural conflation of the different cinemas and cultures that it appropriates. People are attracted to *Kill Bill* for its diffused Asianness, in which the Japanese and Chinese filmic traditions merge into an undistinguished whole, although the hilarious Pai Mei in *Kill Bill: Volume 2* does remind viewers of the racism in Hong Kong cinema against the Japanese. The film is clearly too self-reflexive for us to believe that Tarantino is so confused by the two distinct cinematic cultures as to misread one as the other. Instead, the film has a Generation-X mentality: everything is there to be mocked, including Hollywood itself and the Asian cinemas to which the film supposedly pays tribute.

As a result, neither the Japanese nor the Hong Kong cinemas being credited in *Kill Bill* remained unified. The climatic scene in *Kill Bill: Volume 1* was set in the Japanese restaurant "House of Blue Leaves" but was filmed in Beijing.[9] According to Tarantino, there are three main advantages to this Beijing location: "The Beijing team of master Woo Ping, the Crazy 88; a vividness and invigoration of Chinese cinema that Tarantino aspires to; and shooting in the Chinese way, i.e., lame concept of scheduling" (Turner 2004). Clearly, Tarantino is attracted to the Hong Kong way of filmmaking, from the skilled labor (Yuen Wo Ping and his crews) to daily logistics (the lame scheduling). But the distinct Hong Kong flavors correspond not only to the production logic behind the scene but also the general tone of the film. The architecture of this Japanese restaurant is so un-Japanese (in spite of a few Japanese icons, such as flower arrangements) that it resembles less a Japanese restaurant than the traditional Chinese teahouse or motel (*kezhan*) so often seen in Shaws costume pictures, with flying bodies freely tossed from the second floor to the foyer. Deliberate or not, the film is full of Japanese–Chinese conflation. It inserts a "Shaw Scope" title card in the beginning of the film, but the film is supposed to be an homage to a Japanese filmmaker. Lucy Liu, who is a Chinese American, portrays O-Ren Ishii (Cotton Mouth), Queen of the Tokyo Underworld. Combining Japanese animation (*anime*) and the Hong Kong style of kung fu, *Kill Bill* can be seen as distinguishably American, as it is neither Japanese nor Hong Kong. As James Steintrager claims, regarding the cult phenomenon of Hong Kong cinema in the United States, "we are led to infer that the fan's biggest crime is really that he does not care for the hermeneutic task of understanding the other at all" (2005).

However, I am not condemning this plagiaristic, or parasitic, practice by Tarantino, who seemingly does not "respect" the sources to which he "pays homage," in the same way that Steintrager reminds us to be careful not to use cultural criticism to legitimize a "right" kind of spectatorship as opposed to the "wrong" kinds (Steintrager 2005). It is unproductive and ignorant to hold onto individual cinematic traditions as discrete and independent, as we all know that all national cinemas in the world mutually influence each other constantly. If *Kill Bill* plagiarizes Hong Kong cinema, Hong Kong cinema has often plagiarized Hollywood and other cinemas. Plagiarism is not only an eternal problem of Hollywood, but it is also an eternal problem of cinema as a culture industry, which always works very hard to maintain the pseudo-individualization of its indeed very standardized products. *Kill Bill* is unique largely because it highlights instead of conceals such acts of plagiarism.

While the climatic fighting scene in the Japanese restaurant is distinctly Hong Kong, the Shaws kung-fu style developed in the 1960s and 1970s was highly indebted to Japanese cinema. The two most distinct Hong Kong cinematic entities *Kill Bill* refers to are Shaws and Bruce Lee, which in their own ways are connected to Japan.[10] The 1970s Shaws Tarantino pays homage to was a quintessential dream factory, which produced a steady output of formulaic films in a most efficient and effective way. If Hollywood is famous for recruiting foreign talent to support its empire, Shaws ran the same way during its peak. The studio was engaged in elaborate cooperation with Japanese studios, filmmakers, and talent beginning in the 1950s, and the recruits ranged from masters like Mizoguchi Kenji, who directed *Princess Yang Kwei Fei* in 1955, to some less famous but highly talented Japanese directors, such as Inoue Umetsugu, who were stationed in Hong Kong and produced standardized generic works (Davis and Yeh 2003). In fact, it was the Japanese cinematographer Nishimoto Tadashi who patented the Shaw Scope Wide Screen process (Davis and Yeh 2003: 259), whose title card was shown in the beginning of *Volume 1*. The several rapid zooms in on Master Pai Mei in *Volume 2* that so clearly call viewers' attention to Shaws films was also likely a technique Zhang Che and his generation of Hong Kong filmmakers learned from Japanese period dramas (*jidaigeki*) films and television dramas.[11] Li Hanxiang's famous "bird's eye shot," which so fascinates Tarantino, was clearly borrowed Japanese cinema from early, like Kurosawa Akira's first film, *Sanshiro sugata* (1943).

The films of Bruce Lee also have a strong Japanese dimension. As I mentioned earlier, the "House of Blue Leaves" sequence is modeled after the final scene in *Fist of Fury*, in which the blocking – shifting through the Japanese sliding doors in both scenes – gives both Thurman and Lee different layers of spatial and emotional dimensions. We notice that while *Fist of Fury* is supposedly based upon a strong anti-Japanese sentiment, the film appropriates a lot of Japanese cinematic stylistics, particularly from the samurai films, partly reflecting the practice of Hong Kong cinema at that time. Bruce Lee himself also incorporated Japanese martial arts into his *Jeet Kune Do*. The yellow jumpsuit allegedly represents no specific style of martial art, but it gives the wearer the freedom and power to adapt to any form of fighting, which might also accurately describe Hollywood as a national cinema. In other words, Uma Thurman's gender-ambiguous Bruce Lee look could be seen as "having no style as style." Since

Hong Kong cinema always freely appropriates ideas and expressions from other cinematic or cultural traditions, the sources from which *Kill Bill* plagiarizes are not "original" as such. When advertising *Volume 1* in London, Tarantino explained to British reporters his preferred style of moviemaking: "I like movies about people who break rules, who are mavericks" (BBC 2003). The yellow jumpsuit may represent precisely such an attitude of rule-breaking. But what are the rules to be broken? In what ways can cultural appropriation with such elaborate intertexuality be seen as rule-breaking, or rule-abiding? Or is the question of who is copying whom still meaningful in today's global culture industry, which is fueled by the rapid recycling of ideas and expressions?

Acknowledging its diverse sources of appropriation, *Kill Bill*, however, should not be celebrated as a meta-textual celebration of Hong Kong and Japanese cinema; the films being appropriated are as honored as they are defamed. I must emphasize here that such a "dialogic" system of mutual borrowing is not necessarily egalitarian and receptive, as literary critics such as Mikhail Bakhtin would suggest (Bakhtin 1981). Instead, violence is often involved in any act of appropriation and alternation. According to Thomas Leitch, remakes in the end always deny their originals: "Although remakes by definition base an important part of their appeal on the demonstrated ability of a preexisting story to attract an audience, they are often competing with the very films they invoke" (Leitch 2002: 44). According to Leitch, the fundamental rhetorical problem of remakes is to mediate between two apparently irreconcilable claims: that the remake is just like its model, but better. Leitch calls this paradox disavowal: the combination of acknowledgment and repudiation in a single ambivalent gesture (2002: 53). In spite of the tribute paid, remakes are less dialogic than disavowal.

If *Kill Bill* is a remake paying homage to the Asian films it alludes to, it is also an update and a transcultural rewrite of Asian cinema, with the purpose of serving and entertaining a new generation of American and global audience members. The remake, therefore, implicitly criticizes the original for being outmoded, which in this case would mean that the white woman Uma Thurman is more relevant to today's film viewers than the Asian male Bruce Lee. In other words, by stylistically calling attention to Bruce Lee and his yellow jumpsuit, Tarantino is also calling attention to Bruce Lee's datedness. It is only through Tarantino's remake, or parody, that Bruce Lee can still be "fun." As Leitch comments, many Hollywood remakes of foreign films are imperialistic, as the goal of the remake "is to translate not a language but a culture" (2002: 56). The Hollywood remake tries to tame the uncompromising, difficult, and ultimately unresponsive elements of the original films to accommodate the demands of American consumers. In the case of *Kill Bill*, in spite of the jumpsuit, Thurman is purged of the animalistic nature of Bruce Lee: she kills because her child is killed, while the narcissist Bruce Lee kills often for the sake of self-performance and self-mythologization (Bordwell 2000: 53). Although in *Volume 2* Bill reminds The Bride that she is obsessed with killing, at the end she happily returns to the mother role she has so much desired. In the final scene of *Fist of Fury* Bruce Lee hops at the camera, posing a direct confrontation with the viewers; in contrast, Thurman smiles gently and romantically at the end of each of the two volumes, a gesture that negates all the previous anger she shows in the films.[12]

The kind of transnational cinematic appropriation shown in *Kill Bill* is more than a cobweb of intertextuality that no commercial film production could avoid; it also reveals the necessary blending of cultural specificities in the mutual copying of ideas in today's commercial cinema, upon which Hollywood as a (trans)national cinema is based. Hollywood cinema constantly borrows elements from other national cinemas, but at the same time the cultural identities of these details are deliberately confused, diffused, and ultimately destroyed. These foreign influences, which themselves are not culturally pure to start with, are either concealed by Hollywood packaging or highlighted as cultural gimmicks, marketed for the consumption of viewers all over the world.

Piracy and its debunking of Hollywood's (trans)national myth

Piracy, however, is a production and distribution system outside the control of the US-centric cinemascape, which explains the fierceness of copyright discourse with regard to the criminalization of piracy. Just as Donald Evans did in Beijing, I also picked up a pirated DVD version of *Kill Bill* in an obscure shopping mall in Hong Kong. The pirated DVD might reveal partly how this Hollywood (trans)national identity works. The visual quality of the DVD is quite satisfactory, and its prompt availability indicated that the version was taken from a screener copy, probably leaked during the post-production process. In spite of the good visual and audio quality of the pirated disc – it very much resembles official copies – one major element that defines pirated discs is their ridiculous subtitles. There are two major tasks that fall to Hollywood distributors marketing their films internationally: advertising, and dubbing or subtitling for different markets. While the pirates invest as little as they can in their business, they are the distributors of these pirated films and have to assume these two major duties. In terms of promotion, the pirates usually rely entirely on the official distributors for their advertising. But in order to catch up with the official release, the pirates must work on the dubbing and subtitling themselves, because the screener copies that serve as the master version usually do not have subtitles yet. So the subtitles in the pirated copies are interesting because, first, they are the most obvious components pirates add to the product, and second, they demonstrate how people outside the United States understand Hollywood films.

Predictabily, we run into translations of very poor quality in pirated films. The results are sometimes incredible, with subtitles suggesting little of (or sometimes meanings opposite to) the actual dialogue, thereby subverting the film's original storyline. One very interesting mistranslation in my pirated *Kill Bill: Volume 1* DVD occurred in the scene in which the two fighting women are taking a break in Vernita Green's (Copper Head's) kitchen after Green's daughter comes home from school. The dialogue between the two is as follows:

Green: You bitch, I need to know if you will gonna starting more shit around my baby girl.

The Bride: You can relax for now. I'm not going to murder you in front of your child, OK?

Green:	I guess you are more rational than Bill led me to believe you are capable of.
The Bride:	It's mercy, compassion, and forgiveness that I lack, not rationality.

But the subtitles of the pirated version translate them as:

Green:	You bitch, never want to hurt my daughter.
The Bride:	Can we have a chat? I won't hurt your child.
Green:	I can't believe you have such a temper.
The Bride:	That's my way, passion; not nationality.[13]

This set of subtitles corresponds very little to the actual dialogue, and even suggests wrong information, as The Bride originally says she does not have any compassion while the subtitles of the pirated version suggest otherwise. These kinds of subtitling mistakes are ubiquitous in pirated movies, sometimes making the storylines incomprehensible. But the most astonishing mistake in this clip is the term "nationality" replacing "rationality." The viewers of the pirated disc do know that The Bride is an American, and the nationality she refers to would be her American identity. So she is really saying, "Yes, I am rude, in spite of my American nationality, which is supposed to make me otherwise." Not grasping the dialogue, the interpreter has to rely on prior cultural assumptions – the American people, at least seemingly, are not rude – in order to make sense of the scene. In the film, this beautiful American lady has been too violent to conform to the stereotypical Chinese reading of the American people, for which Hollywood is partly responsible. This subtitle translation demonstrates that no matter how much *Kill Bill* incorporates features of other cinematic traditions to become a global product, it will be received globally as an American product. I think this sense of "Americanness" is important to the numerous illegal viewings of pirated Hollywood films all over the world, as the distinctions among different films are vague, and viewers choose the movies largely according to their nationality (say, Hollywood or Hong Kong) and their genre.

Individual scenes can also produce different meanings for different viewers. There is another noteworthy subtitling mistake in the pirated *Kill Bill*. In the ending scene of the "House of Blue Leaves" sequence, The Bride is engaged in a final fight with O-Ren Ishii in the snowy backyard. Ishii hits The Bride in the back, and The Bride is seriously wounded and dying. Ishii says, "Silly Caucasian girl likes to play with samurai sword. You may not be able to fight like a samurai; but you are going to die like a samurai." But the "pirated" Ishii says, "Like the sun-rising flesh blood, your attack is just like the blazing sun of the summer; because that's your style." Unlike the earlier section, in this scene The Bride's ethnicity/nationality is repressed instead of highlighted in the pirated version. The effect is very different: while the original line presents itself as a self-reflexive meta-criticism of the film, or of Hollywood in general, the pirated version maintains a very poetic general tone, highlighting not the individuality of The Bride, but the general cultural feelings of samurai–kung fu cinema: the "style" mentioned here refers more to the general samurai qua Hollywood style instead of the style of The Bride. While the earlier set of translation mistakes highlights the concealed American identity of the film, this second set of mistakes is based on generic expectations.

But these two sets of subtitling mistakes reveal a common logic to the cultural reception of Hollywood cinema in general – extremely diversified local readings. Subtitling is in fact a very important component in the global circulation of films, specifically in the context of Hollywood being "properly" received globally. No matter how hard Hollywood tries to produce a "universal" cultural commodity, notwithstanding the increasing use of spectacle, the storyline is still largely conveyed through dialogue, which is typically spoken in English. Proper and effective translation seems to be intrinsic to Hollywood's global regime. But pirated films, which lack proper translation, continue to cater to global viewers. At times when the translator or viewer fails to grasp the exact dialogue, he or she adds in his or her own interpretation to give it meaning. In the first set of mistakes, the translator adds his or her readings of American femininity; in the second case while the translator misses the wittiness, or the specific auteur mark, of Tarantino, he or she substitutes a general cultural feeling for the Hollywood representation of Japanese–Hong Kong swordplay. In both cases, the translator relies on his or her own imagination to supply the missing meanings of the American product. These subtitle mistakes reveal that diversified readings are always at work in the reception of Hollywood films, dialectically forging the unified global branding of Hollywood.

What I want to emphasize is that no matter how important such diversified local readings are for allowing Hollywood films to access different markets, they are not allowed to be manifested in the official versions. Translations are standardized around the world, and the distributors generally do not allow regional markets to alter original dialogue according to their own taste and values. The "creative" subtitling of pirated movies is revealing when studied in the context of Hollywood's global marketing, whose homogenizing tendency aims at effacing its transnational receptions. The major Hollywood distributors, like Miramax, both sell American films in other countries and buy the copyrights of foreign films for the US market, very much overseeing and engineering the entire global film flow. While Hollywood distributors seldom alter their American films for screening in different parts of the world,[14] they always alter the foreign films they purchase in order to cater to the American market. A recent Internet petition appeals to Disney (which owns Miramax and Dimension Films) to cease the alteration of the Hong Kong films they distribute, and particularly the irresponsible editing. As the petition claims, "the movies often have footage removed by Disney because they consider it objectionable (violence, drug use, etc.), because it contains Chinese/Asian cultural and/or political references which North American viewers may not fully understand, or (most often) simply because they want to make the movie shorter and/or change its pacing (Klotera *et al.* 2002). In fact, Disney claims exclusive distribution rights to many Asian films not only in the United States but also in many parts of the world, and thus decides how these Asian films should be shown worldwide.[15] However, a major rationale behind the alterations of the original films is their comprehensibility to American audiences, so that the world sees versions of Hong Kong films that supposedly were tailored for American viewers. This hegemony of American taste, obviously, is largely forged, as the distributors often assume that there is only a single American view, which in turn is based on the perceived inability of American audiences to accept any cultural differences. The diversified readings of Hollywood films exemplified by the above-mentioned mistranslations in fact take place not only among different linguistic groups but among the American viewers themselves, and the diversity of the American audience is inevitably sacrificed by Hollywood's (trans)nationality.

Hollywood's transnationality is composed of different kinds of copying, both on the levels of ideas making up the films and the legal and illegal circulation of the final products. Hollywood constantly copies the ideas and expressions of others and claims them as its own, forging a national identity composed of transnational influences. Copyright discourse chooses to be blind to this cultural traffic and violence and instead concerns itself only with the circulation of the final product. Thus, in copyright discourse, film is seen as just a commodity instead of a system of representation. The result is the reification of the final product – the Hollywood film – without consideration of the complex process by which the film incorporates, tames, and in the end covers up its transnational components. This ideological fallacy is governed by a national myth, the myth that the United States is both national and global at the same time, and that it has its own national identity – an identity to be consumed by people all over the world.

5 Movie piracy as a technological threat to Hollywood

As I mentioned in Chapter 4, current copyright discourse tolerates the appropriation of ideas but criminalizes product piracy. While I have discussed idea appropriation extensively in the two preceding chapters, in this chapter and the following, I focus on product piracy. I have argued that acts of copying are essential to any concept and practice of culture, and transcultural productions and their reception especially involve issues of copying. However, if mimesis is culturally productive, product piracy emphatically is not, since it involves no creative or manual manipulations that can be ascribed any cultural value. Product piracy is commonly understood to be nothing but robbery, and it undercuts the most valued aspects of our capitalist system, which protect an individual's property, creativity, and investment. As I mentioned in Chapter 2, parties with vested interests in preventing piracy condemn the practice for being uncivilized and selfish, and such allegedly universal and transcendental moral accusations work to conceal the many power networks and discourses that piracy develops along and within. I do not wish to rescue piracy from legal regulations; I am, however, interested in the cultural and social density of piracy, which is deeply entrenched in and fueled by recent developments of globalization. Rather than taking a simple morally deterministic stance, I explore the context in which movie piracy is situated – an underlying network woven by both discursive and non-discursive elements.

IPR owners can easily and legitimately label these lucrative underground businesses as thieves. But they seldom address the fact that local markets' demand for their products is what makes piracy such a booming business. The so-called victims, who created the demand in the first place, are directly promoting this "robbery," as demonstrated by the fact that many countries in which piracy is rampant – such as those in East Asia, the Middle East, and Latin America – are also the most intensely influenced by Western cultural imperialism (Bettig 1996: 214–21). However, it would be simpleminded to equate copyright owners and pirates with a West – rest dichotomy. In Chapter 6, I will discuss the meanings of movie piracy from the perspective of the sociopolitical problems a developing country such as China currently faces. Here I want to focus on another major factor shaping piracy's geopolitical network: technology. Piracy of videotaped Hollywood films was rampant in Europe in the 1980s. Doubtless Europe has been influenced by Hollywood's cultural imperialism, but movie piracy was popular in Europe at that time also because its countries – particularly the United Kingdom – possessed the then state-of-the-art Video Home System (VHS) technology (Segrave 2003: 145–56). Technology has always been a key factor in shaping movie piracy, which makes use of latest reproduction and distribution techniques to reach the masses. Oftentimes the same technology is utilized by both legitimate copyright holders and pirates, both of whom aim to accrue the greatest possible capital gain.

In fact, copyright discourse has always been transformed and underwritten by technological development. Mass culture, as its name suggests, is characterized by its accessibility to the masses, and it must be accompanied by speed: not only should products reach large numbers of people across nations, but these populations must also receive the products in a timely manner, so that global trends are created. Enhancing accessibility, both in terms of time and space, is possible only with continually updated copying and distribution technologies. As I mentioned in Chapter 1, "fixation" is essential to qualify a work for copyright; without fixation expressions cannot be circulated and reproduced, and profits cannot be made. The technology of fixation concerns not only the producers but also the pirates, who often utilize the same technology to mass produce the same products.

Book piracy, the earliest form of illegal duplication of IP, was impossible prior to the 1400s, when books could only be reproduced by hand. The concept of copyright – the right to copy – became necessary with the invention of the movable-type printing press, which in turn made piracy possible. The evolution of book piracy took another crucial turn with the invention of the photocopier, and computers have made it even easier to duplicate written documents with virtually no loss of quality in successive generations of copies. The history of music piracy also parallels the history of music recording and distribution. While it is very difficult to reproduce vinyl albums on a massive scale, the transition to cassette tapes and later to CDs made music reproduction, and therefore piracy, much easier.

Technological change also characterizes the history of movie piracy. Movie piracy existed in the form of 16mm films before the invention of the VHS and VCR in 1975. With the advent of digital technology in the 1980s, pirates could reproduce all films digitally, which engendered the phenomenon we are examining in this chapter – disc piracy. The latest vehicles for pirated movies are the digital formats circulating on the Internet; these are made possible by new technologies like broadband transmission and peer-to-peer (P2P) file-sharing software. Cyber piracy has attracted much attention in recent IP discussions, to which I will return at the end of the chapter. Recent Hollywood producers even warn that the film industry will soon be crushed if Internet file-sharing piracy continues to grow (Stahl 2003). Because in this book I am investigating copyright in relation to the politics of place, I am less interested in the Internet than in video discs – the form of technology that makes Asia a hotbed of movie piracy. Developed in 1993, VCD – and to a lesser degree DVD, invented in 1997 – represent a key transitional stage for movie piracy. This form of piracy, in contrast to the Internet piracy largely undertaken by the middle-class youth of developed countries, reveals some prominent globalization problems Asia now faces.

In the following pages, I examine the ambivalent meanings of the pirated Hollywood movies circulated in Asia. Movie piracy can be seen as one of the most important underground cultural mediators between the Asian people, who desire modernity, and the United States, which creates, displays, and exports modernity. I am particularly interested in analyzing whether the low-tech apparatus involved in Asian movie piracy demonstrates a new interrogation and understanding of Hollywood's current technological fetishism. We all know that the abundant use of technology secures Hollywood's dominant position in global cinema; the sometimes extremely poor audio and visual quality of the pirated versions of these films, however, present a laborious and alienated form of viewer identification not engineered by Hollywood the producer. This chapter will continue to develop the argument set up in the last chapter to demonstrate how product piracy never equates to perfect copying.

Academic discussions about technology often stray between technology's ideological use and implications and a critique thereof. On the one hand, we have (post)Marxists such as Herbert Marcuse, whose theory of technology hinges almost entirely on the ideological networks underlying technology's use (Marcuse 1941). On the other hand, some contemporary technoculture theorists highlight technology as an essential and inextricable part of humanity that cannot be discussed as an independent instrument, but only as an embodied experience (Mark Hansen 2000). In this chapter, I critically engage with both these positions. Technology, as a cultural mediation in a power-ridden international environment, is still used as an objectified and powerful tool to propagate the universalized meanings of progress, on which the power hierarchy of the modern world order is built. However, such instrumental reasoning and manipulation of technology is challenged by people in different parts of the world who use technology non-discursively and non-politically.

The following analysis is divided into two parts: one descriptive, and the other more speculative. I first provide an overall survey and analysis of the technology involved in Hollywood and in Asian movie piracy in order to understand the underlying disjuncture between them. I then demonstrate how low-tech movie disc piracy, which tries to capture the high-tech content and sensationalism of the Hollywood product, might complicate the relationship between technology and cultural control in the modern world. Owing to the lack of social data about the production and reception of movie piracy in Asia – due to its illegal and highly dispersed nature – this chapter is not a concrete and definite case study of the Third World's subversion of the First World. I am, instead, interested in exploring whether movie piracy can be theorized as a critical interrogation of today's international cultural politics, allowing us to arrive at a more productive understanding of technology as an expression of people's practical and corporeal experience of the material world embedded in, or sometimes superseding, a socially constructed political economy.

Hollywood technological fetishism and VCD piracy

Hollywood is clearly the party most committed to fighting movie piracy, as its interests are directly jeopardized by piracy, in terms of both immediate and future profits. One of the major tasks of MPAA/MPA is to actively fight piracy by promoting IPR legislation and law enforcement around the world. In 2000 alone, the MPA launched over 60,000 investigations into suspected piracy activities and more than

18,000 raids on pirate operations around the world – with the cooperation of local authorities (MPAA 2000). The five largest studios also recently created the Internet-based MovieLink – which allows users to rent and download movies to a PC – with the aim of countering online piracy. The number of pirated movies can be translated into American dollars representing the alleged loss to Hollywood movie producers at present; but it is the future exploitation of the market that concerns global capitalists the most. Increasingly, capitalists in the West see the Asian, and particularly the Chinese market as their future hope, but this hope can be realized only if the West can continue to dictate the rules of the game. The aggressive black market is a serious threat to this rosy business plan.

However, the cultural significance of movie piracy may lie as much in piracy's economic damage as in its threat to the alleged cultural supremacy of the American film industry. Hollywood conglomerates are now the only film establishments that can afford the latest production and exhibition technology, and they also enjoy a prime geographic position, surrounded by the most established digital information industries (A. Scott 2000). It is Hollywood's access to and manipulation of technology that defines its supreme position in world cinema. It is true that Hollywood compels the global masses to desire their products through various marketing and diplomatic means: a century of US diplomatic and economic coercion directly made Hollywood the king of world cinema. But these aggressive marketing strategies are built upon a hierarchical system, and recently only films featuring a large amount of digital imaging are classified as A-films. The continuing international success of these films induces Hollywood to further invest in computer technology,[1] making the constant expansion of this technology almost a vicious circle.[2]

However, these high-tech visual and audio effects are reproduced unfaithfully on most pirated discs circulating in Asia, undercutting Hollywood producers' attempts to use high technology to control and manipulate the desires of global audiences. Control is inherently technological in character, because it is often accomplished through the invention and manipulation of mechanisms that order and regulate activities. The recent blind worship of computer technology in Hollywood is also a form of control, but its aim is not to command physical control of the audience through systematic management, such as distribution tactics or scheduling plans; instead, it engenders a technological fetishism that fuels the fantasies of the audiences. Theodor Adorno, using Karl Marx's concept of fetishism, argues that under the manipulation of the culture industry the exchange values of commodities obscure their use values, therefore they blind us to the labor and the materiality of the products (Adorno 1991: 34). The exchange values of recent Hollywood products are overwhelmingly determined by the amount of the latest computer technology used, so that the quality and the quantity of these technologies directly affect the value of these films and overshadow all other cinematic components. By fabricating reality in order to provide the largest degree of escapism and to habituate the audience to a certain sensory form of desire, technology objectifies the audience's experience of the films to effects that can only be mastered by large film studios. This technological fetishism shared between producers and audiences allows computer effects to dominate the mentality not only of Hollywood but also of global cinema.

As Thomas Schatz demonstrates, Hollywood enjoyed a dramatic windfall in the 1980s and early-1990s, but production costs also shot up tremendously: "The rise in production costs is due largely to two dominant factors: an increased reliance on special effects and the soaring salaries paid to top talent, especially stars" (1993: 26). The huge investments in digital technologies are based on the promise of profit returns, which have often materialized in the last two decades. A blind faith in the direct relation between investment in special effects and revenue return has ruled Hollywood.[3] Novel special effects, more than any other cinematic means, most directly correlate to successful saturation advertising during the pre-screening stage. And this kind of publicity will in turn guarantee high first-weekend box-office returns, sales of tie-in products, TV syndication, and video rentals. Technology can also actually reduce certain production costs by converting exotic locales, stars, and costumes into computer-generated graphics (Hozic 2001). Investment in technology is considered one of the safest and most rational business strategies in today's film industry, and digitalization now promises eternal profits for this risky business of moviemaking.

The never-ending attempts to perfect Hollywood's production technology inevitably require constant technological upgrades on the receiving end, so that viewing equipment, not only in theaters but also in homes, is always racing to catch up with the latest sensations Hollywood films supposedly provide. Sony and Columbia's "hardware–software" alliance in 1989, and Matsushita's acquisition of Universal-MCA the following year, indicate that the home entertainment market is a major consideration in the production of Hollywood. Also, along with the blossoming computer-game industry, state-of-the-art video technology fuels the development of home entertainment, which follows quickly on the heels of theater facilities in its attempts to reproduce the sensory thrills a Hollywood film promises to provide. It is no surprise that in 1993 Sony decided not to globally launch its own new discovery – VCD – when Columbia TriStar Films was producing and distributing blockbusters like *Robocop 3*, whose sensational thrills just could not be captured by the new VCD technology. However, while the media conglomerates in the West chose to reject VCD technology due to its incompatibility with Hollywood's high-concept production and marketing packages, a large number of Asian markets adopted it enthusiastically, bypassing the global distribution network of the conglomerates in order to "steal" enjoyment. Darrell Davis calls the VCD a form of cockroach capitalism precisely because of its proliferation; the VCD has become the major movie carrier in many developing countries within a short period of time (2003: 169–70). This redundant low-end technology presents the fiercest challenge to the high-end products the technology was supposedly designed for.

The VCD is now one of the core technologies in Asian movie piracy. Unlike the earlier generation of video apparatus (VHS and VCR), VCD is an audiovisual technology many people in the West have not heard of. Segrave does not mention VCDs at all in his comprehensive historical account of movie piracy from the invention of cinema to 2001 (2003). It is a 4.72 inch disc that can store still or moving images, two tracks of sound, and digital information files. It was first launched in 1993 and soon became vastly popular in many Asian countries, excepting Japan

(S. Wang 2003: 56; Hu 2004). VCD is now the dominant movie carrier in many Asian countries, including China, Taiwan, Hong Kong, Singapore, the Philippines, Thailand, Vietnam, India, and Malaysia (D. Scott 2003). It is also becoming popular in Latin America and Africa.

The VCD's history dates back to 1982, when Sony and Philips cooperatively developed CD-DA (Compact Disc-Digital Audio, also known as Red Book technology) as the prototype for compact-disc technology. A succession of new technologies have been developed and released by the two companies since then, including the CD-ROM (Yellow Book) in 1985, the CD-I (Green Book) in 1987, the CD-R (Orange Book) in 1992, and the VCD (White Book) in 1993. The VCD first allowed linear MPEG-based video material to be put on a compact disc in a standard format, meaning that a feature-length movie was easily accessible in a form much lighter, cheaper, and smaller than the prevalent VHS. The disc is light and small – extremely convenient for storage and transportation. Its recorded content is accessible in any VCD player connected to a TV, or (unlike a DVD) on a standard PC with a CD-ROM drive, making it the most accessible and cheapest medium of movie viewing available.

The VCD is a unique and interesting cultural phenomenon in our globalization age, as it is a product of Western technological modernity yet represents an Asian experience foreign to the West. Unlike the analog VHS, the digital VCD never caught on in North America, Europe, or Japan, but it was readily accepted in developing Asian communities. We might never be able to find out the real reasons Sony and Philips decided not to launch the VCD globally in 1993, but we do know the consequence of this decision: the major manufacturers of VCD players are not these transnational firms but local brands scattered across Asia. As Kelly Hu demonstrates, unlike most consumer technologies supported by Japanese-Western transnational electronics corporations, the VCD was not disseminated from the First World to Asia, but it has been booming across the Asian region since the mid-1990s (Hu 2004). If, as Appadurai claims, "technology, both high and low, both mechanical and informational, now moves at high speeds across various kinds of previously impervious boundaries" (1996: 34), then the VCD might be the one exceptional mass technology that is still bounded by certain geographical frontiers. Unlike the CD, which utilizes almost the same technology and has become the global standard music carrier, the VCD is popular only in Asian and other developing countries. In fact, one can also argue that it is VCD piracy that led to the replacement of VHS technology, thereby also destroying the traditional video-rental market. In Asia and other developing countries, it is difficult to differentiate between VCDs and piracy as cause and effect. I am by no means suggesting that these countries comprise a homogenous entity; but the fact that the VCD has been widely used only in certain developing countries indicates that there are discursive connections, be they cultural, economic, or technological, among these countries that facilitate their use of VCDs.

In the West, the domestic audiovisual apparatus progressed from VHS tapes to laser discs (LDs) to DVDs in the last two decades, each step representing more or less an advance and a technological breakthrough. In Asia, however, the VCD is on an alternative route, as its widespread usage overlaps with that of the aforementioned three, and it does not follow the teleological path we always assume for the development of technology. In terms of visual and audio quality, the VCD is a technological regression from both VHS tapes and LDs, which were invented much earlier. The VCD uses MPEG-1 compression, with a resolution of 352 × 240 (NTSC) or 352 × 288 (PAL). Although is comparable to VHS resolution, in reality the audio-visual quality of VCDs is usually lower than that of VHS tapes. The major advantage of the VCD is its low cost: about US$0.30 per disc, allowing its retail price to go as low as US$1.00.[4]

The relatively low-tech and medium-priced VCD technology ideally suited most East Asian communities in the early 1990s, when many households were purchasing their first VCRs. It was a time when VHS technology had already penetrated the developed world. In early 1990s, when the VCD was first introduced to the market, VCR penetration in US households was well above 70 percent (MPAA 2000), and was over 40 percent in France (US Department of Commerce 2000). In contrast, until 2001 VCR penetration in Asia-Pacific markets was just over 12 percent (*Screen Digest* 2002). But the VCD replaced the VCR as the first generation of home entertainment technology in many Asian countries. It was almost impossible to persuade the VCR-owning households in the West to reinvest both in hardware and software for what was really a less advanced technology. In many Asian countries, however, consumers prefer VCDs to LDs and DVDs in terms of price and to VHS tapes in terms of accessibility. Since the VCD is digital instead of analog, it also dovetails with the rapidly increasing number of Asian homes with personal computers. Price and accessibility seem to be more important than quality in the Asian home entertainment market, which welcomes an inferior technology the West rejected.

Also, the relatively simple technology involved in the production of the discs and players is comparatively accessible to manufacturers in the developing world. China soon became the largest producer of and market for VCDs. In 1997, sales of VCD players in China accounted for more than 80 percent of the world's total consumption (*Asian Sources Electronics* 1998: 85). The production and consumption of VCD technology has become a locomotive of China's economy. The top three advertisers for China Central Television's (CCTV) prime-time slots in 1998 were all Chinese VCD producers: Idal VCD, BBK VCD, and Shinco VCD. The advertisements earned US$55 million for CCTV that year (Lai 1998). Both the players and the discs are cheap to buy and easy to make. It is simple to duplicate VCDs using relatively low-end computer equipment like CD-ROM burners (in the home), or monoline machines (in factories). The low production costs and great accessibility of VCD technology allow the growth of VCDs to develop almost hand-in-hand with illegal mass reproduction of films. Many people in Asia can finance their own piracy businesses, and the masses can also participate in the consumption of the pirated products with minimal investment in either hardware or technical knowledge. VCD piracy is now so rampant in many Asian countries that markets stocking pirated materials have become major attractions for Western tourists (Golab 1998).

But it would be naïve to separate Western capitalist interests from this rosy picture and consider VCD technology and the associated movie piracy industry an Asian modernization phenomenon. While most of the VCD players are local products, machines for producing the discs are often foreign-made. The inevitable result of this excessive import of machines is overproduction. As Caroline Baines reports: "Strong demand for the product, an excess of CD replication capacity (particularly in China and Hong Kong) and a disregard for copyright laws have resulted in the market being overwhelmed with pirate products" (2001). While most discussions of piracy are centered on the first and third propositions raised by Baines, the issue of disc overproduction is often dismissed as a cause of the strong demand. But in many countries, the importation of the related technology and an excess of CD replication capacity often preceded and caused widespread piracy, which took place in China in the mid-1990s, and in less economically advanced Asian countries in the beginning of the twenty-first century (Esplanada 2004). Excessive production capacity needs a market to absorb their products. Piracy is as much a result of this overproduction as it is its cause.

We can read this scenario from a classical Marxist perspective. Overproduction is internally structured in the development of capitalism as its own crisis, according to Karl Marx. Capitalism has a tendency to overproduce, and this will lead to economic depression. As Marx claims in *The Communist Manifesto*:

> [T]here is too much civilization, too much means of subsistence, too much industry, too much commerce. The productive forces at the disposal of society no longer tend to further the development of the conditions of bourgeois property; on the contrary, they have become too powerful for these conditions.... And how does the bourgeoisie get over these crises? On the one hand by enforced destruction of a mass of productive forces; on the other, by the conquest of new markets, and by the more thorough exploitation of the old ones.
>
> (1986: 229–30)

The Asian pirated movie markets, read from this Marxist perspective, can be seen as both the result of and the solution to the potential crisis of "overproduction." The piracy market is not unassociated with the overall imperialist project of Western capitalism. Marx was not able to anticipate, however, the emergence of multiple distribution networks developing along with various new product reproduction technologies, which are no longer concentrated in the hands of large industrial capitalists. As digital reproduction technology becomes standardized and is diffused internationally, people with different cultural values, norms, and preferences begin not only to desire but also to reproduce the same goods. This standardization of taste as well as the standardization of reproduction technologies further fuel overproduction, on the part of both copyright holders and pirates around the world. As I mentioned, it is difficult to conclude whether the VCD is responsible for the widespread and large-scale movie piracy in Asia, or whether it is the Asian desire for Western entertainment at low prices that is responsible for the extreme success of the VCD format. But we do know that both courses are not unrelated to the easy availability of the related technology, which seems to lead to the overproduction of the discs in the first place.

Therefore, while technological development fuels the continual expansion of Hollywood, the industry also has much fear of technology, specifically its accessibility to pirates. For example, many copyright holders are still hesitant to place their movies and other audiovisual works on broadband because it will open the door to widespread digital piracy (Goldstein 2003: 164–5). Such fear is not simply the result of the "democratic" tendency of the Internet; it was already observable when the VHS was first developed in the 1970s. Major studios like Universal saw the invention of the VCR not as a new distribution venue so much as an easy tool for piracy (Weil and Polansky 1985: 317–31). As it happens, the VCR both facilitated illegal dubbing and increased the films' accessibility, benefiting both the pirates and the official distributors. Video discs are having a similar effect.

We are seeing an increasing popularity in DVDs, both legal and bootlegged, in more affluent Asian societies such as Hong Kong and Singapore, but DVD technology still has not replaced the VCD as the major movie carrier (D. Scott 2003: 62–3). Although the DVD, unlike the VCD, is widely used in the West, geographical differences can also be detected in these products, as they are produced, packaged, and priced differently in Asia than in the West. While a recent Hollywood DVD is typically priced at around US$30 in the West, the official version of the same movie can be sold in Asia for US$10, with less packaging and fewer bonus features. Pirated DVDs, not surprisingly, can be priced as low as US$3, since DVDs can also be produced more cheaply in Asia, partly because of the increase in production and in production capacity (Smiers 2002: 122), and also because of overpricing in the West. It is less the producer than the market that determines the quality and the price of a product.

In this sense, pirated VCD movies – or pirated DVDs or CDs for that matter – are not analogous to Napster or downloaded MP3s. The former is offline and the latter is online; furthermore, their users' demographics are vastly different. Consumers purchasing the discs, be they VCDs, CDs, or DVDs, can bring them home and play them on their regular home-entertainment equipment. These media require almost no technical knowledge on the part of the users, whereas Napster and MP3 users, like computer hackers, belong to a middle-class young generation that is equipped with both knowledge and hardware (Garofalo 1999; Cooper and Harrison 2001). Movie piracy through discs penetrates an audience of more diverse class, age, culture, and geography than that for pirated online material. Also, the new online music and image piracy only needs a virtual distribution network and therefore is basically non-material, while pirated discs are still tangible materials and require real distribution and retail lines. However, sometimes the two systems converge: Malaysia is becoming an export hub for pirated DVDs and VCDs via the Internet, with Kuala Lumpur, Penang, and Johor Bahru as the primary exit points catering to big orders from North America, Europe, Australia, New Zealand, and South Africa. Ordered through the net, the discs are delivered through the courier, express mail and registered mail services (Ghani 2003). The technology involved in the production, distribution, and reception of pirated VCD movies are often primitive yet always highly mobile.

The sense of criminality is also stronger in disc piracy than in web piracy. As Danny Birchall argues, Napster users are an egalitarian community fostering a sense of camaraderie and shared adventure, while traditional video pirates are often labeled as involved "in drug peddling, pornography, forged currency, theft and even terrorism" (Birchall 2000). MPAA special agents describe Asia as a battlefield. Lowell Strong, head of the MPAA's Asian Pacific Bureau, and his team refused to carry out their mission in Macao in the late 1990s. In Strong's words, "Macao is almost lawless.... Gangs run the casinos. The police are corrupt, and they shoot each other. The chief had to leave because of threats on his life. A pirated cassette is not worth getting someone killed" (Golab 1998). Asian movie piracy – with its low-tech and criminal aspects – is stigmatized in the West in the same way that Asia is depicted as uncivilized and lawless in Hollywood films. The hacker, instead, is often romanticized in films like *The Net* (dir. Irwin Winkler, 1995) and *The Matrix* (dir. Andy Wachowski and Larry Wachowski, 1999) as able to outwit evil forces based on an extraordinary relationship to technology.

On top of the intrinsic low quality of the VCD, the ways movies are pirated in general can also be seen as primitive, whether the pirated material is a VCD or a better-quality DVD. The making of pirated discs can be divided into the production and the post-production stages. There are basically two types of pirated VCD movies: the disc version and the theater version. The former are VCD copies of laser discs, DVDs, or "screener" copies of movies (those sent to video-rental stores, cinemas, or even festival judges for preview before they decide to purchase them or recommend them as finalists). The latter is a master copy of the theater version, produced by smuggling a camcorder into the theater and directly recording a new movie, either at a local movie house or in a major city where the film debuted. In turn, many equipment suppliers are proposing new technologies to combat piracy, including developing systems to block camcorder recording and night-vision goggles that would allow security guards to scan the viewing audience for recording equipment (Kemp 2003).

Compared to the disc version, the theater version is inferior in quality, but it can be released almost immediately after the film's opening, and therefore can more effectively benefit from the accompanying blockbuster promotion. Watching movies recorded in theaters is a particularly awkward experience, as the camcorder used to film the movie also captures both aurally and visually the activities taking place in the theater. These incidental happenings can easily alienate audiences from complete absorption in the films. Classical Hollywood's realist style employs certain filmic techniques, such as continuity editing and realistic lighting, in an attempt to create the illusion of reality (Bordwell *et al.* 1985; Currie 1996; Hallam and Marshment 2000). However, when watching pirated films, the sensation created by the transparent background music is often corrupted by coughing, ringing phones, or conversations; we also see the audience taking and leaving their seats. These extraneous activities disrupt the continuities of the narrative. While in the theaters we might still be able to tune out the ambient disruptions and concentrate on the screen and the loudspeakers, these pirated films make such adjustments more difficult since both the cinematic material and any distractions from it come from the same image and soundtrack. The technology of theater piracy fails to reproduce the theatergoer's experience of a film, although it most genuinely and loyally captures the experience of being in a movie theater.

After the movies are either captured at the theater or reproduced from other media, the products have to go though some kind of post-production before they can be sold. This might include subtitling, dubbing in local dialogue, and product packaging.

Subtitling, more often than dubbing, is almost inevitable in pirated Hollywood films. The official VHS or DVD versions of the films usually are not released until months after the film is released in theaters, and the master copy the pirates make from a screener copy almost never has subtitles and is therefore incomprehensible to the Asian masses. I demonstrated in the previous chapter how the pirated *Kill Bill* shows the inability of the translator to understand colloquial American English, and how such inaccurate mediation made the pirated film a different one from the original. As a result, viewers often find the narrative of pirated Hollywood movies difficult to comprehend. In addition to a disjointed story line, careless post-production can also result in unsynchronized voice and image, fuzzy images, and dull sound effects; sometimes one may even discover that the movie on the disc is not the one shown on the cover, or that the disc is simply blank. Pirated VCDs can be seen as a giant, if unintentional, mockery of the original movies. The film's original producers are completely deprived of control over how their products are displayed and consumed.

Piracy's imperfect mimesis

Film technology as experienced by audiences in Asian markets is a broad category that can range from state-of-the-art Hollywood production and exhibition facilities to VCD piracy techniques that reproduce and circulate these high-tech products in illegal, dispersed, and inexpensive ways. Skyrocketing investments in the "production" of Hollywood's blockbusters have been successfully keeping competitors and upstarts from challenging the studios' continual monopolization of the market (Elsaesser 2000). But the decreasing costs of digital "reproduction" of these films also encourage the development of numerous pirate industries around Asia that subvert the Hollywood global reign. In economic terms:

> The cultural industries, like other information industries, are characterized by two inter-related features: within the firm, high fixed costs and low (or even zero) marginal costs – the conditions for natural monopoly – and, at the industry level, the concentration of economic power dominated by a few oligopolistic firms.
>
> (Towse 2001: 39)

As I mentioned in the last chapter, film investors work against all odds to completely manipulate the distribution networks where the real profits are made, which explains today's media conglomeration, and also the flourishing of the lucrative piracy business. In earlier days, a commodity was physical and tangible; piracy involved stealing the materials, which always involves production and material costs. But today piracy requires negligible material investment. The price becomes almost entirely arbitrary because they are pure profits.

We tend to equate technology and control. To David Harvey, for example, new technology means new systems of social and political regulation (Harvey 1989: 145). But the interaction between technology and power can be extremely volatile and contested. The 1998 Digital Millennium Copyright Act (DMCA) in the US, for example, has triggered heated debates around issues of technology's control and the control of technology. The DMCA has two major purposes: to criminalize the production and the dissemination of technology that can circumvent measures taken to protect copyright, and to increase the penalties for copyright infringement on the Internet. The first purpose is particularly controversial, because "for the first time in history, it isn't the copyright violation that is the crime. It is the creation of the technological tools to violate copyright that has become the crime" (D. Clark 2002: 147). While some legal scholars consider the DMCA appropriate for the enforcement of IPR and contractual rights in cyberspace (Kerr 2002), others criticize the DMCA for severely undercutting fair use balances built into copyright law (Lessig 2004). The software and hardware industries were the most vocal opponents of the DMCA, as they argue that it presumes bad faith on the part of the technology industry, and it invites government control of the technology standards-setting process (Clark 2002: 155). The most fundamental issue at stake is whether we can attach human values to technology. As Sheldon W. Halpern demonstrates, some digital technology used to encrypt may also be used to decrypt, so that it can be used to protect and infringe on copyright at the same time (2003: 149). Similarly, both Hollywood and pirates can use the same video disc technologies for their own businesses.

To many Asian pirates, access to digital technologies provides ways to live on, feed off of, and appropriate these controls. While cutting-edge high technology can be an extremely useful tool for social control when it is kept in certain hands, its wide circulation among the masses generates new possibilities that defy the original design. If anything that can be digitalized can be assimilated, such assimilation happens in multiple ways. While our material reality, in all its dimensions, is almost completely invaded and incorporated by the culture industry and its digital representations, these representations can be re-represented and recaptured by different forms of technology to produce different effects and affects. And these multiple forms of affects could threaten the monopoly on aesthetics controlled by the owners of high technology.

But ironically, today's digital movie piracy displays a mimesis that is as imperfect as it can be in our age of virtual reality. Although some pirated video discs feature nearly perfect image and audio capturing, many are obviously inferior in quality to the originals. Every audio and visual detail perfected, and every flaw corrected, by high-tech movies can be undone in the pirating process or in the substandard screening facility. While lousy subtitles often render the storyline incomprehensible, substandard visual quality sometimes makes the viewing of these pirated movies quite a chore. In other words, viewing Hollywood movies in a small and cheap VCD set at home or at humble local theaters makes the moviegoing experience of an Asian viewer completely different than that of viewers in places that have state-of-the-art cinema equipment. While I do not want to go so far as to suggest that VCD piracy subverts Hollywood's pleasure and ideology, it does bring about a laborious and alienated form of identification that Hollywood did not envision.

Walter Benjamin argues that film, with techniques such as close-ups and slow motion, provides the audience with a new capacity and sensitivity to scrutinize modern existence as it consists of disconnected images and fragmented experiences locked up in fragmented spaces (Benjamin 1968: 236–7; Buck-Morss 1989: 268; Taussig 1993: 24–5). But these new ways of seeing, which shocked Benjamin's generation, have now been completely tamed by the commercial film industry, which produces pleasing, rather than surprising, images to anchor the audience's escapist identification. With the aid of new digital technology, Hollywood is now truly able to produce a fantasyland where the fragmentation of daily life is pieced back together. Benjamin might be right that film in its early form allows us to re-examine the underlying logic and absurdities of the reality it claims to capture, but today's mainstream Hollywood productions have long deprived themselves of such power. Pirated movies, on the other hand, offer the audience a chance to re-experience and scrutinize the digital effects and illusionist realism Hollywood fabricates, just as early cinema allowed audiences to see and comprehend hidden details of familiar objects through the means of photographic mechanical reproduction. The reality that piracy reproduces is not the social reality outside the theater that interested Benjamin, but rather the very process of illusion-making Hollywood now so superbly masters and monopolizes. In other words, the act of copying is being emphasized in pirated Hollywood movies, but it self-refers only to the act of copying itself. Benjamin's cinema is politically engaged because it re-presents reality, while pirated movies are also politically suggestive in today's context because they re-present cinema itself. Watching these technically inferior copies, we are reminded of the very power of cinema to fake or reproduce reality, a reminder that indirectly alienates us from the illusion of technological fetishism to which most Hollywood audiences have been habituated.

If the postmodern world constructed by our culture industry is composed of simulacra, of surfaces reflecting surfaces without referring to the *logos*, what is at ideological stake in our representational culture is less the reality that representations claim to capture than the representation technologies that now more than anything else define the materiality of our everyday experience. As Wlad Godzich claims: "We are now inhabited by images that we have not drawn from ourselves, images of external impression that we do not master and that retain all their agential capability without being mediated by us" (Godzich 1994: 169). Technological modes of reproduction are autonomous in themselves – as exemplified in recent Hollywood cinema – and are no longer derived from our discursive reality but have already become our experiential reality.

The most interesting and provocative aspect of the technology of VCD piracy is its ability to steal and rework media, yet this reappropriation mechanism is not fused with ideological intentions and intellectually informed politics. I am not suggesting that we should avoid any political reasoning as a way to understand technology; technology is still utilized, manipulated, and exploited as a powerful tool by those who own it, such as the Hollywood conglomerates. Recognizing the ways technological means may alienate modern subjects in a regulated society, we should also explore how to use the substantive vision of technology to re-interrogate the common instrumental reasoning of technology now ruling the world. The widespread disc piracy of Hollywood films in Asia is an example of a widespread popular cultural activity with no political or intellectual calculation that may serve as an alternative way to reveal the hidden patterns of our ideologically infused entertainment technology.

The utilization and embodiment of technology indeed belongs to the everyday experiential realm of humanity, which cannot be completely controlled either by capitalists with their own financial concerns or by political activists for oppositional politics.

In examining a new form of live and chance video performance, which stresses low-tech analog technique, obsolete computers, and dated software, and is now sprouting up in art galleries and studios of North American cities, Laura Marks argues that these performances are politically dynamic because they challenge virtuality by revealing its "material construction, the social relationships that produced their technology, the economics of their low-tech platforms, and the quirkiness of their human-computer interfaces" (Marks 2001: 309). The artists emphasize the interactions between live performances and electronically mediated images, thereby complicating the relationships between reality and mediation and mocking our mass cultural enterprises that always try to hide these relationships. These avant-garde projects seem to be right on the mark as an escape from technological fetishism, to which Hollywood tries to condition us. But, likely, most of the audience of these art shows were critical of Hollywood to start with; the shows simply reinforce their intellectual stance. To put it another way, unless the audience has knowledge of today's media society's technological control, these artistic protests would mean nothing to them. In what ways, then, can we call these shows political, if the politics is already presupposed?

In both economic and cultural dimensions, the blossoming piracy scene in Asia is fundamentally different from these avant-garde performances in the art galleries and studios of the most modern cities of the world. The artistic performances Marks celebrates are subversive on an intellectual level and attract younger audiences with elitist backgrounds, while pirated movies are watched uncritically by Asian masses yearning to devour First-World entertainment. Most importantly, the heavy aesthetic principles behind Marks' project are auteur driven, in that the participation of the viewers is either conditioned or loosely calculated by the artists. It is true that the audience of the avant-garde video shows is intellectually reminded of the culture industry's technological (im)perfection. But such intellectual activities do not habituate the viewers to a new form of corporeal experience. Instead, the exhibition sites and forms of display already pre-select the audience and require them to understand the works politically and intellectually, a set of circumstances which by no means overlaps or interrogates effectively the mode of pleasure produced by Hollywood cinema.

Laura Mulvey argues that the new digital technology does not pronounce cinema's imminent death; on the contrary, the technology allows us to re-examine and ex-appropriate film time that might point a way to cinema's reorientation in the new century, when time seems no longer to be moving. "As images of convincing realism may now be easily simulated, the vast archive of analogue images now takes on new significance aesthetically, and one might also say philosophically" (Mulvey 2004: 154). But Mulvey still pins her hope on enlightened filmmakers who would turn archival materials to images of the present, so that the meanings of the original can be re-examined. To Mulvey, this interrogation of images is an interrogation of history, and a re-engagement with leftist politics. This aesthetically informed political project, however, works against the intended aim of her paper, in that she wants to break down the binary thinking between fiction and the avant-garde that conditioned her film theories in the 1970s (147). The spectatorship of pirated movies might provide a way for us to conceive of the potentiality of digital technology without privileging the filmmakers over the viewers, which Mulvey's new model also fails to do.

Many viewers of pirated movies are given a degraded experience of today's First World high-tech entertainment. Watching pirated movies, audiences are experiencing only secondhand what an authentic Hollywood cinema experience is supposed to be. They are experiencing, or trying to experience, these dream-making activities, but they often fail to receive the intended effects. Watching the pirated films at home or in a shabby local theater, these audiences have to rely more on their imagination, fantasizing about what "authentic" Hollywood cinema is supposed to be. Unlike the avant-garde shows, pirated movies bring pleasure, but this pleasure is so mediated that it constantly reminds the audience of their "non-present" and "non-participatory" positions. It also constantly reminds the viewer that she or he is not consuming Hollywood in its completeness, thus offering a sense of distance from both the technology and the content.

The practice of watching pirated VCDs is often considered anti-Hollywood. One year after *Titanic* was publicly released in China, Xuanwei Company was made responsible for the film's official video distribution. Knowing that pirated VCDs of the film were already swamping the market, Xuanwei decided to promote the film by advertising the real and authentic "emotions" and "human values" the Hollywood film celebrates. The company also organized an exquisite press party, at which the food, decorations, and clothing were exact replicas of those in *Titanic*, and in so doing displayed the romantic aura of the film (*Zhonghua da huangye* 2001). By linking the authenticity of the official VCD to the authenticity of humanity featured in the film, the company tried to ascribe the aesthetic values to the film which had been contaminated by the morally inferior pirated versions. This promotion campaign was clearly successful, as evidenced by the high sales of the official VCD version. But many Chinese continue to buy pirated copies of this and other Hollywood films, indirectly showing their disinterest in the authentic "Hollywoodness" that the distribution company advertises.

The intellectual reflexivity required by avant-garde video shows does not engage the audience in the experiential dimension, and therefore fails to grasp the non-discursive paths and influences on which technology, or Hollywood's technological fetishism, embarks. The popular consumption of pirated movies, however, participates precisely in the audiences' individual subjectivities, a formation that the Hollywood apparatus also positions itself to engage. The only way to untie the subjectivity that has been corporeally constituted by technology is to engage in a new form of subjectivication. It is the everyday life that defines and is defined by our technological world, and therefore only through the practice of the everyday can we understand technology as "revealing," as Heidegger would say, instead of as a tool (Heidegger 1977). Pirated movies provide a different perception of Hollywood films – one that falls outside the control of the producers.

Today's culture industry is characterized by the producers' strong desire to understand the psychology of their potential customers. They rely on many different means to internalize and construct some notion of audience (Lury 1993; Negus 1999). Hollywood has been eager to investigate and construct their audience, using different marketing strategies to persuade audiences to desire a film they have not yet watched (Altman 1999: 123–43). However, film producers have no access to the audience in the pirate market, from which they generate no profits. Although bootlegged products might at the end help promote the official versions, the producers' lack of information about the viewers also hamper their ability to fully anticipate and manipulate these new markets.

While pirated movies call attention to the false integrity of the original text, they also introduce new ways to conceive the audience. A new concept of cinephile was developed around the act of watching pirated movies. I have observed that people have a greater tendency to share and circulate pirated movies than legal copies, and that owners of pirated VCDs also care less about ownership. This is due in part to the low price of the discs, but also because the discs and their ownership are illegal. The possibility of common good emerges when the concept of "private property" is suppressed. Darrell William Davis and Emilie Yueh-yu Yeh argue that the recent VCD phenomenon in Asia demonstrates a new imaginary transnational community: "The members of this pan-Asian VCD community care more about sharing their consumption pleasures in a virtual world than identifying with a specific national entity" (2004: 241). The VCD community, I would argue, is materialized not only imaginarily, on a transnational scale, but physically, among friends who share pirated films. These circles of audiences realize new practices that were not anticipated by the films' producers. Barbara Klinger demonstrates a new cinephilia developed out of the recent home theater culture, in which the collectors identify with the industry and assume knowledge about both the film and the technology, so that VHS or DVD collectors fetishize the high quality of both the hardware and the content (2001). But in the case of pirated disc, this kind of technophilia is weak, so is the spell Hollywood producers cast on their viewers through digital imaging.

Feng Xiaogong, the most commercially successful film director in China, calls the severe movie piracy situation in the country a reflection of the inferiority of Chinese culture and the baseness of its citizens. He claims that movie piracy does not happen in the United States because the American people naturally see piracy as unethical and equivalent to theft (Tian 2002). Feng criticizes what he sees as the low moral standards of Chinese customers – standards that he naturally judges harshly as they lead to lost profits for his own films. In opposition, Friedrich Kittler and Laurence Rickels criticize precisely this seemingly moral but indeed subservient attitude of the American people toward copyright:

> In America there seems to be greater loyalty to industrial achievement; there's a morality that dictates that one should not hack or patch or copy. The result, it seems to me, is that one is that much more hopelessly surrendered to the industrially determined products.... So there's one guru or prophet who writes the programs, and everyone else is a consumer who doesn't intervene in the process in any serious way.
>
> (1992: 67)

One of the most effective ways to interrogate the power concentrated in the hands of the technology producers and information distributors, as suggested by Kittler and Rickels, is to actively participate in technological processes that reshape the products.

What Kittler and Rickels suggest is that technology is not simply an intellectual enterprise but is ultimately experientially based. In order to reshape the experience and reproduce a new subjectivity, we must grasp technology from within, as individuals who are immediately engaged in technically mediated activities. It is only through the practice of technology that the full potentialities of technology, beyond being just one form of authoritarian technological rationality, can be realized. When Benjamin refers to cinema as potentially liberating, he does not describe this new politics of technology as a new intellectual project that teaches and enlightens the audience (1968: 242). Instead, cinema is considered potentially revolutionary as a tool to undercut the political current of Fascism because cinema can heighten and expand one's perceptions and help us to see what we did not see (236–7). It is not the intellectual dimension but the visceral dimension that is most "political" about technology.

It must be noted that in spite of his high expectations for the new form of mass media, Benjamin does not romanticize it. His ambivalent analysis of people's tactile appropriation of architecture indirectly suggests that the "unconscious optics" of cinema could easily become a means of Fascist control (239–41). While there is a general trend among copyright scholars to read piracy as a strategy to subvert the global information society (Ramasoota 2003), the multivalent meanings of movie piracy cannot be easily reduced to a political project. It is beyond doubt that pirated movies are not designed to be ideological weapons to challenge the global reign of Hollywood cinema. On the contrary, the Asian masses are attracted to these products precisely because they desire the thrilling excitement of Hollywood. The viewers' "tactile appropriation" of pirated movies, which does not involve much intellectual reflection, may only reinforce the manipulations inherent in the original Hollywood films and sustain the tastes and prejudices of the dominant industry. In fact, the more ruthless and widespread the piracy situation is, the more popular the original products have been and/or promise to be. The Asian people's widespread piracy of Hollywood movies only works to prove the products' overwhelming global popularity. As I mentioned, pirated products often serve to introduce the products to a new market before the authentic versions arrive; consumers that currently lack purchasing power are also trained to desire the brand names. Piracy easily fills this gap between consumer desire and purchasing power, although it also allows the pirates to eat up the first wave of profit. Therefore, piracy can be seen as a core component in the globalization chain.

At this moment we can hardly imagine any future of world cinema other than one dominated by Hollywood, with its skyrocketing investments in state-of-the-art digital-imaging technologies. This chapter presents an alternative view of the use of technology, and therefore alternative forms of reception, in cinema not monopolized by the dominating culture industry. The challenges can be read in terms of two hegemonic orders: the one that owns knowledge and information and, more abstractly, the metaphysical order. Raymond Williams argues that new technologies involved in cultural reproduction may become sites of struggle for innovation and diversity, presenting threats to the older social institutions of cultural and social reproduction

(1981: 97). If the invention of book printing ended the church's monopoly on knowledge, as a new means of replicating cultural works piracy also disturbs the established distribution networks of the mainstream film companies. While I do not know if the new reception of Hollywood films via pirated discs will engender a different future for the digitally engineered Hollywood films in Asia, I believe that there are alternative pathways for us to rethink the limits and limitlessness of Hollywood's global reign. Such technological reappropriation, as Heidegger has reminded us, can introduce us to new realm of the performative, which liquidates any "essential" values as truths. By constantly working with technology, we also de-essentialize and humanize technology, calling "us to a fictionalized experience of reality which is also our only possibility for freedom" (Vatimmo 1988: 29).

Today's globalization is made possible largely by the rapid development of communications technology in the last century; actual content is hardly keeping up. We are seeing more and more cable, satellite, and broadband stations fighting to broadcast the same programs, like major sporting events and Hollywood movies, so that "the emphasis [of our global communication system] will ultimately shift to releasing, translating and reconstituting content as widely as possible" (Arup 2000: 257). Piracy, being a reappropriated form of releasing, translating, and distributing Hollywood movies around the globe, might articulate the fictitious dimension of the ideology of Hollywood films. If Hollywood strives its hardest to create some kind of realism, piracy unpacks the coherent form, unleashing the force of the mobility of the symbolic. What is politically significant about movie piracy, then, is both its new distribution possibilities that escape the control of the current copyright holders and its metaphorical nihilist values. If we consider today's global capitalism an extremely potent mechanism that would remove any obstacles to its capacity to serve the interests of property owners and shareholders, piracy can be seen as both the obstacle and the means to destroy obstacles. The relationship between piracy and globalization brings us to the next chapter.

6 The despair of Chinese cinema

Arguably, piracy is active and popular in all developing countries – if not all countries – but among them, China is particularly stigmatized. Its "barbarous" copyright offenses are generally considered a manifestation, among many, of the country's emerging threat to the established world order. According to some estimates, 91 percent of the desktop software used in China in 1999 was pirated (SIIA 2000), and 95 percent of the transactions in audiovisual materials was carried out on the black market (G. Yang 1999). The millions of copies of pirated IP products sold in China can easily be translated into American dollars to represent the alleged loss of the copyright owners. According to an outraged report in *The New York Times*, pirated VCDs of *Dr Seuss' How the Grinch Stole Christmas* were found all over China within a week of the film's debut in the United States, and pirated copies of *Titanic* outsold legitimate ones by about thirty to one. "The [piracy] trade has made it almost impossible to sell legitimate videodiscs [in China], and dampened the lure of Hollywood films in movie theatres" (Smith 2000). The common understanding in the international business world is that this piracy is nothing but robbery, which the Chinese government tacitly ignores, and which the Chinese people fervently and shamelessly support.

This chapter examines the participation of the Chinese state and the Chinese people in the flourishing movie piracy market, but not with the aim of endorsing the stereotypical view of the Chinese people's uncivilized disrespect for IPR. In contextualizing movie piracy in China, I want to further explore whether intellectual property is simply a matter of individual rights and assets that must be protected at all costs. As both concept and reality – cutting across divergent social, cultural, political, and economic discourses – movie piracy in China, as this chapter demonstrates, is largely the result of the global diffusion of consumerism under an unequal distribution of world wealth on the one hand, and specific national politics on the other. Focusing on China's movie piracy as a point of reference, this final chapter engages in the discussion of two major issues concerning cultural control in a globalizing Asia: the internal contradictions of globalization manifested in contemporary (inter-)national cultural politics, and the impacts of globalization on a culture's collective identity, both on the levels of representation and public participation.

To follow up on last chapter's investigation of the local appropriation of global culture, here I want to study specifically how issues and practices of movie piracy are manifested and signified within a specific national scenario. Through a careful reading of the movie piracy situation in China, I want to demonstrate the many levels of conflict between the global and the national; these are often reduced to a degree to facilitate macro theorizations in general discussions of globalization. As I have demonstrated throughout the book, copyright touches on matters related not only to the right to copy but also the right to culture; the violations of copyright within a nation striving for global status crystallize the ambivalent meanings of the right to culture in globalization. To echo the discussion of national sovereignty in the age of globalization in the book's introduction, in this concluding chapter I offer a case study that demonstrates the Chinese state's fear of and desire for globalization, and upon the tensions between the WTO's call for opening markets and IPR protection and the Chinese state's will to control the flow of information and entertainment. I am also interested in exploring the notion of China as a collective agency, which I believe to be a widely circulated assumption about contemporary China that, however, has not been substantiated by careful analysis in scholarly and journalistic discourses. While the West continues to see China as a unified cultural "other" for easy comprehension and political polarization, Chinese intellectuals and politicians also need this notion of a collective agency to realize various national/nationalist projects.[1] Chinese cinema's metamorphosis from a collective public event to a piracy–privacy activity, from a highly controlled mode of production and distribution to a completely underground operation with numerous sites of power and systems of distribution, is one recent social transformation among many that brings the set of cultural problematics created by the dynamics between globalism and nationalism into focus.

Under such dynamics in the new global age, the impossibility of conceptualizing a national cinema, in reference to both production and distribution, implies the increasing difficulties of conceptualizing "Chineseness" as a unified notion in other areas. Following Rey Chow's call for a productive erasure of the concept of a unified Chineseness (1998: 24), I hope that this chapter can help us to reconceive a contemporary China that is no longer a totality moving along a linear historical trajectory. While piracy demonstrates how problematic it is for the state to call for a homogenous Chinese collectivity, this problem also reminds us not to fall into the same ideological trap and fantasize that piracy itself represents the unified action and experience of a "Chineseness" that counters the political hegemony of the state, or that of globalization. Any imagination of a totalizing oppositional collective action and experience is doomed to collapse under the consumerist indifference and fragmentation China is now experiencing. I also hope that this concluding chapter can help us conceive of copyright neither as a positivist legal system nor as a general human right; copyright is tightly embedded in particular geopolitics and cultural conditions that largely concerns cultural scholars.

The current plight of China's film industry, and that of the state

The PRC's recent turn towards marketization by no means suggests the wholesale embracing of a *laissez-faire* capitalism that honors small government and liberalism.

The Chinese state, like many other developing states, has been playing and continues to play a central role in the country's economic reform, which infinitely complicates such seemingly universal terms as capitalism and market. In an essay discussing China's march towards "postsocialism," Arif Dirlik argues that socialism is only a disposable instrument that China employs in the search of wealth and power (1989: 365). Dirlik reminds us that as early as 1951, Benjamin Schwartz already argued that the Chinese communism that took over China in 1949 was just an expression of Chinese nationalism (269). Today's "socialism with Chinese characteristics" can then be seen as a reconnection with the central ideology of the earliest days of the PRC, when socialist ideologies were selectively and strategically used for the empowerment of the state. With national power and autonomy as the highest aims, the "postsocialism" China is now engaging in, as Dirlik concludes, is definitely not a complete embrace of capitalism but, on the contrary, can be envisioned as a new form of socialism that strategically uses capitalism for China's national growth (380–1). Although written more than a decade ago, Dirlik's analysis is still a provocative one, reminding us that capitalism and the market economy have always been severely policed in China, and that the Chinese state by no means would forgo national autonomy and unity for the sake of capitalism. The state is willing to give up and distort many components of capitalism, in the same way as it has socialism, in order to ensure the protection of the ruling power of the Party and the stability of the nation.

However, such efforts are not always effective. In our increasingly globalized world, national unity and state power are becoming more and more difficult to hold on to, a phenomenon not so apparent when Dirlik published his essay in 1989. The Chinese government has constantly found itself caught in the dilemma of both desiring economic development and fearing ideological pluralism, and also on the verge of losing political control of the country in the disarray of a global market economy. The state's position on cinema is an exemplary case: the government holds onto the ideological purity and unity of the national cinema by creating tight restrictions on film production and distribution, but such stringent controls encourage a new form of cinema activity – piracy – which totally evades the control of the government.

In order to understand the current predicament of Chinese cinema, we need to examine its history. As early as the 1930s, the then young and underground Communist Party had already decided to use cinema as its major pedagogical tool to spread its political messages, and it was partly due to its extremely successful cinema campaign – the Left-wing Cinema Movement – that the Party was able to gain popular support in the 1930s and 1940s, which ultimately led to the successful war for Liberation (Pang 2002a). Right after the Party liberated China in 1949, one of the new republic's very first tasks was to solidify its reign over cinema, reorganizing all existing production studios and centralizing the distribution and exhibition network into a highly regulated system (P. Clark 1987: 34–5). All moviemaking production units were moved from Shanghai to Beijing for more effective centralized control. On the distribution level, the China Film Corporation (Zhongguo dianying gongsi) was set up and assigned the role of coordinating with all local production and exhibition units as well as selected foreign distributors to supply films to the Chinese people. The entire movie enterprise, from production to distribution, was under the Party's complete control shortly after 1949, and cinema, more than any other mass media, would become the Party's most powerful propaganda machine in the turbulent years to come.

The power of the China Film Corporation in China's film market was absolute, as it held sole control of film imports, exports, and national distribution (Semsel 1987: 3–6). Under this system, a network of distribution lines was constructed. The China Film Corporation, positioned at the tip of the distribution triangle, purchased completed films from studios and distributed them to several large provincial agencies. These companies dealt with smaller distribution companies at a municipal level, which in turn coordinated with exhibition units in various cities, towns, and villages (Wu 1999: 604). Originally designed to maintain the central government's absolute surveillance, this triangular and hierarchical network gradually evolved into a huge, inefficient, and bureaucratic system detached from the real audience. The China Film Corporation had little idea where its films ended up, and information concerning actual screenings could not be reported back to production houses, as there were just too many agencies involved. Many intermediate distribution companies survived solely on the small profits the films made in local box offices, putting all participants involved in the production–distribution–exhibition line in dire straits.

In spite of the obvious defects of the system and the dangers posed to the national cinema, the state has shown relatively little enthusiasm for relaxing the policy of cinema centralization; other mass media are given more freedom to carry out their own commercial experiments (Zhao 1998). This uneven imposition of control might largely be due to the state's strong conviction of the collectivist ideology and function embodied in cinema. I will return to this point in the last section of this chapter.

Starting in 1993, the government finally began to allow local production units to sell their films directly to regional distributors, but the China Film Corporation continues to hold sole responsibility for the importation of foreign films. At the exhibition level, cinemas can now group themselves into separate cinema chains, but the existing structure has reacted to the changes with a great deal of reluctance. Larger provincial distribution companies have cooperated with some of the smaller ones in their regions and prevented the others from purchasing films directly from the studios, thus continuing to maintain the existing structure in a more or less unaltered mode. Some mainland filmmakers characterize the decade of reform as having achieved nothing but the creation of a number of regional monopolies out of the earlier China Film Corporation's single national monopoly (Kang 2000: 14–15). As a result, most of China's cinemagoers still have no choice in what movies they see, as the films continue to come from the same regional distribution source. The government turns a blind eye to the situation, as the existing structure, however problematic, prevents the formation of a free film market, and this failure indirectly helps the state to maintain its control.

In addition to the flawed distribution network, the production units also are under tremendous pressure. Within the competitive environment where capitalist logic reigns, very few of the film companies in China, which are required to produce "politically correct" films, are making profits. The production manager of Emei Film Studio reported that the total sum of national investment in film production in

1999 was about 300 million RMB,[2] but the total revenue returned was only 30 million RMB – only one-tenth of its investment (K. Li 2000). According to recent web-based research, over 90 percent of the 50,000 interviewees found movie ticket prices to be too high, and they were reluctant to pay such prices to go to the cinema.[3] The national standard price for a movie ticket is 15 RMB, while the price of a pirated VCD can be as low as 5 RMB. In order to survive, some film companies, like Shangdong Film Company and Beijing's Forbidden City Film Company, produce television programs (which are always more profitable) to offset the costs of their films. Some studios, like Nanjing Film Company, cut their production costs immensely; many more rely on government subsidies.

In spite of the general marketization tendency, the majority of China's film companies still rely less on the market than on government aid – which ranges from loans and financial awards to government mass ticket purchasing – for survival. As a result, films have become more and more compliant with official ideology, which further discourages Chinese productions from catering to the tastes and values of the masses. Government funding and involvement, according to Ana M. López (2000), might be important for any national cinema competing with Hollywood; but instead of leading to the examination of structural failures, in reality these interventions usually only provide a protectionist shield against foreign competition or sustain financially deteriorating businesses, and these funding activities only attest to and preserve the structural problems of a failing system. In fact, various kinds of financial aid to the film industry are essential for the government to stay in control. The current dilemma of cinema's position in China – between its roles of political apparatus and commodity – has caused a major headache for film producers, as everyone is caught up in the impossible task of balancing profits and ideology. This predicament has generated a whole set of structural problems that are now leading to the collapse of the national film industry.

Although some individual filmmakers, like Feng Xiaogang and Zhang Yimou, are trying their best to make commercial films for the market, their sporadic success is far from typical. A pure commercial cinema is still only an imagined concept for China's film industry. This irreducible distance between the film industry and its audience directly promotes the popularity of Hollywood and Hong Kong commercial films in China (Pang 2002b). However, the China Film Corporation has been extremely selective in bringing in foreign films; most Chinese audiences can only watch their pirated versions. And the rapid development of the movie piracy industry in China is stunning.

There are now only five agents in China which own the distributions rights of Hollywood films: Shenzhen Laser Program Distribution Company (Shenzhen shi jiguang jiemu chuban faxing gongsi), China Record Company (Zhongguo changpian zonggongsi), China Audio and Video Press (Zhongying yinxiang chubanshe), China Record and Video Press (Zhongguo luyin luxiang chubanshe), and Beijing Oriental Video and Music Company (Beijing dongfang yinying gongsi). Some pirates adopt names that are similar to these official distributors, like Shenzhen Music and Video Press (Shenzhen yinxiang chubanshe). But there are also a number of pirate "brand names" that are famous in their own right among Chinese consumers. Examples include The Great Alliance (Da liangmeng), Live Music (Lakuo yinyue), The Powerful "V" Star (Qiangdang [V] zhuda xing), Discs on Fire (Fashao die), King Films (Wangpai dianying), Golden Warner (Jin huana), and Golden Dragon Visual (Jinlong yingye). These companies are known to be producers of good-quality pirated materials.

Each of these pirate companies has its own editorial direction and image, so that the films or music they choose to pirate are calculated to fit the images of the general brand or specific series. While pirated films are sold mainly on the streets or some temporary stores in Hong Kong and Taiwan, where anti-piracy is fierce, the distribution networks on the mainland are so highly developed that each of these established pirate groups has national distribution and retail lines. For example, a VCD saleslady in Xi'an proudly told a reporter that her shop holds the exclusive right to distribute the products of the pirate brand "Live Music" in the city (Bai 2000). In certain shops, there were also exchange services, in case the customers were dissatisfied with the quality of the discs (Wang 2003: 91). Distributors of very popular Hollywood films allegedly sell more than 10,000 (pirated) copies *per film* in the city of Lanzhou alone (An and Lan 2000: 109). Imagine how many cities like Lanzhou there are in the entire country. Piracy factories are launched by workers laid off by reforming state-owned enterprises or downsizing joint-venture factories (China Hand 2000a). The economies of many villages and towns depend almost entirely on piracy (China Hand 2000b).

The flagrant piracy business is also forcing the official distributors to adapt to the new market environment. The pirates are generally more adventurous and aggressive in terms of marketing strategy. Several years ago, erotic images were seen only on the covers of pirated discs; legitimate companies are increasingly inspired by such practices to package their products accordingly (Youli Zhang 2000). But there are also production houses choosing to invest in higher-quality packaging and additional features to distinguish their discs from pirated copies. Companies have to lower the retail prices of the legitimate VCDs and CDs, to release them faster, and sometimes to forgo theatrical screenings and rely completely on VCDs for exhibition. Allegedly, many film producers themselves are also involved in the piracy business, seeing the pirate market only as an alternative that gives them greater freedom to distribute their works (*Dajiyuan* 2002).

The Hong Kong director Stanley Kwan and his producer Zhang Yongning shot *Lan Yu* (2000), a gay film set in Beijing, with the understanding that the film would not be screened in China. But the knowledge that pirated copies would be seen in China gave them more freedom to conceptualize the film. "Although we won't be able to 'officially' release the film in China, in the end, people will get to see it" (Ng 2002). Unlike their fellow producers, who lament that the piracy market recklessly profits from their investments, many Hong Kong directors, like Wong Kar-wai and Herman Yau, hold positive views of the piracy market, which allows mainland audiences to watch those of their films not officially distributed there (K. Wong 2000; Yau 2000). Thus, a more vigorous and healthy market could not be developed unless censorship were extensively relaxed, which is not likely to happen in the foreseeable future.

The flourishing pirated VCD market gives mainland audiences the chance to watch many films that are prohibited from being screened publicly. For example, to his great surprise, Herman Yau has discovered that he is extremely well known on the mainland, due largely to the popularity of his famous exploitation films like *Taxi Hunter* (*Deshi pan'guan*, 1993) and *The Untold Story* (*Baxian fandian zhi renrou chashaobao*, 1993) (Yau 2000). These films can be circulated only on pirated VCDs, as they are extremely violent and contain illicit material such as rape, murder, and cannibalism. It must be noticed that the pirated VCD market often overlaps with the pornographic movie market. The former is counterfeit while the latter often is not, but they share the same illegal status. In a police raid in Lanzhou, 759 pornographic discs and some cassettes featuring explicit lyrics were seized along with 10,000 pirated VCD and DVD movies (*Gansu xinwen wang*, 2003). The symbiosis between censored materials and pirated movies is seen everywhere in China, mutually reinforcing their illegal status, yet also legitimizing their survival within a vast country ruled by a purist/authoritative government. China's conservative cinema censorship directly fosters the development of a prosperous black market, creating two streams of parallel yet highly divergent exhibition traffic. While the official cinema outlet shows "clean" movies, the prohibited yet more entertaining movies circulate widely on black market VCDs. And it is the black market that more accurately reflects the popular tastes of today's Chinese moviegoers, who also prefer pirated films for their price and accessibility.

In fact, not only Hollywood and Hong Kong commercial films but a large number of European classics are also pirated, so that many Chinese film viewers also have seen the entire corpus of Fellini or Bergman without relying on art theaters or expensive DVD collections (Chen *et al.* 2004: 181–5). Many Sixth-Generation films censored in China for political reasons are also circulated in pirated form. This situation is also referenced in Chinese films themselves. For example, in *Unknown Pleasure* (*Ren xiaoyao*; dir. Jia Zhangke, 2002), there is a scene in which the protagonist sells pirated films to some friends, and the pirated films being sold are precisely those made by the director himself (most of Jia's films are banned in China). As I suggested in Chapter 5, piracy can be productive, particularly within a rigid and hegemonic system, because it challenges the established order. Exact product piracy may not introduce new products or new representations, but it carves out new spaces for change.

As mentioned at the beginning of the chapter, there have been many accusations against the Chinese government for its clandestine support of the piracy industry. However, in reality the PRC has always been concerned about IPR protection, largely due to the double-edged anxiety of yearning to join the international community and fearing the loss of national control. Accession to the WTO had been at the top of government's priority list; this forced the state to comply with international business rules. The United States, a leading source of IP and a net exporter of copyrighted works, has been one of the most strident critics of China's IPR enforcement. From 1994 to 1996, China was put on the priority watch list under Section 301 of the US Trade Act of 1974. Recent WTO negotiations became a political platform for the American government to force China's legal and enforcement systems to comply fully with TRIPs.[4] In a Shanghai municipal court, the MPAA recently successfully sued several Chinese companies for selling illegally copied movies. The companies were ordered to pay MPAA members approximately US$30,000 in damages, to make formal apologies, and to destroy all of their pirated discs (Australian Copyright Council 2004: 6). As one might anticipate, the increasing power of transnational copyright enforcement organizations like the MPAA will continue to be felt in China.

The VCD piracy market weakens the government's of its power of internal control and allows its subjects to experience the world without any filtering. The government can keep an eye even on the unruly Internet, but it remains relatively helpless in screening or blocking the unwelcome messages brought to the Chinese people through pirated movies. Under the dual pressure of outside commercial interests and inside political demands, the PRC is anxious to demolish the piracy market, as evidenced by several large-scale government anti-piracy propaganda campaigns. For example, in 1999 the semi-official Chinese Audio-visual Association (Zhongguo yingxiang xiehui) invited reporters from five major newsgroups in China on a trip to investigate piracy. The event was widely publicized and many articles were published to document the tremendously developed piracy network in the country.

As Daniel C.K. Chow demonstrates, China has demonstrated that it can take swift, effective, and ruthless measures to suppress commercial crimes when a political commitment has been made at the highest levels of government (D. Chow 2000). On the legislative level, the PRC is one of the countries in the world most committed to protecting IPR. Since the 1980s, China has enacted an impressive body of IPR laws and ratified most major international IPR treaties, including the Berne Conventions and the US–China IPR Agreement (Layman and Deringer 2000: 129–39). Law enforcement does not lag behind legislation. Starting in 1997, the government called in the Ministry of Public Security to aid the National Copyright Administration in cracking down on disc pirates. Hundreds of plants have been closed and thousands of people involved in illegal production have been imprisoned. Instances of counterfeiting production in China have decreased dramatically (*Hong Kong Economic Journal*, January 12, 1998).

But it is much more difficult to control retailing. The government has also organized many raids on retail piracy markets, but corruption at the provincial level tremendously reduces the effectiveness of the anti-piracy campaign. The market still flourishes, although many of the discs are no longer "Made in China" but are imported from other areas. In 1997, many pirates moved their factories to Hong Kong and Macau, whence millions of counterfeit and bootleg VCDs were imported back to the mainland each year. In turn the Hong Kong government also started fierce piracy raiding in 1999, and plants moved to other sites in Southeast Asia to continue their business (Ho 2001). Malaysia in particular has emerged as a center of Asian piracy networks, which also extend worldwide (Fadhal 2003; Wang 2003: 85–6). Like transnational corporations that will move anywhere in the world to gain the most favorable business conditions, many pirates also have the transnational mobility to go to places where anti-counterfeiting legislation and enforcement are weak. Within the national space, pirates also try to increase their mobility by situating themselves in advantageous positions. Many of the production plants now operate in ships on the Changjiang River, both to escape arrest and to facilitate shipping (Tang 2001). Surprisingly, these modern pirates choose to model their businesses after their forerunners, who also operated on water. The work the Chinese state must undertake to stop piracy in the vast mainland, and thereby please the international community as well as maintain the control of the nation's information traffic, is much more difficult than most critics would assume.

The state, ultimately, becomes the victim of its own policy. On the one hand, in order to maintain a unified and clean cinematic representation of China, the government forces the national cinema to ignore the tastes of the masses, who now turn to the black market for pirated movies to satisfy their entertainment demands. The shift of the movie market from official to underground channels results in great financial loss to the government in terms of taxation, and the government is also forced to surrender its cultural control to foreign popular cultures, particularly those of Hong Kong and the United States. On the other hand, in spite of its painstaking attempts to please the international business communities, the Chinese government is constantly condemned by the world for its inefficient policy in IPR protection. Peter Feng (Feng Xiang) points out a specific problematic legislative situation in China: IP laws are much more elaborate and developed than those pertaining to private property, making the practice of the former sometimes very abstract and speculative without the support of the latter (Feng 2004: 83–4). While Feng does not further explain the situation, we can interpret this unparallel legal development in light of the country's current economic situation: intellectual properties, in which global corporations are involved, take precedence over private properties, which are of concern to the general Chinese people. The many policies made as a result of the PRC's intense desire to enter the global capitalist order and maintain domestic ideological control take a detour, only to return and haunt the government itself. The concept of national sovereignty leads to our continuing investigation of Chinese national cinema.

Piracy, cinema, and globalization

As illustrated in Chapters 1 and 2, copyright was originally a concept and policy meant to balance public and private interests, granting limited freedom to the public in the form of "fair use" of copyrighted materials on by setting aside a "public domain," and at the same time protecting and rewarding creativity. But recent legal developments are so protective of copyright holders that they can hamper creative freedom and discourage cultural reproduction and dissemination. Copyright has become a form of censorship; the rights of the users are sacrificed to those of the owners. When this criticism of copyright protection is put into a globalized context, the problems are even more obvious. The sheer bulk of very broad and very basic patents and copyrights have created many barriers to the development of national industries.[5] Today's international copyright laws are major and powerful tools that perpetuate and reinforce the historically constructed uneven distribution of global wealth, as the developed world has increasingly become home to the copyright holders, while the developing world houses the users of copyrighted materials.

As mentioned in Chapter 4, although piracy seems to admit no ambiguity in the idea–expression dichotomy, in that it supposedly involves no exercising of creativity, the previous two chapters demonstrate that movie piracy might textually transform certain elements of the original. However, the most significant cultural meanings of movie piracy do not reside in their texts. Movie piracy is a particularly rich phenomenon when read from the receiving end, which involves people's rights and desire to access diverse cultural materials. Movie piracy in China is particularly pertinent to an examination of the relationship between copyright and reception rights, as the country's film distribution does not operate in the ideal "free market" from which the notion of IPR supposedly derives its meaning. The use of today's international copyright laws in a highly regulated market governed by an authoritarian government poses a double threat to cultural diversity, less in terms of the freedom to create than in the freedom to receive. On the one hand, international copyright laws make legitimate video copies very expensive. While constantly attracted by Western entertainment and cultural productions, most Chinese lack the financial means to purchase these commodities. On the other hand, the PRC's tight control of both the production of national cinema and the distribution of international films further stifles the video market and theater screenings. The people are therefore under a dual form of control: the desire for Western commodities and the denial thereof. Desires for imported entertainment are only reinforced, and the inevitable result is piracy, which in turn hampers the development of national cinema. Paul Willemen characterizes two potential types of national cinema: one that benefits the homogenizing top-down project of nationalism and one that opposes it (Willemen 1994: 212). In China, piracy threatens both of these possibilities.

James Donald and Stephanie Hemelryk Donald argue that some Chinese films manifest a publicness – a shared experience of the cultural present – to provide spectators "an inventive, creative and mundane engagement with the dense symbolic now [they] inhabit" (Donald and Donald 2000: 127). In her own book, Stephanie Hemelryk Donald more elaborately demonstrates how Chinese cinema in the 1980s successfully constructed an imaginary space for people to observe, experience, and reflect upon rural dislocation in the wake of economic reform (Donald 2000: 67–83). According to Donald and Donald, although this engagement takes place through the individual viewing experience of different spectators, a publicness is created by the films, since they establish a public memory through which the audience is reminded of the present and its predicaments. Donald and Donald's reading of contemporary Chinese cinema is a moving one, as it gives cinema a very specific and important political position to allow people to perform counter-hegemonic cultural activities. However, the film texts Donald and Donald refer to are the canonical Fifth-Generation texts, such as *The Big Parade* (*Da yuebing*, 1985), *Red Sorghum* (*Hong gaoliang*, 1987), and *Yellow Earth* (*Huang tudi*, 1984), whose directors shared a loosely connected ideological agenda. These films might indeed define a singular and unified viewing experience, which Donald and Donald celebrate. However, entering the late 1990s, with the Chinese film industry on the verge of complete collapse, and the Chinese people clearly preferring to watch pirated movies from Hollywood and Hong Kong, Donald and Donald's specific reading of the national cinema seems no longer applicable.

While we can no longer imagine how Chinese cinema could embody any subversive ideology or forms of people's collective anti-hegemonic action, neither can we imagine the state using cinema so conveniently as an ideological mouthpiece. The government's present embarrassing position in relation to its film industry indirectly reveals the state's flawed conception of cinema as a representation of collective Chinese consciousness. Cinema has always been dear to the CCP, mostly due to the medium's publicness and therefore its usefulness as a means of publicity. When made in an intelligent way, a film text can be a powerful tool to indoctrinate the audience in any form of ideology, but it is the collective viewing experience that most effectively promotes the ideological infiltration. Public film screening can be seen as a collective ritual, which has much more power than the film text alone. And it is the publicness of cinema, instead of its visual and audio features, that most uniquely defines its political position.[6]

However, movie piracy belongs to the private sphere, in contrast to the public sphere traditionally occupied by cinema. In the West, the introduction and quick popularity of video rental in the 1970s "democratized" cinema's previously Fordist consumption patterns and unsettled the public sphere formed by movie watching.[7] The age of video rental, however, never reached China, as movie piracy swept the nation before Blockbuster could do so. Still used to the public-screening rituals of cinema, in the 1990s the Chinese audience was suddenly introduced to the disarray of movie piracy. The public movie-watching experience suddenly became domesticated and intractable. Experiencing the outside world through film is now an activity belonging to individual time and space. Individuals can now relax at home, taking their time and making their own choices as to which part of the "West" and which aspects of "modernity" they want to consume. Recent research on Beijing film audiences indicates that most Beijingers go to the cinema fewer than five times a year, while over 60 percent of the interviewees watch at least one film a week at home – probably mostly on pirated VCDs (Dai 1999: 90–1). Very few Chinese watch movies in theaters, and the activity is now almost exclusively performed by couples on dates. In fact, the flourishing pirated VCD market is publicly acknowledged in the country: most of China's film magazines introduce and analyze films not screened in China but available only in VCD and DVD formats, and many of these films are pirated. The new movie culture introduced by piracy developed more rapidly and created greater cultural disturbances than the video culture that started in the West in the 1970s – piracy is destructive to the status quo largely because it is illegal. In this case, no one group is in control of the films being pirated, distributed, and watched, and no one identifiable form of power – political, civil, or commercial – can manipulate movie-watching activities in China, as numerous people participate in piracy due to the minimal technology and low costs involved. It is this implication of "privacy" that most threatens the PRC's governing ideology, which demands unity and harmony to legitimate its own rule.

The flourishing of VCD piracy and the failing Chinese film industry might demonstrate that scholars can no longer define the watching of Chinese cinema as "political" in its usual sense. If watching pirated movies is, in fact, political, its meaning might ultimately reside in being non-political. The political aspects of pirate cinema in contemporary China, if any remain, no longer lie in its mass production of a sense of collective identity but precisely its opposite, that film-watching has now become an activity distanced from any form of control. If Linda Williams is right in her argument that contemporary cinema disciplines the audience into a docile body (L. Williams 2000), movie piracy is non-disciplinary. Spectators of pirated movies do not need to follow the time-scheduling of theater screening and television broadcasts, nor do they need to return the films to video rental stores.[8] Pirated movies cannot control nor be controlled by any identifiable source of power.

Movie piracy in China, therefore, might be seen as a classic example of Michel de Certeau's "strategy vs tactics" model, in which a top-down "strategy" transforms the uncertainties of history into stability that sustains one's own power, while the bottom-up "tactics" respond to the strategy as transitory and non-cohesive, able to subvert its organization and rationality (de Certeau 1988). But there are major differences between de Certeau's theorization and China's actual piracy scene, and movie piracy is far from a romantic form of guerrilla warfare to fight hegemony. Obviously, it is naïve to assume that piracy is an egalitarian effort by the people to oppose some authoritative policy, because what the people desire is entertainment from commercial Hong Kong and Hollywood films, which are hegemonic in their own discursive structures. The popular commercial films being pirated are often invested with various forms of prejudices, ranging from racism, chauvinism, and homophobia to capitalist greed. The so-called tactics involved in piracy are neither humanistic nor democratic in nature but are carried out by their own system of exploitation, through which gangster tycoons earn astronomical profits. Most frighteningly, piracy demonstrates the potent penetrating power of capital (gained by the pirates instead of by Hollywood studios) to break down barriers to capital's expansion; in our case what is being challenged is the ideological control of the now mighty Chinese state. Unlike de Certeau's "tactics vs strategy" model, in which the former are just feeble disturbances in the inexorable domination of the latter, the flourishing piracy market seems to suggest that the force opposing despotism is now gaining an upper hand and overthrowing the state's control. On the other hand, it would also be a mistake to consider piracy as solely governed by capitalist logic, in which the free market provides the ultimate regulations, since piracy operates outside any legal system. As the capitalist market cannot survive without the protection of a powerful system of legislature and enforcement, the criminal pirate market's violence and unmanageability only harm the orderliness of capitalism. Although movie piracy sanctifies the culture industry by circulating its products to areas beyond its usual scope of control, the culture industry is very vocal in its fight against piracy, as this industry has the most to lose. Or so it claims.

Therefore, the cultural meanings of movie piracy in China are not its implications of (anti-)capitalist will and discipline but its dissemination and disorder. Movie piracy can be seen as the largest crime collectively committed by the Chinese people against the authority of both the state and capitalism. But this piracy by no means creates a self-empowerment of the people, as it does not promote the development of a cinema or a new culture belonging to the Chinese people in the new global era. Movie piracy does not provide for the cultivation of a healthy and vigorous film industry in China, much less one that can survive foreign competition. The decreasing ticket revenues of the nation directly hamper the film industry's ability to reinvest, which causes the national cinema to lose its competitiveness with foreign industries.

The most powerful aspect of movie piracy in the context of contemporary Chinese culture is its fluidity and disorder – the fact that no major political or commercial party can singlehandedly condition the people's everyday life. Piracy demonstrates a lack of authorship, and a lack of authority, rules, and discipline. Trying to tackle the increasingly impossible project of theorizing a national Chinese cinema, particularly in view of the inclusion of Hong Kong and Taiwanese productions, Chris Berry suggests a performative model of collective agency, through which Chinese films can exceed the problematics of a unified collectivity:

> Rather than arguing for the total abandonment of the concept of national agency in regard to national cinema, [we should] argue for recasting national cinema as a multiplicity of projects, authored by different individuals, groups, and institutions with various purposes, but bound together by the politics of national agency and collective subjectivity as constructed entities.
>
> (1998: 132)

While Berry's proposal can help us to rethink Chinese cinema as a fluid and noncoercive entity, this model is based on a pluralistic and productive film scene that has the capacity to incorporate projects with different styles, contents, and ideologies, which can hardly apply to mainland cinema at the moment. A more pressing question among filmmakers at present maybe how official culture should respond to the "enemy" piracy culture, which is as pluralized and as mobilized as one can imagine.

Like many other phenomena caused by globalization, piracy is created and participated in by many local and international players who are both architects and victims. But the case of movie piracy does not simply show the evil impacts of globalization in a developing country like China. The internal contradictions of globalization revealed here do not rest on simple unidirectional West/non-West hegemonies and appropriations, but are more specifically generated within a (post)Socialist state trying hard to hold on to ideological control of its people in a globalizing age. The contradictions of globalization are shown here less as defects of a coherent structure than as responses of a government and a people to the threats and lures of globalization. The Chinese state is particularly caught in the dilemma between ideological control and economic activities, as the country's economic success is a major pillar legitimizing the state's authoritative sovereignty. Almost all legal and illegal commercial activities taking place in the country are directly or indirectly linked to the topsy-turvy political reality cocooned in layers of ideological contradictions. The Party's immense desire for national power, as prophesized by Schwartz and Dirlik, only makes these ideological contradictions of the Chinese state more apparent and unsolvable.

Not One Less and collective Chineseness

The case of movie piracy in China proves not only the difficulties of political control but also the increasing impossibility of defining a national cinema/identity. An interesting case in point that can demonstrate this predicament is the cinema market in May 1999, when North Atlantic Treaty Organization (NATO) bombed Belgrade's Chinese Embassy. At a time when China's collective anger towards the United States was at its highest, Zhang Yimou's *Not One Less* (*Yige dou buneng shao*) received the highest box-office receipts in all major Chinese cities that month, and ultimately became the highest-grossing domestic film of the year.[9] The film describes the dogged journey of a 13-year-old substitute teacher traveling all the way from a remote rural village to the bustling and alienated city in search of a dropout student who is not much younger than the teacher. After much misery, the young teacher finds herself being interviewed on a television news program about her trip to the city and the plight of rural education. Her ardent and tear-jerking story touches many hearts in the city. The missing boy is finally reunited with the faithful teacher and the village through a collective effort by the people and the media. The title *Not One Less* clearly suggests the film's collectivist ideology, and it can be seen as a sentimentalist representation and celebration of the traditional populist ethos of mutual help and the unyielding loyalty of the authorities to the people.

In February 1999 – when the film was finishing its post-production – media coverage focused on the purchase of the national distribution rights to the film by newly established semi-government organization China Film Group (Zhongguo dianying jituan), who bid an extremely high 11.8 million RMB (Cao and Yi 1999) – showing the government's high-profile approval of the film's ideology. The film was officially released in late April, 1999, and an accompanying nationwide campaign used the film to promote rural education and national cinema. With such obvious support from the government, the film found itself (very soon after its public release) embroiled in the furious anti-American sentiments spreading rapidly across the nation. During this time when the government, through the mass media, was organizing the entire nation to say no to the United States, this film conveniently became a part of the ideological machine shaping and endorsing the sizzling nationalist sentiments of the time. Its success at the box office demonstrates the audience's strong participation in the civil-cum-state nationalist campaign. All these historical and political factors combine to make the film one of a handful of contemporary Chinese films that have enjoyed the endorsement of both the government and the people. Its success also revived a cultural legacy in which films provide a public space and crystallize collective emotions in China, even at the turn of the twenty-first century.

Very interestingly, a large-scale anti-piracy campaign was launched at the same time: for the first time in history a series of highly publicized raids was organized to hunt down pirated copies of this single film (Sina 2003). The government clearly gave the message that the film belonged to the official culture, and its healthy message should not be contaminated by pirated versions. There are reports that the film's box-office record was not a faithful reflection of audience opinion, as the number of government-purchased tickets surpassed the number of individual tickets sold (Cao and Yi 1999). Although the film was more popular than many other "main melody" (state-sponsored) films, the success of the film as an event film that displays the collective emotions of the people was not purely egalitarian but partly constructed.

Underlying this national campaign for a unified Chinese cinema was the pirate movie market, which, at that time, was flooded with Hollywood films such as

Armageddon, *Saving Private Ryan*, and *Antz*, which are loaded with overt US-centric ideologies. *Antz*, for example, clearly presents a strong condemnation of communist regimes, which are described as advocating collectivist ideology for their own political interests. In other words, *Antz* criticizes precisely the kind of collectivist ideology glorified by *Not One Less*. It is impossible to verify whether it was the American *Antz* or the authentically Chinese *Not One Less* that captured a larger Chinese audience around the time when NATO bombed the Chinese embassy. However, it is clear that the wide circulation of pirated movies complicates not only the state's top-down media control but also the formation of any unified collective experience of the people from the bottom up. Even with the government's tight control of cinema, movie piracy nevertheless gives the Chinese masses a tremendous range of choices. Complete control of the film market is impossible. In the age of piracy, any structured form of cinematic identification with nationalism is at stake, whether it is authoritative or egalitarian. And the success of *Not One Less* in crystallizing the collective Chinese emotions remains a rare and fleeting example in a contemporary Chinese cinema pushed hard by the government, yet tremendously corroded by piracy.

In fact, the volatile relationship between Zhang Yimou, the director of *Not One Less*, and the Chinese state is an interesting yet typical example of the confusing ideological stance of the government toward cinema. While some of Zhang's prior Fifth-Generation films, like *Judou* (*Judou*) and *To Live* (*Huozhe*) were banned in China, and he himself was seen as a political dissident, he is now embraced by the state as its prodigy, or even its mouthpiece, which is clearly observed in the national distribution privileges his most recent films, *Hero* (*Yingxiong*, 2002) and *House of Flying Daggers* (*Shimian maifu*, 2004), enjoyed. *Hero*, premiered in the Great Hall of the People, monopolized almost the entire national film market in the 2002 Christmas holiday season, so was the case of *House of Flying Daggers* in 2004 Summer. With the accompanying media frenzy, the films have enjoyed box-office success around the country. Similar situations also happen with the Sixth-Generation directors. Zhang Yuan's production *Seventeen Years* (*Guonian huijia*, 2000) was triumphantly promoted by the government as a national educational film that all Chinese students should watch, but his erotically and politically provocative *East Palace, West Palace* (*Donggong xigong*), made just three years earlier, was not allowed to be shown until recently.[10] While the Chinese government no longer stigmatizes individual filmmakers as troublemakers and exhibits an astonishingly and unpredictably wide range of responses to different works by the same filmmaker, the filmmakers themselves also seem to hold no stable political stance and are willing to compromise much more than we expect. We can celebrate such phenomena as kinds of postmodern pluralism that resist grand narratives; it is, however, precisely this kind of chaos manifested in Chinese cinema that make Berry's wish for the healthy development of Chinese cinema difficult to realize.

The film *Not One Less* also provides us an example with which to understand a new imagined embodiment of collective Chineseness: television. When the substitute teacher finally arrives in the city, she is too feeble to search the entire area for one missing person. In the end, she successfully persuades the manager of a television station to allow her to announce her search on television. The program rouses the entire city, and people rally to help her to find the student. The film postulates a new public experience for Chinese people: television watching, which might now replace cinema in its position of representing the collective Chinese experience. While *Not One Less* may be the most representative recent film to glorify cinema's function in forging a collective Chinese identity, in the end the narrative relies on television to fulfill this ideological aspiration.

As Zhang Yimou would know very well, television production is much more profitable than moviemaking in China, partly because the government exerts a fierce, singlehanded, centralized control of cinema, but gives television relative commercial freedom. In today's China, in spite of the intense television regulation procedures, "television drama production still exhibits a greater degree of freedom and flexibility than cinema, which is subject to the administrative centralization of state power" (Yin 2002: 36). For television, centralized censorship is replaced by regional inspection. While non-television companies can produce television dramas, television companies are also allowed to accept non-state funding, investment from foreign and overseas enterprises, as well as joint funding arrangements (Yin 2002: 36). Such relatively lax controls are only a dream for film companies. As statistics show, the development of cinema lags far behind that of other media under China's open-market policy. In 1985, 127 feature films were produced, yet annual film production in 1998 dropped to 82 films (National Bureau of Statistics 2000: 711). However, the number of hours of television programs increased from 6,957 to 118,343 within the same thirteen-year period (National Bureau of Statistics 2000: 712), representing a seventeen-fold increase. Rapid development can also be seen in traditional print media such as books (a 311 percent increase), magazines (a 174 percent increase), and newspapers (a 141 percent increase) in the same period (National Bureau of Statistics 2000: 714), demonstrating that the mass media, in spite of the government's ideological control, on the whole flourish under economic reform. Watching television is becoming the favorite pastime of the Chinese people, so it is not surprising to see *Not One Less* replacing cinema with television to represent a newly imagined collective Chinese experience.

But this new rendering of Chinese collectiveness through television is by no means "public" in its traditional sense. The television episode featured in *Not One Less* was clearly modeled after CCTV's *Time and Space of the Orient* (*Dongfang shikong*) and *Interviews in Focus* (*Jiaodian fangtan*), arguably the two most popular television programs in the late 1990s. The two programs were so popular that they attracted a surge of imitators who created interview programs in the same style, which focused on revealing and sentimentalizing the lives of ordinary people. These programs, although presented as such, could by no means be considered news programs, since they did not report on or investigate incidents and individuals of current public interest. The people being interviewed and explored were always the ordinary and the common – many viewers could personally identify with them. There were no big stories to tell, no social themes guiding the programs; these programs aimed at presenting a quasi-realistic, although largely sentimentalized, manifestation of ordinary lives (J. Zhang 1999: 1–36). In other words, the popularity of these interview programs may in fact harm the development of Chinese journalism, as people conceive of news programs not as media to interrogate public issues and supervise the government but only as a forum to expose and come to terms with an individual's personal life. The audience is inscribed within their own horizons and emotions, rather than encouraged to participate in the public sphere. If *Not One Less* is really trying to demonstrate a new publicness evolving in China, this publicness is introverted and, in the end, privatized.

As writer Su Tong describes television culture in 1990s China:

> Those watching television have no fervent devotion to the machine. Lazily they lie on the sofa, with sunflower seeds and a cup of green tea at hand, their eyes and ears are captured by the television screen and sound. At this moment, Bill Clinton and Andy Lau, Xing Zhibin and Maggie Cheung, Hangtian airplanes and Huiyuan fruit juice obtain an astonishing chance for equality.[11]
>
> (1999: 64)

Su Tong's description seems to suggest that if television can unify China, it produces a stabilizing effect, which flattens hierarchy and reduces meanings into unstable yet equivalent floating signifiers. This sense of indifference differs greatly from the fervent reception of the media in the previous decade when television was first popular on a mass level. Even for the television historical dramas so popular in China around the fiftieth anniversary of the PRC in 1999, the reception is not unified. Although most of these dramas spread ideologies of people's loyalty to and the ultimate righteousness of emperors or high-level government officials, the audience's frenzy lies less in the collective yielding to authority than in individual viewers' personal identification with the power being celebrated. A mainland audience comments on the popularity of these television series in a disdainful tone: "When watching these dramas, most audiences identify themselves with the major characters and reveal their desire for power" (Fang 2001: 43). According to this view, in spite of the vast popularity of this television genre, collective yielding is replaced with personal will to power, as the identification resides more in the power-holders than in the docile subjects, and the resulting effects do not forge, but challenge, any nationalist projects.

There are now 3,593 television stations operating in China, the highest number of any country in the world (H. Zhang 2001: 27). Although programs repeat on different stations, the diversity of television content now offered to Chinese people is hard to ignore. China's situation is also different from that of the developed world, where concentrated media ownership and control results in, to use Edward Herman's terminology, "marginal" or "meaningless" diversity (Herman 1983: 135–46). While the numerous cable-television stations are owned by a handful of conglomerates in the United States, those in China are not yet united by mergers and acquisitions. In addition to the high number of television stations, there are 2,049 newspapers, 8,149 magazines, and more than 3,500 radio stations operating in China (H. Zhang 2001: 29). Any fantasy of a single collective Chinese experience consolidated by the mass media is obsolete and unconvincing. Cinema might have failed to dominate the public experience of the Chinese people, but no other form of mass media can succeed at this impossible task either. These media might be less policed by the government, and therefore economically more vigorous, but the impact of market diversification on these media is more obvious. In other words, tight ideological control, as in cinema, leads to piracy, while looser regulation, as in television, brings forward uncontrollable market diversification and complacent consumerist ideology. In both cases, a unified national identity manifested through mass media is a myth.

The presumed reading of China as a collective entity – in which all Chinese share a singular collective history and identity – is not only a fiction created for political manipulation, but is also a concept widely circulated among scholars of contemporary Chinese culture. Most studies are informed by phenomena before the 1990s that characterized the PRC when it might still be possible to speak of collective experiences and attitudes. But the 1990s saw an increasing de-politicization of people's everyday lives as the nation achieved a more stable political and economic condition. The pluralization of the "Chinese experience" not only reflects a late-capitalist globalized fragmentation of life in China, but it is also a fact of political reality. To my mind, after June Fourth there could no longer be any major national event – not even the accession to the WTO or the 2008 Olympics – that could mark a linear historical progression of China; massive political meetings and decisions are gradually losing their meaning in the people's lives, as are any collectivist ideologies the national cinema supposedly embodied. With the double reinforcement of economic stability and political authoritarianism, China has now gradually entered a phase where complacency and indifference are the sociopolitical norm, notwithstanding the lingering nationalist sentiments now taking pains to try to unify disparate walks of life.

Movie piracy and globalization

Movie piracy, therefore, is only one cause and manifestation, among many, of a disunited Chineseness. In the age of consumerist globalization, both the state's desire for hegemonic control and scholars' and artists' fascination with collective egalitarian reactions are doomed to go bankrupt, a phenomenon easily observed in the current Chinese cinema scene, which has been detrimentally affected by piracy. In fact, piracy is a unique case of cultural disarray among many other activities as a demonstration of the characteristics of globalization, as piracy is engendered by globalization but remains outside of, or even subversive to, globalization's control and interests. The products of globalization do not always serve to maintain the mechanism's interests and continuing expansion. Being caught in the power network of China merging with the world, and of an authoritarian government struggling to cope with globalization, piracy reveals itself as an interesting force that threatens both the prevalent political ideology of the Chinese state and the emerging global order. Yet the people are not necessarily empowered, nor is any concept of a unified Chineseness.

I mentioned in the book's introduction that Sassen identifies a new global legal regime developed to communicate between global capitalism and state sovereignty. She believes that this new legal regime helps negotiate the interests of and conflicts between the global and the national, thereby facilitating the practices of global economy on various national levels (Sassen 1996: 25–6). Sassen is correct in pointing out the intended functions of this legal regime, which ensures the effectiveness of the global order in various national contexts, but she might have seen the collaboration as too smooth, and she idealizes the hurried participation of docile nation states in economic globalization through the implementation of these laws. The conflicts and the collaborations between the global and the national are performed on many more levels. The case of movie piracy in China demonstrates some serious tensions between the global order and individual states, in spite of the tremendous attraction to the former on the part of the latter.

But the piracy situation should not be interpreted as a simple antagonistic relationship between local consumption and the global market economy. As I have been trying to show in this book, the criminal and the official interact in many ways, ranging from fierce competition to mutual supports. As we can see, many times the pirate and the legal markets comply with each other to promote the formation of a single global market, comprising the dominant Hollywood as the global center, and minor regional film industries, like Hong Kong's and India's, which serve alternative tastes. Pirated and original films can be read as dialectic manifestations of a single cinematic world order. In a way, movie piracy can be seen as demonstrating a key thesis of Hardt and Negri's: "Contrary to the way many postmodernist accounts would have it, however, the imperial machine, far from eliminating master narratives, actually produces and reproduces [ideological master narratives] in order to validate and celebrate its own power" (2000: 34).

However, while I agree that there is a hegemonic world order we cannot get away from, I also want to keep a critical distance from the aggrandizement of this world order as omnipotent, which might lead to an affirmation of the status quo, for which Hardt and Negri have been criticized (Tracy 2002). If we follow Hardt and Negri's logic, all exceptions to copyright discourse are parts of a biopolitical machine. This might be a valid description of the design of the copyright legal regime, which includes and tolerates specific exceptions. But actual happenings in the cultural domain, where mutual copying and piracy take place in numerous forms, do not conform to this description and therefore do not legitimize the totality of the copyright system, either from the perspective of enforcement or infringement. The question we must address, then, is the formulation of copyright as a contingent and incomplete system, which, as has hopefully been clear by now, is more complicated than both Sassen's model of "global–national" and the "Empire" model of Hardt and Negri. I hope that my book's humble contribution to the development of copyright discourse will point out the danger of conceptualizing any system as totalizing and invincible, particularly in relation to the realm of culture.

Notes

Introduction

1 René Girard is probably the anthropologist who is keenest on exploring issues related to mimesis. To summarize his thoughts very briefly; he argues that human beings are mimetic in nature, and we desire what others desire. This mimetic desire, however, creates competition and the impossibility of differentiating one from the other. Only through the lynching of a scapegoat can social order be restored, and differences be observed (1978).

2 Walter Benjamin argues that we are seeing the decay and the resurgence of the mimetic faculty of human beings in modern times. The canon most relevant to the mimetic faculty is language, which, according to Benjamin, is the highest level of mimetic behavior that, however, has also liquidated the magic of mimesis (1978: 336). Julia Kristeva discusses the connection between mimesis and language via the mother–child relationship: the child's mimetic desire for the mother before the castration complex is both nonobjective and yet always already in a world of difference (1987: 21–35). Similarly, the mimetic feature of language is also based on the logic of difference. The concept of mimesis brings Jacques Derrida to his formulation of the sign, which pretends to a sameness which it offers only in its difference (1981: 173–285).

3 I am not, however, dichotomizing the UN and the WTO as two organizations having two completely different rationales. As I will demonstrate in Chapter 1, both have offices dealing with IP, and they have similar objectives.

4 Piracy, of course, is not equal to guerrilla-style subversion of the copyright regime. We will discuss in detail the complex relationship between piracy and Hollywood films in Chapters 4 and 5.

1 Expressions, originality, and fixation

1 I will keep my references minimal for factual information. But I must acknowledge that my IP knowledge is based largely on secondary sources instead of the text of actual laws, which are sometimes incomprehensible to non-experts such as myself. I have tried to carefully cross-refer the information being recorded here, but if my discussion of these legal concepts is inaccurate or outdated, such errors are solely my responsibility.

2 WIPO's origin can be dated back to the Paris Convention for the Protection of Industrial Property of 1883, but its later development has been largely influenced by the Berne Conventions.

3 Ten countries signed this agreement: Belgium, France, Germany, Haiti, Italy, Liberia, Spain, Switzerland, the United Kingdom, and Tunisia, many of which were the greatest colonial powers of the time, so that the first Berne Convention immediately extended to a significant part of the world.

4 Nonobvious invention refers to an invention that would not have been anticipated by someone skilled in a particular field. So if someone invents a device that many in a profession would

find it very easy to develop with existing knowledge, she or he cannot register the product for a patent.

5 Works of authorship that fall within this definition may include literary works (including computer programs); musical works and accompanying lyrics; dramatic works and dialogue; pantomimes and choreographic works; pictorial, graphic, and sculptural works; sound recordings; and motion pictures and other audiovisual works. Tangible media, accordingly, may include printed books, musical CDs, paintings, and films.

6 There are, however, many cases that demonstrate that the courts are eager to protect satire and parody, both as entertainment and as social and literary criticism. I will talk more about the concept of "fair use" in the next chapter. But the reality is many artists and investors choose to avoid any dubious situations that might lead to expensive litigation.

7 The public domain is the body of works in which no person or organization has any proprietary interest. Such works are considered part of the public's cultural heritage, and anyone can use and build upon them without restriction. Chapter 2 will discuss the concept in detail.

8 The United States was one of the last major countries to sign the Berne Conventions (it did not do so until 1989) largely because of the movie industry's opposition to its moral rights clause (article 6bis). This created much embarrassment for US trade officials, who could not insist that foreign governments accede to the Berne Conventions until the United States itself became a signatory.

2 Copyright's limits and ethics

1 In addition to "fair use," different national laws also permit certain exceptions to copyright, allowing, for example, libraries, archives, and educational and nonprofit groups to make copies of copyrighted works for limited purposes.

3 Violence and New Asian Cinema

1 John Woo mentioned how much he liked this film, but he did not remember the name of the film (*Godamongdirectors*, year unknown). Based on Woo's description, I believe it to be *Narazu-mono*.

2 See the many film reviews on the film available on the Internet, including those on YesAsia, Learning Thai, and MoovGoog.

3 He made a TV documentary entitled *When Cinema Reflects the Times: Hou Hsiao-Hsien and Edward Yang* (1993) (Milestone Films and Video 1996).

4 See the director's profile on the DVD version of the film.

4 Copying *Kill Bill*

1 For some relevant data, see Balnaves, Donald, and Donald 2001: 33–43.

2 This particular title card, together with its jingle, was seen in almost every Shaw production in the 1970s. I thank those scholars around the world in the CULTSTUD-L who responded to my inquiry and confirmed that the title card was seen in many regional versions of *Kill Bill: Volume 1*.

3 Detailed discussion of the tensions between Golden Harvest and Shaws regarding this case can be found in Liang Liang 2004 and G. Yang 2004.

4 In the American version of *Kill Bill: Volume 1*, only one of Sophie's arms is chopped off, whereas both of her arms are lost in the supposedly more violent Asian version of the film.

5 I believe the former is included in all regional versions, but the Japanese tribute is included only in the East Asian version.

6 This is only a general view, which does not mean the "idea–expression" dichotomy is not applicable to cinematic copyright issues. In fact, there is a growing tendency toward content protection, which might place the entire media industry in jeopardy. In the famous *Kroft* case (1977), the US Ninth Circuit Court of Appeals introduced the concept of "total concept and feel" to determine that a TV production had plagiarized McDonald's TV commercials. This case concerns many copyright critics, as it can be seen as idea protection that opposes basic copyright principle (Vaidhyanathan 2001: 112–16).

7 However, Hollywood distributors alone are responsible for the films' advertising, from which the pirates benefit.

8 There are many new websites and numerous Internet dialogues that trace the intertextual cobweb of *Kill Bill*, demonstrating the specific appeal of the film to the cinephiliac Desser describes (forthcoming).

9 The ending titles of *Kill Bill: Volume 1* clearly state, "Produced with the assistance of China Film Co-Production Corporation."

10 Note that Bruce Lee did not make any films with Shaws; he is the Golden Harvest prodigy, although the head of Golden Harvest, Raymond Chow, had been production manager at Shaws, which demonstrates the unbreakable links between the two companies.

11 These zoom-in shots are also frequently seen in spaghetti Westerns, but the Hong Kong filmmakers most likely pilfered it from Japanese sources, as the new 1970s Hong Kong action films are in general very much indebted to the influence of Japanese cinema and television. I thank Darrell Davis for this observation.

12 This final scene of *Kill Bill: Volume 1* can be compared to that of *Alien* (dir. Ridley Scott, 1979). See Creed 1990.

13 The subtitles in the pirated DVD have both English and Chinese versions. I am quoting the English version, on which the Chinese subtitles are based.

14 Of course, there are always exceptions, which oftentimes are promotional gimmicks rather than real considerations of cultural differences; for example, the Asian version of *Kill Bill* is supposed to be more violent than the Western version. Sometimes the films have to be re-edited to pass specific national censorships.

15 In fact, Disney sometimes purchases the distribution rights to certain films in parts of the world in which they have no intention of showing the films, in order to minimize competition with Disney's own productions.

5 Movie piracy as a technological threat to Hollywood

1 In 2002, the three Hollywood films with the highest international box-office returns were *Harry Potter & the Chamber of Secrets* (US$604,608,624), *The Lord of the Rings: The Two Towers* (US$576,430,919), and *Spider-Man* (US$418,001,475). In 2003 they were *The Lord of the Rings: The Return of the King* (US$741,859,899), *Finding Nemo* (US$525,030,441), and *The Matrix Reloaded* (US$457,023,240) (Box Office Mojo International, 2005). All of these films rely heavily on digital effects.

2 The average movie-ticket price in the US rose from US$5.80 in 2002 to US$6.03 in 2003. It is very likely that most of the increase was due to computer technology (NATO Statistics 2004).

3 In reality the studios also produce a steady output of smaller films that often emerge as surprise hits. But the random successes of these individual films are too difficult to predict and control, and reliance on these films does not suit today's corporate management strategies in Hollywood, which demand steady and stable incomes.

4 In 2001, the worldwide average wholesale prices for a DVD and a VHS tape were US$15.20 and US$7.50, respectively, compared with only US$2.70 for a VCD. At the consumer level the equivalent prices were US$20.70 for a DVD, US$11.90 for a videocassette, and US$4.80 for a VCD. In many Asian pirate markets the retail price of a VCD can be considerably less (*Screen Digest*, 2002).

6 The despair of Chinese cinema

1 For the popular but problematic description of a unified Chineseness from both sides, see, for example, Gertz (2000) and Song *et al.* (1996).
2 At present, US$1 is approximately equivalent to 8 RMB.
3 This research was conducted by China's Sina web in November 2000 (Sina 2000). According to recent statistics provided by the New China News Agency, the standard movie ticket price equals 2 percent of the Chinese average monthly income, while the corresponding figures in the United States and India are 0.5 and 0.25 percent respectively (*Mingpao*, 2000).
4 Recent WTO negotiations triggered hot debates within China's film circles. People worry that with the government's promises of raising the quotas for imported films and allowing a larger share of foreign investments in China's film market, Hollywood will soon dominate the entire national film market.
5 For a discussion of biotechnological products, see Barton (1998).
6 On two different ways to relate cinema to the public sphere, that is, cinema as an activity and cinema as text, see Miriam Hansen (1991) and Dissanayake (1996).
7 However, as Richard Dienst reminds us, this visual "democratization" ultimately benefits the entertainment conglomerates that profit from this immense expansion in the volume of overall televisual time (1994: 165–6).
8 There have always been VCD rentals throughout Asia, but sales dominate the VCD culture and economy, probably due to the discs' low price and high degree of durability.
9 For the May 1999 box-office records in major Chinese cities, see *Zhongguo dianying shichange* (1999: 38).
10 My thanks go to Dai Jinhua, who reminded me of the similar case of Zhang Yuan.
11 Andy Lau and Maggie Cheung are famous Hong Kong movie stars, and Xing Zhibin was arguably China's most popular female television news anchor in the 1990s.

Bibliography

Abbas, Ackbar. 1997. *Hong Kong: Culture and the Politics of Disappearance*. Minneapolis, MN: University of Minnesota Press.

Adorno, Theodor. 1991. *The Culture Industry*. London: Routledge.

Alford, William P. 1995. *To Steal a Book is an Elegant Offense: Intellectual Property Law in Chinese Civilization*. Stanford, CA: Stanford University Press.

Althusser, Louis. 1971. *Lenin and Philosophy and Other Essays*. London: New Left Books.

Altman, Rick. 1999. *Film/Genre*. London: BFI.

An Guang and Lan Ping. 2000. "Gansu Sheng daoban dianying guangpan zhuangkuang diaocha" (The Study of Pirated Movie Discs in Gansu Province), *Dianying Yishu*, 3: 109–10.

Appadurai, Arjun. 1996. *Modernity at Large: Cultural Dimensions of Globalization*. Minneapolis, MN: University of Minnesota Press.

Aristotle. 1970. *Poetics*. trans. Gerald F. Else. Ann Arbor, MI: University of Michigan Press.

Arup, Christopher. 2000. *The New World Trade Organization Agreements: Globalizing Law Through Services and Intellectual Property*. Cambridge: Cambridge University Press.

Asian Sources Electronics. 1998. "Prices Plummet below $100 as Format Matures," *Asian Sources Electronics* 28. 6 (July): 84–6.

Auerbach, Erich. 1953. *Mimesis: The Representation of Reality in Western Literature*. trans. Willard R. Trask. Princeton, NJ: Princeton University Press.

Australian Copyright Council. 2004. *Copyright Update* 4. 1 (February).

Bai, Wei. 2000. "Anfang Xi'an Chengdu yinxiang shichang" (Visiting the Audio–Visual Market in Xi'an and Chengdu), *Zhongguo yinxiang* (China's Music and Video) 2. 46: 52–3.

Baines, Caroline. 2001. "Media Manufacturing within the Asia Market," *Asian Market Survey*, http://www.opticaldisc-systems.com/2001MarApril/AsianMarket32.htm; accessed March 1, 2002.

Bakari, Imruh and Mbye B. Cham, eds. 1996. *African Experiences of Cinema*. London: BFI.

Bakhtin, Mikhail. 1981. *The Dialogic Imagination: Four Essays*. ed. Michael Holquist, trans. Caryl Emerson and Michael Holquist. Austin, TX: University of Texas Press.

Balnaves, Mark, James Donald, and Stephanie Hemelryk Donald. 2001. *The Global Media Atlas*. London: BFI.

Barthes, Roland. 1977. *Image-Music-Text*. trans. Stephen Heath. New York: The Noonday Press.

—— 1991. *The Responsibility of Forms: Critical Essays on Music, Art, and Representation*. trans. Richard Howard. Berkeley, CA: University of California Press.

Barton, John H. 1998. "International Intellectual Property and Genetic Resource Issues Affecting Agricultural Biotechnology," in *Agricultural Biotechnology in International Development*, eds Catherine L. Ives and Bruce M. Bedford. Oxon, New York: CAB International, 273–84.

Bazin, André. 1967. *What is Cinema?* trans. Hugh Gray. volume 2. Berkeley, CA: University of California Press.

BBC News. 2003. "Tarantino Defends *Kill Bill* Violence," October 3, http://news.bbc.co.uk/1/hi/entertainment/film/3157596.stm; accessed May 1, 2004.

Beard, Joseph. 2001. "Clones, Bones and Twilight Zones: Protecting the Digital Persona of the Quick, the Dead and the Imaginary," *Berkeley Technology Law Journal* 16 (Fall): 1165–271.

Ben-Atar, Doron. 2004. *Trade Secrets: Intellectual Piracy and the Origins of American Industrial Power*. New Haven, CT: Yale University Press.

Benjamin, Walter. 1968. "The Work of Art in the Age of Mechanical Reproduction," in *Illuminations*, ed. Hannah Arendt, trans. Harry Zohn. New York: Schocken Books, 217–51.

—— 1978. "The Mimetic Faculty," in *Reflections: Essays, Aphorisms, Autobiographical Writings*, ed. Peter Demetz, trans. Edmund Jephcott. New York: Schocken Books, 333–6.

Berry, Chris. 1998. "If China Can Say No, Can China Make Movies? Or, Do Movies Make China? Rethinking National Cinema and National Agency," *Boundary 2: An International Journal of Literature and Culture* 25. 3 (Fall): 129–50.

Bettig, Ronald V. 1996. *Copyrighting Culture: The Political Economy of Intellectual Property*. Boulder, CO: Westview Press.

Birchall, Danny. 2000. "Thieves Like Us," *Sight and Sound*, October, 32–4.

Bloom, Harold. 1973. *The Anxiety of Influence: A Theory of Poetry*. London: Oxford University Press.

Bordwell, David. 2000. *Planet Hong Kong: Popular Cinema and the Art of Entertainment*. Cambridge, MA: Harvard University Press.

—— 2002. "Ripples on Nearby Shores: Contemporary Taiwanese Cinema as Regional Influence," Talk delivered at Hong Kong University of Science and Technology, March 25.

Bordwell, David, Janet Staiger, and Kristin Thompson. 1985. *The Classical Hollywood Cinema: Film Style and Mode of Production to 1960*, New York: Columbia University Press.

Box Office Mojo International. 2005, http://www.boxofficemojo.com/intl/; accessed January 13, 2005.

Brenner, Susan W. 2003. "Complicit Publication: When Should the Dissemination of Ideas and Data be Criminalized," *Albany Law Journal of Science and Technology* 13: 273–429.

Buck-Morss, Susan. 1989. *The Dialectics of Seeing: Walter Benjamin and the Arcades Project*. Cambridge, MA: The MIT Press.

Cao Baoping and Yi Ren. 1999. "Cong *Yige Dou Buneng Shao* kan dianying shushi" (Reading cinema narrativity from *Not One Less*), *Dianying yishu* (Film art) 268 (May): 77–81.

Carter, Cynthia and C. Kay Weaver. 2003. *Violence and the Media*. Buckingham and Philadelphia, PA: Open University Press, 2003.

Castells, Manuel. 1996. *The Rise of the Network Society*. Maldan, MA: Blackwell.

Chakravarty, Sumita S. 2003. "The Erotics of History: Gender and Transgression in the New Asian Cinema," in *Rethinking Third Cinema*, eds Anthony R. Guneratne and Wimal Dissanayake. New York and London: Routledge, 79–90.

Chen Guanzhong, Liao Weitang, and Yan Jun. 2004. *Boximiya Zhongguo* (Bohemian China). Hong Kong: Oxford University Press (China).

China Hand. 2000a. "Ch 10-Property/licensing-Sec 1: The IPR Climate," October 8, http://www.eiu.com; accessed June 15, 2001.

—— 2000b. "Ch 10-Property/licensing-Sec 3: The Pirates Strike Back," October 8, http://www.eiu.com; accessed June 15, 2001.

Chow, Daniel C.K. 2000. "Counterfeiting in the People's Republic of China," *Washington University Law Quarterly* 78. 1 (Spring): 1–54.

—— 2003. *The Legal System of the People's Republic of China in a Nutshell*. St. Paul, MN: West Group.

Chow, Rey. 1995. *Primitive Passions: Visuality, Sexuality, Ethnography, and Contemporary Chinese Cinema*. New York: Columbia University Press.

—— 1998. "On Chineseness as a Theoretical Problem," *Boundary 2: An International Journal of Literature and Culture* 25. 3 (Fall): 1–24.

Chua, Beng Huat. 2004. "Conceptualizing an East Asian Popular Culture," *Inter-Asia Cultural Studies* 5. 2 (August): 200–1.

Clark, Drew. 2002. "How Copyright Became Controversial," in *Copy Fights: The Future of Intellectual Property in the Information Age*, eds Adam Thierer and Clyde Wayne Crews Jr. Washington, DC: Cato Institute, 147–61.

Clark, Paul. 1987. *Chinese Cinema: Culture and Politics since 1940*. Cambridge: Cambridge University Press.

Clarke, Eric. 2000. *Virtuous Vice, Homoeroticism and the Public Sphere*. Durham, NC and London: Duke University Press.

Cohen, Julie E., Lydia P. Loren, Ruth G. Okediji, and Maureen A. O'Rourke. 2002. *Copyright in a Global Information Economy*. New York: Aspen Law and Business.

Cohen, Tom. 1994. *Anti-Mimesis from Plato to Hitchcock*. Cambridge, UK: Cambridge University Press.

Cook, Curtis. 2002. *Patents, Profits & Power: How Intellectual Property Rules the Global Economy*. London: Kogan Page.

Cooper, Jon and Daniel M. Harrison. 2001. "The Social Organization of Audio Piracy on the Internet," *Media, Culture & Society* 23. 1: 71–89.

Crary, Jonathan. 2001. *Suspensions of Perception: Attention, Spectacle, and Modern Culture*. Cambridge, MA: The MIT Press.

Creed, Barbara. 1990. "*Alien* and the Monstrous-Feminine," in *Alien Zone: Cultural Theory and Contemporary Science Fiction Cinema*, ed. Annette Kuhn. London: Verso, 128–41.

Crofts, Stephen. 1993. "Reconceptualizing National Cinema/s," *Quarterly Review of Film and Video* 14. 3: 49–67.

CULTSTUD-L (Cultural Studies listserv), http://mailman.acomp.usf.edu/mailman/listinfo/cultstud-l; accessed May 2004.

Currie, Gregory. 1996. "Film, Reality, and Illusion," in *Post-Theory: Reconstructing Film Studies*, eds David Bordwell and Noël Carroll. Madison, WI: The University of Wisconsin Press, 325–46.

Curti, Andrea M. 2001. "The WTO Dispute Settlement Understanding: An Unlikely Weapon in the Fight against AIDS," *American Journal of Law and Medicine* 27: 469–85.

Dai, Degang. 1999. "Dui Beijing dianying guangzhong guangying qingkuang de diaocha baogao" (A Report on Current Beijing Audience), *Beijing Dianying Xueyuan xuebao, The Journal of Beijing Film Academy* 33: 92–7.

Dajiyuan. 2002. "Dalu daoban yezhe yu quannei renshi koujie fandaoban lan shang jia lan" (Pirates Cooperating with the Media Industry: The More and More Difficult Anti-piracy Campaign), April 6, http://www.epochtimes.com; accessed April 6, 2002.

Davis, Darrell William. 2003. "Compact Generation: VCD Markets in Asia," *Historical Journal of Film, Radio & Television* 23. 2: 165–76.

Davis, Darrell W. and Emilie Yueh-yu Yeh. 2003. "Inoue at Shaws: The Wellspring of Youth," in *The Shaw Screen: A Preliminary Study*, ed. Wong Ain-ling. Hong Kong: Hong Kong Film Archive, 255–71.

—— 2004. "VCD as Programmatic Technology: Japanese Television Drama in Hong Kong," in *Feeling Asian Modernities: Transnational Consumption of Japanese TV dramas*, ed. Koichi Iwabuchi. Hong Kong: Hong Kong University Press, 227–47.

Debord, Guy. 1995. *The Society of the Spectacle*. New York: Zone Books.

de Certeau, Michel. 1988. *The Practice of Everyday Life*. trans. Steven Rendall. Berkeley, CA: The University of California Press.

—— 1997. *Culture in the Plural*. trans. Tom Conley. Minneapolis, MN: University of Minnesota Press.

Deleuze, Gills and Félix Guattari. 1994. *What is Philosophy?* trans. Hugh Tomlinson and Graham Burchell. New York: Columbia University Press.

Derrida, Jacques. 1978. *Writing and Difference*. trans. Alan Bass. Chicago, IL: The University of Chicago Press.

—— 1981. "The Double Session," in *Dissemination*. trans. Barbara Johnson. Chicago, IL: The University of Chicago Press.

—— 1998. "Faith and Knowledge: The Two Sources of 'Religion' at the Limits of Reason Alone," in *Religion*, eds Jacques Derrida and Gianni Vattimo. Stanford, CA: Stanford University Press. 1–78.

—— 2001. *On Cosmopolitanism and Forgiveness*. trans. Mark Dooley and Michael Hughes. London and New York: Routledge.

Desser, David. Forthcoming. "Hong Kong Film and the New Cinephilia" in *Hong Kong Connections: Transnational Imagination in Action Cinema*, eds Meaghan Morris, Siu-leung Li, and Stephen Ching-kiu Chan. Hong Kong: Hong Kong University Press.

Dienst, Richard. 1994. *Still Life in Real Time: Theory After Television*. Durham, NC: Duke University Press.

Dirlik, Arif. 1989. "Postsocialism? Reflections on 'Socialism with Chinese Characteristics'," in *Marxism and the Chinese Experience: Issues in Contemporary Chinese Socialism*, eds. Arif Dirlik and Maurice Meisner. New York and London: M.E. Sharpe, 362–84.

—— 2003. "Global Modernity? Modernity in an Age of Global Capitalism," *European Journal of Social Theory* 6. 3: 275–92.

Dissanayake, Wimal. 1996. "Cinema and the Public Sphere: The Films of Oshima Nagisa," in *In Pursuit of Contemporary East Asian Culture*, eds. Xiaobing Tang and Stephen Snyder. Boulder, CO: Westview, 139–56.

Dolor, Beting Laygo. 2004. "Asian Cinema Revisited," *Manila Standard*, April 21.

Donald, James and Stephanie Hemelryk Donald. 2000. "The Publicness of Cinema," in *Reinventing Film Studies*, eds Christine Gledhill and Linda Williams. London: Arnold, 114–29.

Donald, Stephanie Hemelryk. 2000. *Public Secrets, Public Spaces: Cinema and Civility in China*. Lanham, MD; Boulder, CO; New York; Oxford: Rowman and Littlefield.

Eley, Geoff. 1992. "Nations, Publics, and Political Cultures: Placing Habermas in the Nineteenth Century," in *Habermas and the Public Sphere*, ed. Craig Calhoun. Cambridge, MA: MIT Press, 289–339.

Elias, Stephen. 1999. *Patent, Copyright and Trademark*, ed. Lisa Goldoftas. Berkeley, CA: Nolo Press.

Ellickson, Lee. 2002. "Preparing to Live in the Present: An Interview with Hou Hsiao-hsien," *Cineaste* 27. 4 (Fall): 13–20.

Elsaesser, Thomas. 2000. "The Blockbuster: Everything Connects, but Not Everything Goes," in *The End of Cinemas as We Know It: American Film in the Nineties*, ed. Jon Lewis. New York: New York University Press.

Else, Gerald F. 1986. *Plato and Aristotle on Poetry*. Chapel Hill, NC: University of North Carolina Press.

Epstein, Richard A. 2004. "Liberty versus Property? Cracks in the Foundations of Copyright Law," John M. Olin Law and Economics Working Paper no. 204.

Esplanada, Jerry E. 2004. "VRB 'success story' Cited but RP Still Piracy Hotspot," Inquirer News Service. July 21, http://www.inq7.net/ent/2004/jul/22/ent_2-1.htm; accessed October 26, 2004.

Evans, Donald. 2003. Speech presented in the American Chamber of Commerce, Beijing, October 28. Quoted in Chow Chung-yan, "China Will Take More Imports from US," *South China Morning Post*, October 29, 2003.

Fang, Lei. 2001. "Zhiyi 'lishiju' de lishiguan" (Questioning the historical sense in "historical dramas"), *Dianshi yanjiu* (TV Research) 134 (October): 43.

Feinsod, Mark L. 1996. "A Conversation with 'Maborosi' Director, Hirokazu Kore-Eda," http://www.indiewire.com/people/int_kore-eda_hiro_2_960905.html; accessed May 31, 2004.

Feng, Peter (Feng Xiang). 2003. *Intellectual Property in China*. 2nd edn. Hong Kong: Sweet and Maxwell Asia.

—— 2004. *Zhengfa biji* (Notes on Politics and Law). Nanjing: Jiangsu Renmin Chubanshe.

Fishman, Stephen. 1996. *The Copyright Handbook: How to Protect and Use Written Works*. Berkeley, CA: Nolo Press.

Foucault, Michel. 1977. "What is an Author?" in *Language, Counter-memory, Practice: Selected Essays and Interviews*, ed. Donald F. Bouchard, trans. Donald F. Bouchard and Sherry Simon. Ithaca, NY: Cornell University Press, 113–39.

Frankena, William K. 1973. *Ethics*. 2nd edn. Englewood Cliffs, NJ: Prentice-Hall.

Frow, John. 2000. "Public Domain and the New World Order in Knowledge," *Social Semiotics* 10. 2: 173–85.

Fuller, Graham. 2001. "Wong Kar-wai: Interview," *Interview* 31. 2 (February): 96–7.

Gabardi, Wayne. 2000. *Negotiating Postmodernism*. Minneapolis, MN: University of Minnesota Press.

Gaines, Jane M. 1992. *Contested Culture: The Image, the Voice, and the Law*. London: BFI.

Gallagher, Thomas. 2002. "Copyright Compulsory Licensing and Incentives," *Copyright in the Cultural Industries*. Cheltenham: Edward Elgar, 85–98.

Gansu xinwen wang. 2003. "Lanzhou chachao yiteda fanhuang wodian" (Raiding a Big Pornographic Material Market in Lanzhou), June 19, http://www.gs.chinanews.com.cn/news/2003–06–19/1/4298.html; accessed July 1, 2003.

Garofalo, Reebee. 1999. "From Music Publishing to MP3: Music and Industry in the 20th Century," *American Music* 17. 3: 318–53.

Gateward, Frances. 2003. "Youth in Crisis: National and Cultural Identity in New South Korean Cinema," in *Multiple Modernities: Cinemas and Popular Media in Transcultural East Asia*, ed. Jenny Kwok Wah La. Philadelphia, PA: Temple University Press, 114–27.

Gertz, Bill. 2000. *The China Threat: How the People's Republic Targets America*. Washington, DC: Regnery Publishing.

Ghani, Fadhal Ilahi Abd. 2003. "Klan Export Hub for Pirated DVDs and VCDs," *Malay Mail*, September 9, 2003; accessed through LexisNexis, January 13, 2005.

Girard, René. 1978. *To Double Business Bound: Essays on Literature, Mimesis, and Anthropology*. Baltimore, MD: Johns Hopkins University Press.

Godamongdirectors. Year Unknown. "Voyager Essay," http://www.godamongdirectors.com/woo/faq/wooessay.html; accessed June 10, 2004.

Godzich, Wlad. 1994. "Languages, Images, and the Postmodern Predicament," in *Materialities of Communication*, eds Hans Ulrich Gumbrecht and K. Ludwig Pfeiffer. Stanford, CA: Stanford University Press, 355–70.

Golab, Jan. 1998. "Video Cop: Motion Picture Association of America Battles Bootlegging of Videos," *Los Angeles* 43. 2 (February): 36.

Goldstein, Paul. 2003. *Copyright's Highway: From Gutenberg to the Celestial Jukebox*. Stanford, CA: Stanford University Press.

Gomery, Douglas. 2000. "Hollywood as Industry" in *American Cinema and Hollywood: Critical Approaches*, eds John Hill and Pamela Church Gibson. London: Oxford University Press, 19–29.

Gunning, Tom. 1989. "An Aesthetic of Astonishment: Early Film and the (In)credulous Spectators," *Art & Text* 34: 31–45.

—— 1994. "The Whole Town's Gawking: Early Cinema and the Visual Experience of Modernity," *Yale Journal of Criticism* 7. 2: 189–201.

Habermas, Jürgen. 1989. "The Public Sphere: An Encyclopedia Article," in *Critical Theory and Society: A Reader*, eds Stephen E. Bronner and Douglas M. Kellner. New York: Routledge, 136–42.

—— 1997. "Modernity: An Unfinished Project," in *Habermas and the Unfinished Project of Modernity: Critical Essays on the Philosophical Discourse of Modernity*, eds Maurizio Passerin d'Entrèves and Seyla Benhabib. Cambridge, MA: The MIP Press, 38–55.

Hallam, Julia and Margaret Marshment. 2000. *Realism and Popular Cinema*. Manchester: Manchester University Press.

Halpern, Sheldon W. 2003. "Copyright Law and the Challenge of Digital Technology," in *Image Ethics in the Digital Age*, eds Larry Gross, John Stuart Katz, and Jay Ruby. Minneapolis, MN: University of Minnesota Press, 143–170.

Hamelink, Cees J. 2003. "Cultural Rights in the Global Village," in *Cultural Rights in a Global World*, eds Anura Goonasekera, Cees Hamelink, and Venkat Iyer. Singapore: Eastern Universities Press, 7–25.

Hammond, Stefan and Mike Wilkins. 1996. *Sex and Zen & A Bullet in the Head*. New York: Fireside.

Hansen, Mark. 2000. *Embodying Technesis: Technology Beyond Writing*. Ann Arbor, MN: The University of Michigan Press.

Hansen, Miriam. 1991. *Babel and Babylon: Spectatorship in American Silent Film*. Cambridge, MA: Harvard University Press.

—— 1994. "Early Cinema, Late Cinema: Transformations of the Public Sphere," in *Viewing Positions: Ways of Seeing Film*, ed. Linda Williams. New Brunswick, NJ: Rutgers University Press, 134–54.

Hardt, Michael and Antonio Negri. 2000. *Empire*. Cambridge, MA: Harvard University Press.

Hart-Davis, Guy. 2001. *Internet Pricay [sic] Exposed*. San Francisco, CA: SYBEX.

Hartnick, Alan J. 2004. "Intellectual Property; The Other Side: Copywrongs and Copyleft," *New York Law Journal* 117 (June 18): 3.

Harvey, David. 1989. *The Condition of Postmodernity: An Enquiry into the Origins of Cultural Change*. Oxford, UK: Blackwell.

Heidegger, Martin. 1971. *On The Way to Language*. trans. Peter D. Hertz. New York: Harper & Row.

—— 1977. "The Question Concerning Technology," *The Question Concerning Technology and Other Essays*. trans. William Lovitt. New York: Harper Torchbooks.

—— 1996. *Being and Time: A Translation of Sein und Zeit*. trans. Joan Stambaugh. Albany, NY: State University of New York Press.

Herman, Edward. 1983. "Diversity of News: 'Marginalizing' the Opposition," *Journal of Communication* 35. 3: 135–46.

Hernandez, Eugene. 2004. "Magnolia Gets Thai Action Hit 'Ong-Bak: Thai Warrior'," http://www.indiewire.com/biz/biz_040604ongbak.html; accessed January 31, 2005.

Higson, Andrew. 2000. "The Limiting Imagination of National Cinema," in *Cinema and Nation*, eds Mette Hjort and Scott MacKenzie. New York: Routledge, 63–74.

Hitchcock, Lori D. 2002. "Transnational Film and the Politics of Becoming: Negotiating East Asian Identity in *Hong Kong Night Club* and *Moonlight Express*," *Asian Cinema* 13. 1 (Summer): 67–86.

Ho, Sam (Assistant Director, Asia/Pacific Anti-Piracy Operations, Motion Picture Association International). 2001. Interview with the author. July 4.

Hong Kong Economic Journal (Reporter Unknown). "Dalu daoban guangdie qingkuang yousou shoulian" (The Situation of Pirated Disks in the Mainland is Weakening), *Hong Kong Economic Journal*, January 12, 1998.

Hozic, Aida A. 2000. "Hollywood Goes on Sale; or, What Do the Violet Eyes of Elizabeth Taylor Have to Do with the 'Cinema of Attractions'?" in *Hollywood Goes Shopping*, eds David Desser and Garth S. Jowett. Minneapolis, MN and London: University of Minnesota Press, 205–21.

—— 2001. *Hollyworld: Space, Power, and Fantasy in the American Economy*. Ithaca, NY and London: Cornell University Press.

Hu, Kelly. 2004. "Chinese Re-makings of Pirated VCDs of Japanese TV Dramas," in *Feeling Asian Modernities: Transnational Consumption of Japanese TV dramas*, ed. Koichi Iwabuchi, Hong Kong: Hong Kong University Press, 205–26.

Hutcheon, Linda. 1989. *The Politics of Postmodernism*. London: Routledge.

IMDbPro.com. 2004. "Business Data for Ong-bak," http://www.imdb.com/title/tt0368909/business; accessed January 31, 2005.

Jalladeau, Alain. 2000. "Asia's Magic Lantern," http://www.unesco.org/courier/2000 10/uk/doss11.htm, accessed June 7, 2000.

James, Stan. 2004. "Festival Will Feature Best Asian Films," *The Advertiser*, January 23.

Jameson, Fredric. 2002. *A Singular Modernity: Essay on the Ontology of the Present*. London: Verso.

Jaszi, Peter. 1994. "On the Author Effect: Contemporary Copyright and Collective Creativity," in *The Construction of Authorship: Textual Appropriation in Law and Literature*, eds Martha Woodmansee and Peter Jaszi. Durham, NC: Duke University Press, 29–56.

Jayasuriya, Kanishka. 1999. "Symposium: The Rule of Law in the Era of Globalization: Globalization, Law, and the Transformation of Sovereignty: The Emergence of Global Regulatory Governance," *Indiana Journal of Global Legal Studies* 6 (Spring): 425–56.

Johnston, Donald F. 1978. *Copyright Handbook*. New York and London: R.R. Bowker Company.

Kamalipour, Yahya R. and Kuldip R. Rampal. 2001. "Introduction," in *Media, Sex, Violence, and Drugs in the Global Village*, eds Yahya R. Kamalipour and Kuldip R. Rampal. Lanham, MD: Rowman and Littlefield, 1–5.

Kang, Jianmin. 2000. "Zhendui wenti xunqiu tupo" (Looking for Breakthrough from the Core of the Problem), *Dianying yishu* (Film Art) 3. 272: 13–15.

Kemp, Stuart. 2003. "Piracy Top Priority at Cinema Expo: Four-day Convention Concentrates on Copyright Theft," *The Hollywood Reporter*, June 27.

Kerr, Orin S. 2002. "A Lukewarm Defense of the Digital Millennium Copyright Act," in *Copy Fights: The Future of Intellectual Property in the Information Age*, eds Adam Thierer and Clyde Wayne Crews Jr. Washington, DC: Cato Institute, 163–70.

Kittler, Friedrich and Laurence Rickels. 1992. "Spooky Electricity," *Artforum*, December: 66–70.

Klinger, Barbara. 2001. "The Contemporary Cinephilia: Film Collecting in the Post-Video Era," in *Hollywood Spectatorship: Changing Perceptions of Cinema Audiences*, eds Melvyn Stokes and Richard Maltby. London: BFI, 132–51.

Klotera. 2002. "Appeal to Miramax: Web Alliance for the Respectful Treatment of Asian Cinema: Our Purpose," http://alliance.hellninjacommando.net/purpose.htm; accessed December 1, 2004.

Kristeva, Julia. 1987. *Tales of Love*, trans. Leon S. Roudiez. New York: Columbia University Press.

Lai, Iris. 1998. "Idal VCD Snaps up Prime Commercial Slot at CCTV Auction," *Media: Asia's Media and Marketing Newspaper* 6 (February): 12.

Landes, Joan B. 1988. *Women and the Public Sphere in the Age of the French Revolution*. Ithaca, NY: Cornell University Press.

Landes, William M. 2003. "Copyright," in *A Handbook of Cultural Economics*, ed. Ruth Towse. Cheltenham, UK: Edward Elgar, 132–42.

Landes, William M. and Richard A. Posner. 2003. *The Economic Structure of Intellectual Property Law*. Cambridge, MA: The Belknap Press of Harvard University Press.

Larochelle, Gilbert. 1999. "From Kant to Foucault: What Remains of the Author in Postmodernism," in *Perspectives on Plagiarism and Intellectual Property in a Postmodern World*, eds Lise Buranen and Alice M. Roy. New York: State University of New York Press, 121–30.

Layman, Jeffrey and Freshfields Bruckhaus Deringer. 2000. "IPR Protection after WTO: Copyright Law and Enforcement under the TRIPs Agreement," in *China WTO: Shaping the Future*, ed. David Packer. Hong Kong: Asia Law and Practice. 129–319.

Learning Thai. 2004, http://www.learningthai.com/movies/ong_bak.php; accessed June 20, 2004.

Leitch, Thomas. 2002. "Twice-told Tales: Disavowal and the Rhetoric of the Remake," in *Dead Ringers: The Remake in Theory and Practice*, eds Jennifer Forrest and Leonard R. Koos. Albany, NY: State University of New York Press, 37–62.

Lessig, Lawrence. 2001. *The Future of Ideas: The Fate of the Commons in a Connected World*. New York: Random House.

—— 2004. *Free Culture: How Big Media Uses Technology and the Law to Lock Down Culture and Control Creativity*. New York: Penguin.

Li, Ding-Tzann. 1998. "A Colonized Empire: Reflections on the Expansion of Hong Kong films in Asian Countries," in *Trajectories: Inter-Asia Cultural Studies*, ed. Kuan-Hsing Chen. London: Routledge, 122–41.

Li, Kangsheng. 2000. "Shenceng wenti zaiyu shichang" (Buried Problems in the Market), *Dianying yishu* (Film Art) 3. 272: 10–11.

Liang, Lawrance. 2005. "Welcome Address," Contested Commons/Trespassing Publics: A Conference on Inequalities, Conflicts and Intellectual Property, January, New Delhi.

Liang, Liang 2004. "Breaking the Sky and Wrecking the Earth, Fighting Through East and West" (Tiancan dique dapian dongxi), http://tw.music.yahoo.com/news/ctnews/20040225/110300.html; accessed May 1, 2004.

Liao, Binghui. 1991. "Ji long you ya de sheyingshi" (A Photographer who can Neither Listen nor Talk), in *Xin dianying zhi si: Cong "Yiqie wei mingtian" dao "Beiqing chengshi"* (The Death of New Cinema: From *All For Tomorrow* to *City of Sadness*), eds Mizou and Liang Xinhua. Taipei: Tangshan Chubanshe, 129–34.

López, Ana M. 2000. "Facing up to Hollywood," in *Reinventing Film Studies*, eds Christine Gledhill and Linda Williams. London: Arnold, 419–37.

Lury, Celia. 1993. *Cultural Rights: Technology, Legality and Personality*. London and New York: Routledge.

McCalman, Philip. 2004. "Foreign Direct Investment and Intellectual Property Rights: Evidence from Hollywood's Global Distribution of Movies and Videos," *Journal of International Economics* 62. 1: 107–23.

McChesney, Robert W. 1999. *Rich Media, Poor Democracy: Communication Politics in Dubious Times*. Urbana, IL: University of Illinois Press.

McJohn, Stephen M. 2003. *Intellectual Property: Examples and Explanations*. New York: Aspen.

Mackintosh, Paul St John. 1996. "*Maborosi,*" *The Times Literary Supplement* 4867 (July 12): 21.

McSherry, Corynne. 2001. *Who Owns Academic Work?: Battling for Control of Intellectual Property*. Cambridge, MA: Harvard University Press.

Manovich, Lev. 2001. *The Language of New Media*. Cambridge, MA: MIT Press.

Marcuse, Herbert. 1941. "Some Social Implications of Modern Technology," in *Studies in Philosophy and Social Science* 9.3; reprinted in *Technology, War, and Fascism*, ed. Douglas Kellner. London and New York: Routledge, 41–65.

Marks, Laura U. 2001. "Live Video," in *The End of Cinema as We Know It: American Film in the Nineties*, ed. Jon Lewis. New York: New York University, 305–15.

Marx, Karl. 1975. *Early Writings*. New York: Vintage Books.

—— 1986. "The Communist Manifesto" in *Karl Marx: A Reader*, ed. Jon Elster. Cambridge: Cambridge University Press.

Marx, Karl and Friedrich Engels. 1970. *The German Ideology*. New York: International Publishers.

Mason, Phil. 2002. "Dancing to a New Beat," http://www.totaldvd.net/features/genre/200203 Eastern.php; accessed June 7, 2004.

Medosch, Armin. 2005. "Tales of the Commons," Paper presented to "Contested Commons, Trespassing Publics: A Conference on Inequalities, Conflicts and Intellectual Property." New Delhi, January.

Melberg, Arne. 1995. *Theories of Mimesis*. Cambridge: Cambridge University Press.

Mikuriya, Kunio (Deputy Secretary-General of the World Customs Organization). 2004. "Speech given to World Custom Organizations's Regional Forum in Shanghai," November 23. Reprinted in http://english.people.com.cn/200411/23/eng20041123_ 164884.html; accessed November 26, 2004.

Milestone Films and Video, 1996. "Press Kit of *Maborosi*," http://www.milestonefilms.com/pdf/Mabarosi.pdf; accessed January 13, 2005.

Miller, Arthur R. and Michael H. Davis. 1983. *Intellectual Property: Patents, Trademarks, and Copyright in a Nutshell*. St. Paul, MN: West Publishing.

Miller, Toby, Nitin Govil, John McMurria, and Richard Maxwell, 2001. *Global Hollywood*. London: BFI.

Mingpao. 2002. "Dianying shichang xian jianjia zhan" (Battle for Lowering Ticket Price Now Taking Place in Movie Market), December 16.

—— 2004. "Changxiao yunchengshu faxian wuyuan maopai huo" (5 Dollar Bootlegged Popular Fortune-telling Books are Discovered), December 12.

Mitchelson, Ronald L. and James O. Wheeler. 1994. "The Flow of Information in a Global Economy: The Role of the American Urban System in 1990," *Annals of the Association of American Geographers* 84. 1: 87–107.

MoovGoog, 2004. "Ong-Bak," http://www.mallasch.com/movies/review.php?sid = 110; accessed January 31, 2005.

MPAA (Motion Picture Association of America). 2000. "2000 Economic Data," http://www.mpaa.org/useconomicreview/2000Economic/slide.asp?ref = 27; accessed December 1, 2003.

—— 2004. "Anti-Piracy," http://www.mpaa.org/anti-piracy/index.htm; accessed October 15, 2004.

Mulvey, Laura. 2004. "Passing Time: Reflections on Cinema from a New Technological Age," *Screen* 45. 2 (Summer): 142–55.

Mustonen, Mikko. 2003. "Copyleft – the Economics of Linux and other Open Source Software," *Information Economics and Policy* 15. 1: 99–121.

National Bureau of Statistics, People's Republic of China compile. 2000. *China Statistical Yearbook 2000*. Beijing: China Statistics Press.

NATO (National Association of Theatres Organization). 2004. Statistics, Average U.S. Ticket Prices, http://www.natoonline.org/statisticstickets.htm; accessed January 14, 2005.

Negt, Oska and Alexander Kluge. 1993. *Public Sphere and Experience: Toward an Analysis of the Bourgeois and Proletarian Public Sphere*. Minneapolis, MN: University of Minnesota Press.

Negus, Keith. 1999. *Music Genres and Corporate Cultures*. London and New York: Routledge.

Netanel, Neil Weinstock. 1996. "Copyright and a Democratic Civil Society," *Yale Law Journal* 106 (November): 283–464.

Ng, Fiona. 2002. "Interview: Love in the Time of Tiananmen: Stanley Kwan's *Lan Yu*," indieWIRE, February 7, http://www.indiewire.com/people/int_Zhang_Yongning_020725.html; accessed December 1, 2003.

Nix. 2004. "A Nixfilm.com Review of Ong-bak 2003," http://www.nixflix.com/reviews/ongbak.htm; accessed May 20, 2004.

Nornes, Abe Mark and Yeh Yueh-yu. 1998. "Violence: Seen and Unseen," http://cinemaspace.berkeley.edu/Papers/CityOfSadness/violence.html; accessed May 29, 2004.

Nowell-Smith, Geoffrey and Ricci, Steven, eds, 1998. *Hollywood and Europe*. London: British Film Institute.

Olson, Scott Robert. 1999. *Hollywood Planet: Global Media and the Competitive Advantage of Narrative Transparency*. Mahwah, NJ: Lawrence Erlbaum Associates.

Pang, Laikwan. 2002a. *Building a New China in Cinema: The Chinese Left-wing Cinema Movement, 1932–37*. Lanham, MD: Rowman and Littlefield Publishers.

—— 2002b. "The Global/National Position of Hong Kong Cinema in China," in *Media in China*, eds Stephanie Hemelryk Donald, Michael Keane, and Yin Hong. London: Routledge Curzon, 55–66.

—— 2002c. "Masculinity in Crisis: Films of Milkyway Image and Post-1997 Hong Kong Cinema," *Feminist Media Studies* 2. 3 (Fall): 325–40.

Panitchpakdi, Supachai. 2001. "Balancing Competing Interests: The Future Role of the WTO," in *The Role of the World Trade Organization in Global Governance*, ed. Gary P. Sampson. Tokyo, New York, and Paris: United Nations University Press.

Patterson, Lyman Ray. 1968. *Copyright in Historical Perspective*. Nashville, TN: Vanderbilt University Press.

Pax, Salam. 2003. "Shortcuts: People: Observations: Curiosities: Diversions: Blue Movies in Baghdad," *The Guardian*, July 8: 4.

Petty, Scott. 2004. "Just Do It: House Committee Works up a Sweat (of the brow) and Approves Database Protection Bill," *Intellectual Property Today*, March 24. http://www.kslaw.com/library/articles.asp?1178; accessed January 12, 2005.

Picker, Randal C. and Alan Charles Rual. 2001. "European Union Database Developments: An Update on the Status of Intellectual Property Protections for Factual Compilations," http://www.sidley.com/cyberlaw/features/eu_database.asp; accessed July 26, 2004.

Plato. 1974. *The Republic*. trans. Desmond Lee. Harmondsworth: Penguin.

Ramasoota, Pirongrong. 2003. "Balancing the Scruples of Copyright and Piracy in a Globalized Information Society" in *Cultural Rights in a Global World*, eds Anura Goonasekera, Cees Hamelink, and Venkat Iyer. Singapore: Eastern Universities Press, 123–38.

Randall, Marilyn. 1999. "Imperial Plagiarism," in *Perspectives on Plagiarism and Intellectual Property in a Postmodern World*, eds Lise Buranen and Alice M. Roy. New York: SUNY, 131–40.

—— 2001. *Pragmatic Plagiarism: Authorship, Profit, and Power*. Toronto: University of Toronto Press.

Rees, Gavin. 2001. "Getting Busy with the Miike," Guardian Unlimited, http://film.guardian.co.uk/interview/interviewpages/0,6737,458009,00.html; accessed June 23, 2004.

Richards, Thomas. 1991. *The Commodity Culture of Victorian England: Advertising and Spectacle, 1851–1914*. London: Verso.

Richie, Donald. 2001. *A Hundred Years of Japanese Film*. Tokyo: Kodansha.

Rinzler, Carol E. 1983. "What's Fair about 'Fair Use'?" *Public Weekly* 223. 14: 26–8.

Robertson, Roland. 1992. *Globalization: Social Theory and Global Culture*. London: Sage.

Rose, Mark. 1988. "The Author as Proprietor: *Donaldson v. Becket* and the Genealogy of Modern Authorship." *Representations* 23 (Summer): 51–85.

Rothman, William. 2001. "Violence and Film," in *Violence and American Cinema*. ed. J. David Slocum. New York: Routledge, 37–46.

Russell, Mark. 2004. "Dialogue: Park Chan-wook," The Hollywood Reporter.com, http://www.hollywoodreporter.com/thr/awards/cannes/feature_display.jsp?vnu_content_id = 1000511737; accessed June 23, 2004.

Samuelian, Kristin Flieger. 1998. "'Piracy is Our Only Option': Postfeminist Intervention in *Sense and Sensibility*," in *Jane Austen in Hollywood*, eds Linda Troost and Sayre Greenfield. Lexington, KY: University Press of Kentucky, 148–58.

Sassen, Saskia. 1991. *The Global City: New York, London, Tokyo*. Princeton, NJ: Princeton University Press.

—— 1994. *Cities in a World Economy*. Thousand Oaks, CA: Pine Forge Press.

—— 1996. *Losing Control? Sovereignty in an Age of Globalizaion*. New York: Columbia University Press.

—— 1998. *Globalization and Its Discontents*. New York: New Press.

Schatz, Thomas. 1993. "The New Hollywood," in *Film Theory Goes to the Movies*, eds Jim Collins, Hilary Radner, and Ava Preacher Collins. New York and London: Routledge, 8–36.

Scott, Allen J. 2000. *The Cultural Economy of Cities: Essays on the Geography of Image-producing Industries*. London: Sage Publication.

Scott, David. 2003. *Asia Pacific Video: Market Assessment and Forecast* (A *Screen Digest* Report). London: Screen Digest Limited.

Screen Digest. 2002. "World Regional Video Markets Compared Disc Business Gathers Pace," November 1. http://global.factiva.com/zhtw/arch/display.asp; accessed December 1, 2003.

Segrave, Kerry. 2003. *Piracy in the Motion Picture Industry*. Jefferson, NC, and London: McFarland & Company.

Sell, Susan K. 2003. *Private Power, Public Law: The Globalization of Intellectual Property Rights*. Cambridge: Cambridge University Press.

Semati, M. Mehdi and Patty J. Sotirin. 1999. "Hollywood's Transnational Appeal Hegemony and Democratic Potential?" *Journal of Popular Film & Television* 26. 4 (Winter): 176–89.

Semsel, George Stephen, ed., 1987. *Chinese Film: The State of the Art in the People's Republic*, New York and Westport, CT, London: Praeger.

SIIA (Software and Information Industry Association). 2000. "Report on Global Software Piracy," http://www.siia.net/piracy/pubs/piracy2000.pdf; accessed December 1, 2002.

Sina (Xinlang wang). 2000. "Diaocha biaoming jue daduoshu wangmin renwei muqian guonei dianying piaojia guogao" (Research Shows Most Web Visitors find the National Film Ticket Price too High), http://ent.sina.com.cn/m/c/22840.html; accessed January 14, 2005.

—— 2003. "*Yige dou buneng shao*" (Not One Less), http://living.sina.com.cn/yige/; accessed December 9, 2004.

Slocum, J. David. 2001. "Violence and American Cinema: Notes for an Investigation," in *Violence and American Cinema*, ed. J. David Slocum. New York: Routledge.

Smiers, Joost. 2002. "The Abolition of Copyrights: Better for Artists, Third World Countries and the Public Domain," in *Copyright in the Cultural Industries*, ed. Ruth Towse. Cheltenham: Edward Elgar, 119–39.

Smith, Craig S. 2000. "A Tale of Piracy: How the Chinese Stole the Grinch," *New York Times*, December 12.

Söderberg, Johan. 2002. "Copyleft vs. Copyright: A Marxist Critique," *First Monday* 7. 3 (March), http://firstmonday.org/issues/issue7_3/soderberg/index.html; accessed December 7, 2004.

Song Qiang, Zhang Zangzang, Qiao Bian, Tang Zhengyu, and Gu Qingsheng. 1996. *Zhongguo keyi shu bu* (China Can Say No). Beijing: Zhonggua Gongshang Linahe Chubanshe.

Sprigman, Chris. 2002. "The Mouse that Ate the Public Domain: Disney, The Copyright Term Extension Act, and *Eldred V. Ashcroft*," *FindLaw's Legal Commentary*, http://writ.news.findlaw.com/commentary/20020305_sprigman.html; accessed March 5, 2002.

Stahl, Lesley. 2003. "Pirates Of The Internet," CBS Sixty-Minutes Special, http://www.cbsnews.com/stories/2003/10/31/60minutes/main581153.shtml; accessed November 2, 2003.

Stam, Robert. 2000. *Film Theory: An Introduction*. London: Blackwell.

Starr, Paul. 2004. *The Creation of the Media*. New York: Basic Books.

Steintrager, James A. 2005. "An Unworthy Subject: Slaughter, Cannibalism and Postcoloniality" in *Masculinities and Hong Kong Cinema*, eds Laikwan Pang and Day Kiu-mui Wong. Hong Kong: Hong Kong University Press, 155–74.

Stock, Ann Marie, ed., 1997. *Framing Latin American Cinema: Contemporary Critical Perspectives*. Minneapolis, MN: University of Minnesota Press.

Streeter, Thomas. 1994. "Broadcast Copyright and the Bureaucratization of Property," in *The Construction of Authorship: Textual Appropriation in Law and Literature*, eds Martha Woodmansee and Peter Jaszi. Durham, NC and London: Duke University Press.

Strong, William S. 1993. *The Copyright Book: A Practical Guide*. Cambridge, MA: The MIT Press.

Subway Cinema. 2004, http://www.subwaycinema.com/frames/iss.htm; accessed May 20, 2004.

Sum, Ngai-Ling. 2003. "Informational Capitalism and U.S. Economic Hegemony: Resistance and Adaptations in East Asia," *Critical Asian Studies* 35. 3: 373–98.

Su Tong. 1999. "Dianshi shidai" (The Television Era), in *Richang Zhongguo – Jiushi niandai laobaixing de richang shenghuo* (Everyday China – The Daily Life of the Common People in the 1990s), eds Wu Liang and Gao Yu. Nanjing: Jiangsu Meishu Chubanshe.

Tang Zaiyang. 2001. "Dalu duo zai Changjian chuanshang daokao" (The Mainland Pirates Hiding in Ships of Changjian), *Lianhe wanbao*, July 20.

Taussig, Michael. 1993. *Mimesis and Alterity: A Particular History of the Senses*. New York, London: Routledge.

Taylor, Charles. 2004. *Modern Social Imaginaries*. Durham, NC: Duke University Press.

Teo, Stephen. 1997. *Hong Kong Cinema: The Extra Dimension*. London: BFI.

Thompson, Elizabeth. 2001. "Sex and Cinema in Damascus: The Gendered Politics of Public Space in a Colonial City," in *Middle Eastern Cities: 1900–1950: Public Places and Public Spheres in Transformation*, eds Han Chr Korsholm Nielsen and Jokob Skovgaard-Petersen. Aarhus, Denmark: Aarhus University Press, 89–111.

Tian Daoyuan. 2002. "Feng Xiaogang buzai mai daobang" (Feng Xiaogang Doesn't Buy Pirated Products Anymore), *Duowei zhoukan* (Chinese Newsweek) 96 (March), http://www.chinesenewsweek.com/96/literautre/7681.html; accessed March 1, 2003.

Tomlinson, John. 1999. *Globalization and Culture*. Chicago, IL: University of Chicago Press.

Towse, Ruth. 2001. *Creativity, Incentive and Reward: An Economic Analysis of Copyright and Culture in the Information Age*. Cheltenham, UK and Northampton, MA: Edward Elgar.

Tracy, James F. 2002. "Empire," *Journal of Communication Inquiry*, 26. 3 (July): 330–6.

Truffaut, François. 1954. "On a Certain Tendency of the French Cinema," *Cahiers du cinéma*; reprinted in *Movies and Methods I*, ed. Bill Nichols. Berkeley, CA: University of California Press, 1976, 224–37.

Turner, Matthew. 2004. "Kill Bill Interview: With Quentin Tarantino and Uma Thurman," http://www.viewlondon.co.uk/home_feat_int_killbill2.asp; accessed May 1, 2004.

Udden, James. 2002. "Hou Hsiao-hsien and the Question of a Chinese Style," *Asian Cinema* 13. 2 (Fall/Winter): 54–75.

U.S. Department of Commerce. 2000. National Trade Data Bank, http://www.tradeport.org/ts/countries/france/isa/isar0022.html; accessed November 3, 2001.

Vaidhyanathan, Siva. 2001. *Copyrights and Copywrongs: The Rise of Intellectual Property and How it Threatens Creativity*. New York: New York University Press.

Vattimo, Gianni. 1988. *The End of Modernity: Nihilism and Hermeneutics in Postmodern Culture*, trans. Jon R. Snyder. Baltimore, MD: The Johns Hopkins University Press.

Wang, Shujen. 2003. *Framing Piracy: Globalization and Film Distribution in Greater China*. Lanham, MD: Rowman & Littlefield.

Washburn, Dennis. 2001. "The Arrest of Time: The Mythic Transgressions of *Vengeance is Mine*," in *Word and Image in Japanese Cinema*, eds Dennis Washburn and Carole Cavanaugh. Cambridge: Cambridge University Press, 318–41.

Wasser, Frederick. 1995. "Is Hollywood America? The Transnationalization of the American Film Industry," *Critical Studies in Mass Communication* 12. 4 (1995): 423–37.

Weaver, James and Jacob Wakshlag. 1986. "Perceived Vulnerability to Crime, Criminal Victimization Experience, and Television Viewing," *Journal of Broadcasting and Electric Media* 30. 2: 141–58.

Weber, Max. 1968. *Economy and Society: An Outline of Interpretive Sociology*. Guenther Roth and Claus Wittich, eds, New York: Bedminster Press.

Weil, Ben H. and Barbara Friedman Polansky, eds. 1985. *Modern Copyright Fundamentals: Key Writings on Technological and Other Issues*. New York: Van Nostrand Reinhold Company.

Weisser, Thomas, ed. 1994. *Asian Trash Cinema: The Book*. Miami, FL: ATC/ETC Publications.

Wikipedia, a free-content encyclopedia, http://en.wikipedia.org/wiki/Main_Page.

Willemen, Paul. 1994. *Looks and Frictions: Essays in Cultural Studies and Film Theory*. Bloomington, IN: Indiana University Press; London: British Film Institute.

Williams, Alan. 2002. "The Raven and the Nanny: The Remake as Crosscultural Encounter," in *Dead Ringers: The Remake in Theory and Practice*, eds Jennifer Forrest and Leonard R. Koos. Albany, NY: State University of New York Press.

Williams, Linda. 2000. "Discipline and Fun: *Psycho* and Postmodern Cinema," in *Reinventing Film Studies*, eds Christine Gledhill and Linda Williams. London: Arnold, 351–78.

Williams, Raymond. 1977. *Marxism and Literature*. Oxford and New York: Oxford University Press.

—— 1981. *Culture*. London: Fontana Press.

Wollen, Peter. 1998. "Tinsel and Realism," in *Hollywood and Europe: Economics, Culture, National Identity 1945–1995*, eds Geoffrey Nowell-Smith and Steven Ricci. London: British Film Institute, 129–34.

Wong, Kar-wai. 2000. "Interview," *Meiri xinbao* (Daily News), November 26.

Wong, Lawrence Ka Hee, Director, Film-Physical Production, Shaws, 2003. Interview by the author, December 17.

Woodmansee, Martha. 1984. "The Genius and the Copyright: Economic and Legal Conditions of the Emergence of the 'Author'," *Eighteenth-Century Studies* 17. 4: 425–28.

Wu, Yigong. ed., 1999. *Shanghai dianying zhi* (An Account of Shanghai's Cinema). Shanghai: Shanghai Shehui Kexue Yuan.

Yang, Deli. 2003. *Intellectual Property and Doing Business in China*. Amsterdam: Pergamon.

Yang, Guang. 1999. "95percent of the Audio-Video Market is out of Control according to Statistics," http://www.fzen.com.cn/991206/8_4.html; accessed November 1, 2002.

—— 2004. "The story of Hong Kong's cinema tycoon Run Run Shaw" (Xianggang yingcheng daheng Shao Yifu chuangqi). http://www.hebnet.net/mag7/n26/colart12112. htm; accessed May 1, 2004.

Yau, Herman L.T. 2000. Hong Kong Film Director. Interview with the author. October 31.

YesAsia, http://us.yesasia.com/en/prodRvListPage.aspx?pid = 1003201171&section = videos& code = c&; accessed June 6, 2004.

Yin, Hong. 2002. "Meaning, Production, Consumption: The History and Reality of Television Drama in China," in *Media in China: Consumption, Content and Crisis*, eds Stephanie Hemelryk Donald, Michael Keane, and Yin Hong. London: RoutledgeCurzon, 28–39.

Zhang, Haichao. 2001. *Dianshi Zhongguo: Dianshi meiti jingzhen youshi* (Television China: The Favorable Conditions of the Competitiveness of Television). Beijing: Beijing Guangbo Xueyuan.

Zhang, Jinli. 1999. *Jiemi Zhongguo dianshi* (Unravel the Secrets of Chinese Television). Beijing: Zhongguo Chengshi.

Zhang, Youli. 2000. "Zhengban zuocheng daoban yan – Yinxiangye de beiai yu wunai" (Official Discs Pretending to be Pirated Discs: The Tragedy of the Visual Industry), *Zhongguo yinxiang* 1. 45: 33.

Zhao, Yuezhi. 1998. *Media, Market, and Democracy in China: Between the Party Line and the Bottom Line*. Urbana, IL: University of Illinois Press.

Zhongguo dianying shichange (China Film Market) 1999. July.

Zhonghua da huangye (China's Big Yellow Page). 2001. "Taitan nike hao zhengban VCD Zhongguo shichang tuiguang gongguan anli" (The Case Study of the Marketing Strategies of *Titanic*'s Official VCD in China). http://fjt.infoscape.com.cn/gate/big5/www.chinabig. com.cn/zhs/business/relation/school/cases/010820_01.htm; accessed December 1, 2004.

Index